D1174636

OXFORD STUDIES IN THE
HISTORY OF ART AND ARCHITECTURE

General Editors

ANTHONY BLUNT FRANCIS HASKELL CHARLES MITCHELL

ARCHITECTURAL SCULPTURE IN ROMANESQUE PROVENCE

ALAN BORG

WITHDRAWN-UNL

OXFORD

AT THE CLARENDON PRESS

1972

Oxford University Press, Ely House, London W. 1

GLASGOW NEW YORK TORONTO MELBOURNE WELLINGTON
CAPE TOWN IBADAN NAIROBI DAR ES SALAAM LUSAKA ADDIS ABABA
DELHI BOMBAY CALCUTTA MADRAS KARACHI LAHORE DACCA
KUALA LUMPUR SINGAPORE HONG KONG TOKYO

© OXFORD UNIVERSITY PRESS 1972

PRINTED IN GREAT BRITAIN
AT THE UNIVERSITY PRESS, OXFORD
BY VIVIAN RIDLER
PRINTER TO THE UNIVERSITY

NA
3549
.A3P762

Acknowledgements

MANY people helped me in the preparation of this book, and I am extremely grateful to all of them. My work was greatly facilitated by the staffs of various museums and libraries in France, England, and the United States. M. Félix Paknadel of the Université d'Aix-Marseille and Mr. Christopher Crockett kindly took some of the photographs for me. Numerous individuals contributed ideas, suggestions, and criticisms, and I thank them all collectively. The following call for especial mention: my wife, Anne, who not only contributed ideas, but also edited the text and drew the diagrams and the map; Professor Bertrand Davezac of Indiana University; Professor Whitney Stoddard of Williams College; Professor Peter Lasko of the University of East Anglia; Professor George Zarnecki and Dr. Peter Kidson of the Courtauld Institute; and Dr. Rosalie Green of the Index of Christian Art, Princeton University. Above all, I am indebted to Christopher Hohler, Reader in the History of Art at the Courtauld Institute.

Contents

List of Plates

List of Text-figures

Abbreviations

B.M.	*Bulletin Monumental.*
C.A.	*Congrès Archéologique.*
Duprat	Duprat, E. (ed.), *Cartulaire du chapitre de Notre-Dame-des-Doms*, vol. i (*1060–1263*), Avignon, 1932.
G.C.N.	Albanès, J.-H., and Chevalier, U. (eds.), *Gallia Christiana Novissima. Histoire des archevêchés, évêchés et abbayes de France*, 1899–1920, 7 vols.
Hamann, *St. Gilles*	Hamann, R., *Die Abteikirche von St. Gilles und ihre künstlerische Nachfolge*, Berlin, 1955, 3 vols.
Labande, *Études*	Labande, L. H., *Études d'histoire et d'archéologie romane. Provence et Bas-Languedoc*, Avignon–Paris, 1902.
Labande, *Arles*	Labande, L. H., 'Étude historique et archéologique sur S. Trophime d'Arles du IVe au XIIIe siècle', *B.M.*, 1903, 1904.
Labande, *Vaison*	Labande, L. H., 'La Cathédrale de Vaison', *B.M.*, 1905, pp. 253–321.
Labande, *Avignon*	Labande, L. H., 'L'Église Notre-Dame-des-Doms d'Avignon des origines au XIIIe siècle', *Bulletin Archéologique du Comité des travaux historiques et scientifiques*, 1906, pp. 282–365.
Labande, *Aix*	Labande, L. H., and Agnel, A., 'S. Sauveur d'Aix. Étude critique sur les parties romanes de cette cathédrale', *Bulletin Archéologique du Comité des travaux historiques et scientifiques*, 1912, pp. 289–344.
Lasteyrie, *Études*	Lasteyrie, R. de, *Études sur la sculpture française au Moyen Âge. Fondation Eugène Piot, Monuments et mémoires*, vol. viii, 1902.
Pourrière	Pourrière, J., *Recherches sur la première cathédrale d'Aix*, Paris, 1939.
Revoil	Revoil, H., *L'Architecture romane du Midi*, Paris, 1874, 3 vols.
Sautel	Sautel, J., *Les Chapelles de campagne de l'archevêché d'Avignon et de ses anciens diocèses*, Avignon–Lyon, 1938.
Stockhausen, *Die Kreuzgänge*	Stockhausen, H. A. von, 'Die romanischen Kreuzgänge der Provence; I, Die Architektur; II, Die Plastik', *Marburger Jahrb. f. Kunstwiss.*, vol. vii, 1933; vol. viii–ix, 1936.

Introduction

PROVENCE is at once one of the best-known and one of the least-known regions of France. Each year its sea-coast attracts holiday-makers in their thousands, the majority of whom reach their destination by travelling through the inland heart of Provence. For road travellers this used to mean the old *R.N.* 7, and in the interminable summer traffic jams some waiting motorists may have been able to enjoy the beauty of the surrounding countryside or to study the exterior of an ancient parish church or rural chapel. A few no doubt despaired of the traffic, and plunged off into the hills to find a less direct but infinitely more enjoyable route to the sea. Now, however, the motorway carries all this traffic at a uniform speed down the Rhône valley, and most tourists never have a chance to see Provence at less than 70 m.p.h. This state of affairs is welcomed by many who, like myself, cherish the outstanding and frequently stunning natural beauty of the region. Despite the inevitable and almost always ugly penetration of modern civilization, it is still possible to echo the sentiments of the great twelfth-century troubadour Peire Vidal: 'There is no land that can compare with that from the Rhône to Vence, between the sea and the Durance.'[1]

Yet the medieval monuments in which Provence abounds have received comparatively little recent attention from art historians. In comparison with the regional schools of Burgundy, Normandy, or Poitou, that of Provence has been largely ignored, apart from a continuing discussion of the sculpture at and associated with S. Gilles. There has been no overall attempt at a systematic study of the school, nor has any Provençal building been the subject of a detailed monograph within recent years. One reason for this is doubtless that the main Provençal school has, by tradition and repetition, come to be regarded as *retardataire*, and since, rightly or wrongly, art historians are still most concerned with the *avant-garde* of any particular epoch, Provence has tended to get left out. Yet, even if the traditional view of Provençal Romanesque is the correct one (and, if my conclusions are accepted, it is not) it would hardly seem a valid reason

---

[1] See J. Anglade, (ed.), *Les Poésies de Peire Vidal* (Paris, 1913), no. XIX. This is a well-known poem, which opens with the words 'Ab l'alen tir vas me l'aire / Qu'eu sen venir de Proensa'. The second verse contains the following lines, paraphrased above: 'Qu'om no sap tan dous repaire / Com de Rozer tro qu'a Vensa, / Si com clau mars e Durensa, / Ni on tan fis jois s'esclaire.'

for such neglect. I am not implying that no recent work at all has been done, for there are several dedicated French scholars who are continually enlarging our knowledge of specific monuments. However, there has been little attempt to investigate further the accepted frame of reference for Provençal Romanesque, as it was established in the early part of this century by L. H. Labande.

It must be said at once that Provençal buildings present several peculiar and difficult problems for the art historian. In the first place the upper parts of all the major churches, where the majority of the decoration occurs, are almost totally inaccessible. There are no passage-ways in walls, no tribunes, and no galleries (the baroque gallery at Notre-Dame-des-Doms, Avignon, is a rare and welcome exception). Moreover, the interiors are naturally dark, since windows are scarce, and the gloom is often worsened by coats of post-medieval paint. The exteriors are for the most part equally difficult to get at, since they are usually encased in a solid mass of later domestic building—the worst examples probably being the former cathedrals of Cavaillon and Apt. It is sometimes possible to undertake hair-raising sorties over the roofs, but even so large areas usually remain invisible.

Another problem is presented by the masonry itself. All scholars have commented upon the beautiful ashlar masonry of the majority of Provençal churches; it is this feature which, perhaps more than anything else, gives them their 'Roman' appearance. In the present century, since the fundamental studies of Labande, such masonry has been accepted as a sign of mature Provençal Romanesque, and dateable to the second half of the twelfth century. At the same time, rough unshaped masonry made up of smaller stones—the so-called *petit appareil*—is regarded as earlier, although it is difficult to date accurately. Such a simple formula is obviously highly superficial, and it is generally admitted that rough and inexpertly constructed walls can in fact date from any epoch, including the nineteenth century. Taken on its own, it is rash to conclude anything, particularly any indication of date, from the existence of *petit appareil*. If, as happens all too rarely in Provence, we have *petit appareil* alongside good ashlar facing in the same building, we are probably justified in asserting that two different periods are represented, but we should not necessarily assume that the more competent masonry is the later. While this statement would no doubt be widely accepted, the suggestion that really first-class masonry could be produced in Provence before the mid-twelfth century is somewhat heretical. Nevertheless, one is led inescapably to this conclusion through the study of the architectural decoration.

Another feature further complicates the picture; this is the absence of that stock-in-trade of the architectural historian, the masonry break. Whether this is due to the original skill of the Provençal builders, or whether it is the result of the efforts of subsequent restorers, or a combination of the two, it remains true that there are disastrously few clear breaks in masonry in major Provençal churches. This fact has led many scholars to assume out of hand that a particular building is a unified structure, despite other evidence to the contrary. In the case of several of the major buildings this other evidence is considered in the course of this study, but it may here be noted that a strong argument against the supposed unity of the major Provençal churches is indirectly provided by the minor buildings, the parish churches and the rural chapels. Any number of these are quite clearly and undeniably the work of different periods, for example at Valréas, where aisles were added in the thirteenth century, at La Baume-de-Transit, where the trefoiled apse is manifestly later than the nave, at Donzère (apse rebuilt), at Goudargues, at Notre-Dame-du-Groseau, Malaucène, at La Madeleine, Bédoin, at Notre-Dame-d'Aubune, at Pernes, at Venasque (parish church), at S. Jacques-l'Erémitage, Cavaillon, and so on. In all these cases the breaks in the construction of the building are visible not only in the decoration, but also in the masonry. However, it would be strange indeed if such care was taken to repair, restore, and extend the rural chapels, while the major buildings remained exactly as they were originally designed. In fact, as I shall show, the cathedrals and major churches were equally subject to change. These changes were more skilfully concealed, and sometimes it is only the decoration which reveals their extent, but they were nevertheless made, and were sometimes radical.

A similar problem is that of the masons' marks, which abound in Provençal buildings. For Labande these could be taken as an indication of date, but the problem is more complex than he allowed. He himself observed that all the marks visible in Notre-Dame-des-Doms, which he dated *c.* 1140–60, could be found at Le Thor, dated *c.* 1200. Such a temporal range makes it highly improbable that an individual sign belonged to an individual mason, and once this is admitted, there is no reason why a particular sign should not date fifty years before as well as fifty years after *c.* 1150. Indeed, as Professor Crosby has observed, several of the masons' marks visible at S. Denis can also be found at Pompeii. The mark probably belonged not to an individual but to a family or to a shop, and as such is in a sense timeless. A thorough study of *all* Provençal marks, taking account of their epigraphical characteristics as well as their alphabetical significa-tion, might perhaps allow some more definite conclusions, but until this is done no deductions can be made with safety. For these reasons I have therefore decided to rule out any attempt to date buildings on the basis of these marks, although a particular group of marks in a particular part of a building, and their absence elsewhere, can be a useful guide to the extent of a given building campaign.

The medieval art historian has, if he is lucky, two basic means of approach. One is the monument itself, which he can analyse and dissect; the second is the documents relating to the monument. Ideally, the information gleaned from both these sources should lead to the same conclusions. Unfortunately this has not happened for Provence, and many of the major buildings are dated later than the documents say they should be. If he is forced into a corner, the art historian can always explain this on the grounds that documents disappear more quickly than monuments, but, while this is undoubtedly true, the position in Provence must be regarded as exceptional. We have numerous documents relating to churches in the eleventh and early twelfth centuries, all of which were apparently destroyed without trace some fifty to a hundred years later and completely rebuilt. Because of this apparent dichotomy, I have for the most part begun by ignoring the documentary evidence and analysing the building alone. After this analysis I have then referred my conclusions to the documents. This of course is a reversal of the traditional 'History and Description' procedure, but it does, I think, help to clarify the situation.

The original starting-point for this study was the problem of the nave capitals in Provence, and this indeed remains a central theme. In the course of discussing these capitals other aspects of the decoration were drawn in, but the picture remains far from complete; many facets have had to be excluded to keep the book at a reasonable length. There are several buildings which are mentioned more or less briefly in the text, but which in fact deserve to have a monograph devoted to them alone. Such are the cathedrals of S. Paul-Trois-Châteaux and Cavaillon, the churches of Bourg-S. Andéol and Pernes, and so on. Many other monuments are in need of more material aid—the beautiful hilltop chapel at Venéjan is in a state of ruin, and in danger of collapse, though it could still be saved, while the actual ruins such as Alleyrac, the Chapelle Barbara, or S. André-de-Rosans, are decaying rapidly. S. Christophe-de-Vachères collapsed completely when an aircraft passed through the sound barrier directly overhead. Such monuments are not perhaps the most elaborate or the most beautiful of Provençal churches, but their decay and disappearance are an irretrievable disaster.

Bourg
St. Andéol

St.-Paul-
Trois-Châteaux

St. Restitut

Rosans

Goudargues

Rhône

Aygues

Vaison-la-Romaine

Malaucène

Mont Ventoux

Orange

Sarrians

Carpentras

Pernes-les-
Fontaines

Venasque

Avignon

Le Thor

Simiane

Nîmes

Sénanque

Tarascon

Cavaillon

Apt

Beaucaire

St. Gabriel

St. Rémy

Les Alpilles

Montagne du Lubéron

St. Gilles

Silvacane

Durance

Montmajour

Arles

Salon

Montagne
Ste. Victoire

Étang de
Vaccarés

Aix-en-Provence

Les Stes.
Maries

Étang
de
Berre

Chaîne de L'Étoile

MEDITERRANEAN SEA

0   5   10   15   20   25 Miles

0   5   10   15   20   25   30   35   40 Km

Marseille

La Ste.-
Baume

Fig. i. Map of Provence

1   *The Historical Background*

IT is difficult to fix the limits of medieval Provence with any precision. The boundaries were never laid down in any very certain fashion, and in any case they were frequently changing. What was and was not Provence also depended upon who you were, where you lived, and what territory you or your overlord happened to be claiming at the time. Perhaps the most satisfactory definition is the ecclesiastical one, laid down by the papal decree of 5 May 450, as a result of the jurisdictional disputes between the metropolitan sees of Arles and Vienne, whereby the primacy of the former was recognized in the ecclesiastical provinces of Arles, Aix, and Embrun. The province of Arles contained the cities of Toulon, Marseille, Avignon, Cavaillon, Carpentras, Orange, S. Paul-Trois-Châteaux, Vaison, and Die; dependant on Aix were Apt, Sisteron, Gap, Riez, Fréjus, and Antibes; dependant on Embrun were Nice, Vence, Glandèves, Senez, and Digne.[1] By and large the western limits of this territory were marked by the left bank of the Rhône, although south of Tarascon the diocese of Arles extended across the Rhône to include the communes of Beaucaire, Fourques, Arles-en-Camargue, and Les Saintes Maries-de-la-Mer.[2] The western boundary continued northwards, coincident with the limits of the dioceses of Avignon, Orange, S.-Paul-Trois-Châteaux and Die, as far as S. Laurent-en-Royans. The northern boundary stretched from S. Laurent to S. Jean-d'Herans in the diocese of Die, and, passing into the province of Aix, the northern and eastern limits were defined by the diocese of Gap, with Guillaume-Peyrousse marking the north-eastern extremity. The eastern limit continued in the province of Embrun, along the boundaries of the dioceses of Embrun and Nice, as far as Monaco. The southern limit was determined by the coastline between Monaco and Les Saintes Maries.

The limits of the ecclesiastical provinces and the limits of 'l'école romane de Provence'

---

[1] The standard sources of reference for the early medieval history of Provence are G. de Manteyer, *La Provence du premier au douzième siècles* (Paris, 1908), and E. Duprat, *La Provence dans le haut moyen âge (406–1113)* (Marseille, 1923). See also C. L. De Vic and J. Vaissete, *Histoire générale Languedoc* (Toulouse, 1874–92), 14 vols. Also the various articles in *Provence Historique*, the *Annales du Midi*, etc., together with the subsequent notes to this chapter.

[2] For the precise limits see Manteyer, op. cit., pp. 163–98, and also M. Achard, *Géographie de la Provence* (Aix, 1787), vol. i, and abbé M. Constantin, *Paroisses de l'ancien diocèse d'Arles* (Aix, 1898). The western boundary extended across the Rhône to include smaller areas of territory at several other points.

were not the same, and the former was somewhat more extensive than the latter. In 1945, J. Vallery-Radot attempted to define more precisely the limits of the school, and the majority of the monuments studied in this essay are situated within the limits of the 'domaine' which he established.[3] Nevertheless, it is worth bearing in mind these wider limits, even though they did not really define a social, economic, or artistic unit, and only to a limited extent a political and administrative one.

By the end of the ninth century the disintegration of the Carolingian empire had given rise to two semi-independent regions in what is now south-eastern France, the kingdoms of Burgundy and of Provence. The latter had been entrusted by Charles the Bald to his brother-in-law Boson in 875. Boson's son Louis, known as the Blind (the result of an ill-fated Italian escapade, when his eyes were put out by a rival, Berengar, at Verona), lived a sightless and comparatively powerless life in Provence from 905 until his death in 928. Real power lay already in the hands of the local counts, one of whom, Hugh, was to become King of Lombardy in 926. It was in the hope of consolidating his Italian position that Hugh, around the year 933, ceded Provence to Rudolph II of Burgundy. Provence thus became part of the enlarged Kingdom of Burgundy, and was to remain so throughout the period here under consideration. In fact this kingdom, formed by political accident, and without any geographic or historic unity, was never much of a reality. However, the situation was further changed by the death of Rudolph III of Burgundy in 1032, when his inheritance passed, not altogether legally, to the Emperor Conrad II.

The acquisition of the kingdom of Burgundy by the Empire inevitably affected the course of development in Provence, and it brought the region directly into the disputed field of imperial–papal relations. In the eleventh and twelfth centuries the power of the Emperor, especially to bestow benefits on his faithful supporters, was fully realized in Provence, but many, particularly the clergy, found the price too high. Equally, while the Emperor could give, he could normally only threaten to take away, and this essential weakness helped to determine much of the course of Provençal politics.

The counts of Provence in the eleventh century were the descendants of a mid-tenth century count Boson, who had bequeathed his authority to his two sons, William and Roubaud. It was Count William who, around the year 972, finally rid Provence of the Saracens. After this victory he bore the title of the Liberator, and, no doubt aided by the power and prestige which his military success afforded him, he introduced a rule of order and organization. However, under his descendants and Roubaud's, this unity disappeared and authority was dispersed between the numerous branches of the family. This development was encouraged by the predominance of an allodial rather than a feudal system of landholding; this system, which was widespread throughout the Midi and Catalonia, and which largely derived from the strong traditions of Roman and Visigothic law, inevitably tended to weaken any effort to exert centralized control.[4]

[3] J. Vallery-Radot, 'La Domaine de l'école romane de Provence', *B.M.* (1945), pp. 5–63.

[4] Regarding the significance of the allodial system in southern France, see A. R. Lewis, *The Development of Southern*

The descendants of William and Roubaud ruled over Provence throughout the eleventh century, with each holding an individual countship, and with one bearing the title of Marquis—although this conferred only nominal superiority. However, by the end of the century the two lines were represented only by females, and almost inevitably this situation resulted, by way of marriages, in the involvement of 'foreign' families in the affairs of Provence, notably the houses of Barcelona and Toulouse, whose rivalry was to characterize much of the twelfth century.[5] The daughter of Roubaud, Emma, had married William, Count of Toulouse, and this line was represented by Raymond of S. Gilles, who became Marquis in 1094. Raymond died in the Holy Land in 1105, and four years later his eldest son, Bertrand (whose legitimacy was anyway open to question), also left for the Crusade, assigning his lands and titles to his brother, Alphonse Jourdain—or rather to a council to administer during Alphonse's minority.

The situation was complicated by the descendants of William the Liberator, who had himself produced two lines. One was represented by Alix, who married Ermengaud, Count of Urgel, and a member of the house of Barcelona, *c.* 1080. This marriage produced William of Urgel, who styled himself Marquis of Provence and Count of Forcalquier, after the death of Raymond of S. Gilles in 1105. The other branch was represented by Cecile, who married Bernard Atton, Count of Béziers and Carcassonne. However, Cecile's claims were usurped by her aunt, Gerberge, who married Gilbert, Count of Gevaudan, and the daughter of this marriage, Douce, in turn married Raymond Berengar, Count of Barcelona, thus bringing another and more powerful branch of the Catalan house into Provence (3 February 1112).

The results of this complicated situation need not be followed here in detail.[6] In effect it was only a magnification of the divisive tendencies which were already apparent in the eleventh century in the rivalries of the various local counts. In the twelfth century these conflicting claims and rivalries frequently resulted in warfare. When Alphonse Jourdain attained his majority in 1119, he found that his uncle, William IX, Count of Poitiers, had usurped his inheritance; in the ensuing civil war Alphonse was supported by Bernard Atton (married to Cecile), while Count William naturally found an ally in Raymond Berengar of Barcelona. Few details of this war are known, although it appears to have been waged fiercely and with considerable destruction—we hear of a siege of Orange in which the cathedral was badly damaged, as well as the more well-known outrages at S. Gilles.[7] Agreement was eventually reached in September 1125,

French and Catalan Society, 718–1050 (Texas University, 1965). The influence of Roman law may be illustrated by the fact that a Provençal summary of the Justinianic Code, entitled *Lo Codi*, was drawn up *c.* 1149 for the judges of the Arles region. See C. H. Haskins, *The Renaissance of the Twelfth Century* (New York, 1962) (Meridian Books edition), p. 209. For a detailed study of the revival of Roman Law see M.-L. Carlin, *La Pénétration du droit romain dans les actes de la pratique Provençale (XIᵉ–XIIIᵉ siècles), (Bibliothèque d'histoire du droit et droit romain*, vol. xi, Paris, 1967).

[5] See C. Higounet, 'La rivalité des maisons de Toulouse et de Barcelone pour la prépondérance méridionale', *Mélanges . . . dédiés à la mémoire de Louis Halphen* (Paris, 1951), pp. 313–22. This study emphasizes the importance of the struggle in a European context.

[6] For the political history of the period see primarily V. L. Bourrilly and R. Busquet, *La Provence au moyen âge (1112–1481)* (Marseille, 1924), and P. Fournier, *Le Royaume d'Arles et de Vienne* (Paris, 1891).

[7] Bourrilly and Busquet, op. cit., p. 10.

when control of territory north of the Durance, together with the châteaux of Beaucaire and Valabrègue, passed to Alphonse Jourdain. The remainder, between the Alps, the Durance, the Rhône and the sea went to Raymond Berengar of Barcelona.

The presence of the house of Barcelona was firmly established in Provence by the 1125 settlement. In the following years Raymond Berengar further strengthened his position by introducing institutional and governmental features derived from his Spanish possessions, bringing order to an area which had lacked any firm centralized control for over a century. The link with Spain was further emphasized on the ecclesiastical side; many of the dependencies of S. Victor at Marseille were in Catalonia, including the important house of Ripoll, where Raymond Berengar was buried in 1131.[8] This connection was maintained throughout the century, as for example when, in 1139, William, Archbishop of Arles, was empowered by Innocent II to administer the vacant see of Tarragona.[9] Equally, some Spaniards came to occupy high positions in the Provençal church, such as Berengar, Bishop of Orange.[10] In addition, the links between Provence and the western Midi and Catalonia were reflected in the general social conditions. It was these links which made it both easy and natural for the barons who followed Raymond of S. Gilles on the crusade to be styled Provençals, to distinguish them from their northern French and Norman companions—even though the majority of the southern contingent did not, strictly speaking, come from Provence. By the same token, the inhabitants of Provence proper could recognize in Raymond Berengar an attitude and an understanding similar to their own—and this was something they could never find in the Emperor.[11]

On the death of Raymond Berengar, his inheritance was divided equally between his two sons, confusingly named Raymond Berengar and Berengar Raymond, with the latter holding Provence. The two brothers co-operated closely, supporting each other against their opponents[12] and maintaining the links between their two regions. Consequently both were involved in the most serious Provençal disturbances of the mid-twelfth century, the Les Baux wars. Raymond of Baux was an old crusading companion of Raymond of S. Gilles, and later he appears to have been on excellent terms with Raymond Berengar the Elder. However, in the quarrel between Berengar and Alphonse Jourdain, Raymond of Baux sided with the latter, and was one of those excommunicated in 1121 for his part in the attacks on S. Gilles. Clearly Raymond had a turbulent and unruly nature, but his quarrel with Berengar had its foundations in the growing political ambitions of the house of Baux—ambitions which now had some

---

[8] On S. Victor see the *Recueil des actes du Congrès sur l'histoire de l'abbaye S. Victor de Marseille, 29–30 janvier, 1966* (*Provence Historique*, vol. xvi, fasc. 65, July/Sept. 1966), especially E. Baratier, 'La fondation et l'étendue du temporel de l'abbaye de St. Victor', pp. 395–441.

[9] *G.C.N.*, iii, nos. 535, 537.

[10] The epitaph on his tombstone, preserved in the Musée de la ville d'Orange, opens with the words: 'Nobilis Hispanus Presul Berengarius hujus Urbis in hoc modico conditus est tumolo.'

[11] See Lewis, op. cit., for a detailed study of the unifying factors in the society of the Midi.

[12] Thus Raymond Berengar stepped in to settle a renewed dispute between Alphonse Jourdain and Berengar Raymond in 1134. See Bourrilly and Busquet, op. cit., p. 14.

ground, for Raymond had married Etiennette, the sister of Douce, so becoming the brother-in-law of Raymond Berengar. In the succeeding years the quarrel between the two was carried on more or less continuously, frequently breaking out into skirmishes or longer campaigns, particularly after the death of Raymond Berengar the Elder (whose sons carried on his policies and his quarrels). Berengar Raymond died in 1145, leaving only a young son (inevitably called Raymond Berengar), and in the following years Raymond Berengar of Barcelona carried on the struggle with Baux, until Berengar's death in 1162. Again, the details of these wars need not be given, but one detail of the peacetime campaign is worth noting. Raymond of Baux made a serious effort to enlist imperial support for his claims, and in 1145 he obtained a diploma from Conrad III, acknowledging his position and granting him several important privileges, amongst them the right to establish a mint at Arles. No doubt Conrad's action was intended to show that, in his role as King of Burgundy, he exercised real power in Provence, and that those who were prepared to acknowledge his suzerainty could expect real rewards. In fact the lords of Baux, whose imperial loyalty was based only on political expedience, were to learn that they could trust neither the reality nor the constancy of the rewards. Conrad's diploma was confirmed by Barbarossa shortly after his accession, but the two Raymond Berengars, realizing that Frederick was indeed an emperor to be reckoned with, put their own case before him in 1162. With the prospect of support from this powerful house, both in financial terms and in recognition of Antipope Victor IV, the Emperor had no hesitation in brushing aside Conrad's diploma and recognizing Raymond Berengar III as Count of Provence.

On the death of Raymond Berengar III in 1166, his inheritance passed to Alphonso II, King of Aragon (eldest son of Raymond Berengar, count of Barcelona, who had died in 1162). However, he was challenged by Raymond V, Count of Toulouse, who attempted to reassert his line's ancient claims to Provence. Alphonso secured the support of the majority of local Provençal counts, as well as of the clergy, and after an obscure struggle Raymond V abandoned his claims in a financial deal in 1176. In the remaining years of the twelfth century Provence was relatively peaceful, although there remained numerous localized disputes, which flared into violence from time to time. Alphonso was represented in the region successively by his brothers, Raymond Berengar and Sancho, and Sancho's son, Alphonso. It was only after this Alphonso's death in 1209 that involvement in the Albigensian wars brought a return to more general unrest.

THE CHURCH IN PROVENCE

The annexation of the Kingdom of Burgundy by the Empire was probably initially welcomed by the church. From their point of view, the higher clergy were probably thankful for a sovereign who was far removed from the incessant rivalries of the local counts, and who might be prevailed upon to defend the church from their constant depredations. From the imperial point of view, the Provençal clergy was a potentially valuable ally. Thus when Henry III went to Rome for his coronation in 1046 he was accompanied by the Archbishops of Arles, Besançon, and Lyon—a real, though premature demonstration of an alliance between the Emperor and his Burgundian clergy.

That this alliance was largely stillborn was partially the result of the eleventh-century reform of the church.[13] The efforts of Gregory VII and his legates, notably Hugh of Die, met with a largely favourable response from the clergy of the region. In the first half of the eleventh century the Provençal church had undoubtedly been in a lamentable condition.[14] Its most obvious fault was its increasingly secular nature, largely occasioned by what Professor Lewis has termed the 'new militarism' of lay society,[15] and reflected in the proliferation of castles. The castle had become the political and administrative unit, and possession of a castle was nine points of the law in the surrounding country-side. Unscrupulous lay lords tended to establish castles on or near ecclesiastical property, and this forced the church to retaliate, and so partake itself of the militarist rule. However, the organization of the Peace and Truce of God established an alternative approach which was welcomed by the church, and which naturally opened the way for the Gregorian reform.[16]

Councils at Avignon in 1060, 1063, and 1080 mark the progress of these reforms, and although the deposition of a few simonaical and recalcitrant bishops was necessary, notably Aicard of Arles and Ripert of Gap, the opposition of the clergy was remarkably small. The local counts on the other hand were largely united in resisting reform, regarding a strengthened church as a potentially dangerous rival. Certainly the reforms did not lessen the determination of the bishops to defend and increase their temporal domains, and in other ways too the reforms were far from perfect. Certain families preserved their control of the local see, with the right to dispose of it to one of their members, but by and large the bishops and archbishops were elected regularly by the chapter alone. However, it was perhaps partially as a result of the slight latitude allowed in the interpretation of the canons of reform that the Provençal clergy was to remain faithful and constant in its support of the papacy. Also, from the time of reform, and especially from the establishment of the regular chapters, the Provençal church enters a period of great prosperity.[17]

At the same time the Popes themselves were not distant, unseen figures, as the emperors were. Provençal delegates figure prominently at the Roman councils of 1123, 1139, 1179, and 1215, and in addition there were numerous visits by individual bishops

---

[13] For an excellent study of the ecclesiastical development of the region see B. Bligny, *L'Église et les ordres religieux dans le royaume de Bourgogne aux XIe et XIIe siècles* (Paris, 1960).

[14] For a particular study, see N. Didier, *Les Églises de Sisteron et de Forcalquier du XIe siècle à la Révolution* (Paris, 1954), ch. 1.

[15] Lewis, op. cit., chs. 12 and 13. The militarism was not necessarily new, but it was perhaps more obvious, cf. G. Duby, 'Les Villes du Sud-Est de la Gaule du VIIIe au XIe siècle', *La Città nell'alto medioevo* (Centro Italiano di Studi sull' alto Medioevo) (Spoleto, 1959), pp. 231–76.

[16] The movements of the Peace and Truce of God were of course centred in the Auvergne and south-western Languedoc, and the extent of their influence in Provence requires further investigation.

[17] Some details of the rise in prosperity of the church of Avignon, and the part played by the chapter, are given below, Ch. 3, pp. 39–43. One study, M. Fontana, *La Réforme grégorienne en Provence orientale* (Publications de la Faculté des Lettres d'Aix, Travaux et Mémoires viii) (Aix, 1957), was not available to me.

to the papal presence.[18] Equally, papal visits to Provence, resulting either from choice or necessity, became relatively commonplace.[19] The highest point in this amicable relationship was probably marked by the pontificate of Adrian IV, whose links with Provence dated from his time at S. Ruf in the 1130s.[20] However, throughout the twelfth century there was a continuing series of papal bulls granting or confirming possessions and privileges to the Provençal churches.

Papal friendship and support inevitably made the Provençal clergy less dependent on the emperor, if not overtly hostile to him. Archbishops and bishops were in no hurry to fulfil their obligations as vassals to such a distant suzerain—as is witnessed by the complaint of Lothair against Bernard Garin, archbishop of Arles, in 1136.[21] At times, if the emperor became too pressing, it was necessary to make a submission to him, and this normally resulted in the granting of an imperial diploma, confirming possessions, privileges, and regalia, such as that of Conrad III to Arles in 1145.[22]

This state of affairs was somewhat altered by the accession of Frederick Barbarossa, whose energetic policies called for a more positive attitude on the part of the Provençal clergy. The Emperor's initial successes left them with little opportunity but to toe, at least nominally, the imperial line. However, as far as possible, they held themselves in reserve, unwilling to give any very firm demonstration of support for the Emperor. The Archbishop of Arles pleaded sickness as his reason for not attending the Diet of Besançon, although the Bishop of Avignon was present. Arles sent a representative to the Council of Pavia, and the Bishops of Avignon and Cavaillon were present at Lodi. The year 1162 was one of the high points in Frederick's career; the victor at Milan, he received the homage of Raymond Berengar III and the submission of all the Provençal clergy. For them, as for Alexander III, the Emperor's power must have seemed irresistible. At the same time the Provençal church reaped some of the benefits of victory, in the form of imperial donations and confirmations.

Nevertheless, the settlement of the peace of Venice was welcomed with relief by the Provençal church. The subsequent coronation of Frederick as King of Burgundy, which took place on 30 July 1178, in S. Trophime at Arles, was the signal for a major turn-out of the Provençal episcopate. Besides the Archbishop of Arles, Raymond of Bollène, who performed the ceremony, the Archbishops of Aix and Vienne were present, together with the Bishops of Avignon, Carpentras, Cavaillon, S. Paul-Trois-Châteaux, and Vaison. Most of the local aristocracy were also there, with the exception of the count, Raymond Berengar III, who no doubt did not wish to be seen submitting to

---

[18] Bourrilly and Busquet, op. cit., p. 170.

[19] The following may be mentioned: Urban II, 1095, 1096; Gelasius II, 1118; Calixtus II (Guy of Vienne), 1119; Innocent II, 1130, 1132; Alexander III, 1162, 1165; and almost certainly Eugenius III in 1147 on his way to Lyon. See A. Potthast and P. Jaffé (eds.), *Regesta Pontificum Romanorum ab condita ecclesia* (Berlin, 1875, and Leipzig, 1885-8).

[20] This is despite the fact that Adrian's time at S. Ruf was not altogether happy. His biographer, Boso, relates that after a while the brothers came to regret having elected a foreigner to rule over them (Adrian was of course English). The resulting dispute was only settled by the intervention of Pope Eugenius. See H. K. Mann, *The Lives of the Popes in the Middle Ages*, vol. ix (London, 1914), p. 239.

[21] *G.C.N.*, iii, no. 531.

[22] Bourrilly and Busquet, op. cit., p. 171.

anyone in the heart of his own domains. However, this demonstration by the clergy must be seen as a thankful recognition of the peace, rather than an endorsement of any of Frederick's former policies. In the following years the relationship between the Emperor and the Provençal church remained calm, since neither Frederick, nor his son Henry VI, were able to regain the position vis-à-vis the papacy which had existed in 1162. This was no doubt a relief for the Provençal clergy themselves, who had little real interest in international affairs of this sort; moreover, the cost of international involvement normally exceeded the fringe benefits (in the form of papal or imperial gifts and confirmations).

Relations with the counts of Provence were always of more pressing concern for the church than relations with the Emperor. Many bishops were active as councillors and arbitrators in local disputes, and they consistently exploited these functions to expand and consolidate their own positions. To some extent the almost constant involvement of the higher clergy in comital affairs continued to work against the well-founded aims of the Gregorian reforms. Perpetually active at court, bishops seldom had fixed residences, and appeared in their dioceses only at irregular intervals. The chapters of canons were of course designed to run affairs in the absence of the bishop, but the latter, primarily concerned with the protection of his own territorial interests, too often regarded the chapter as an adversary rather than a collaborator; some examples of the resulting disputes are given in the course of this essay.[23] This was not always the case, and there are some notable exceptions—the Archbishops of Arles, for example, seem to have been on good terms with their chapters throughout the twelfth century. In addition the relations between bishops and their chapters tended to improve in the second half of the twelfth century, when an increasing number of prelates emerged from the ranks of the chapters themselves.

It is the chapters of canons, with their new wealth and authority, which must be regarded as the instigators of much of the building activity during this period. Provençal Romanesque, the chief monuments of which are the great city cathedrals, was a canonical achievement. It is notable that in this region the great abbeys produced very little in the way of building; Montmajour remained unfinished; S. Victor was refurbished, but not rebuilt in any grandiose fashion, and it seems hard to believe that the present small church was once the head of an order which could rival Cluny in its influence. Perhaps the most striking of all is the Cluniac house of S. Gilles, planned so magnificently but apparently never finished, which remains today as a monument to the uncertainty, financial insecurity, and general malaise of monasticism. Only the great Cistercian abbeys of Le Thoronet, Silvacane, and Sénanque can rival cathedrals such as S. Trophime, Arles, or Notre-Dame-des-Doms, Avignon, and they are of course largely free of decorative embellishment.[24] Yet it is difficult to discover the explanation for the lack

---

[23] See below, Ch. 3, pp. 40–41.

[24] For the Cistercian buildings in Provence, see M. Aubert, *L'Architecture cistercienne en France* (Paris, 1948), 2 vols., and the relevant articles in *C.A.* (1909, 1932, 1963).

of fulfilled artistic development in the major Provençal houses, for during the eleventh and first half of the twelfth centuries they were undoubtedly prosperous. Richard, abbot of S. Victor (1079–1108), was an energetic supporter of the Gregorian reform, and under his direction the prestige of the Marseille house grew steadily. Its dependancies were scattered throughout the Midi, and have already been noted as one of the features linking Provence with the house of Barcelona. The enjoyment of continuing papal favours, expressed in donations and confirmations, and numerous generous concessions from local benefactors, gave S. Victor an enormous territorial wealth, which reached its highest point in the mid-twelfth century,[25] and a similar prosperity was enjoyed by the other great Provençal abbeys, such as Lérins and Montmajour.[26] The twelfth century also saw the propagation and expansion of the new military orders, the Templars and Hospitallers, and the latter, first established at S. Gilles, were widely represented in Provence. This expansion, more military than ecclesiastical, which was most noticeable in the second half of the twelfth century, was of course paralleled by the penetration of Cistercian austerity into the region and it was at this same time that a decline set in for the older houses, notably S. Victor, which by the end of the century was rapidly losing its prestige and was heavily in debt to the Jews.

The new orders were undoubtedly partially responsible for the decline of the old houses, but the strength of the regular canons must be regarded as a major contributory factor. Economically the canons were in a better position than the monastic orders, for their possessions, acquired relatively recently and rapidly, tended to be grouped in the immediately surrounding region, instead of being widely scattered, and consequently their domain was easier to administer efficiently.

While the canonical movement can be seen as the strongest and most successful development, there were other, external forces which inevitably reflected upon the church. The pilgrimages to S. Gilles and to the shrine of Mary Magdalen in the Sainte-Baume were undoubtedly influential in bringing men, and of course money, to the region. The origins and early evolution of both these cults is largely obscure, but they do not seem to emerge before the mid-eleventh century. Their subsequent growth benefited from the fact that pilgrims bound for Rome (or, from the south, for Santiago) passed through Provence, and therefore could easily be persuaded to visit these shrines.[27] An equally obscure but perhaps equally significant growth was that of heresy. Peter the Venerable was shocked by its magnitude in the dioceses of Embrun and Gap in the 1130s, and it seems probable that, although we have little information about it,

---

[25] See B. Guérard (ed.), *Cartulaire de l'abbaye de St. Victor de Marseille* (*Collection des cartulaires de France*, vol. ix), Paris, 1857, 2 vols., and n. 8 above.

[26] A factor in all this is certainly the financial involvement of the major traditional houses. Lay society tended to see them as lax, idle, and rich, and the obvious source of financial aid. There were various ways of applying pressure for loans, and monastic treasuries were frequently depleted in this way.

[27] I am grateful to Mr. C. Hohler for pointing out to me that the cults of both S. Gilles and Mary Magdalen depend to some extent on northern influences. It seems entirely possible that the legend of Mary Magdalen arrived in Provence from Vézelay, rather than the other way round; the rhyming office of S. Gilles was written by Fulbert of Chartres, and the legend itself may have developed in the north.

Waldensians, Petrobrusians, and Cathars provided one of the major problems for the Provençal clergy throughout the twelfth century. Their failure to meet this problem is witnessed by the fact that the Albigensians provided both the name and the excuse for the thirteenth-century crusade.

Nevertheless, the picture that emerges of the Provençal church in the eleventh and twelfth centuries is one of a relatively efficient organization, which was designed to run, and succeeded in running, smoothly without too much supervision or interference from the highest ranks. In general terms, and with of course any number of individual exceptions, it does not appear to have been excessively spiritual, but nor was it unduly corrupt. While it produced few men of international standing, it did produce many who were prepared to work to maintain and increase the independence and authority of the church in general, and of their own position in particular.

THE ECONOMY

Because of its geographical position, Provence has always been a commercially active centre, since it provides one of the obvious links between the Mediterranean and the north. In the medieval period, as also today, the prosperity of the commercial sector therefore depended very largely upon the efficacy of the lines of communication.[28] On the map of France it appears that Provence possesses a valuable natural asset, the river Rhône; however, the nature of this river makes it somewhat unsatisfactory for commercial traffic, on account of its very strong current. Even after the invention of the steam engine it proved difficult to tow loaded barges upstream, and in the Middle Ages, when only man- or horse-power was available, it must have been extremely arduous. What traffic the Rhône carried was mostly downstream, and it is probable that many barges were broken up and sold for lumber once they had made the journey, instead of being returned.[29]

Much more suitable for commercial transport were the surviving Roman roads.[30] Four main highways entered Provence. The first of these was the Via Domitia, which ran from Spain through Gallia Narbonensis to the Rhône. The crossing of the Rhône was apparently made by ferry at Beaucaire. There were two roads connecting Provence with Italy; the Via Aurelia, which was the coast road from Arles to Genoa, and the route over the pass of Mons Matrona (Mont Genèvre). In addition, there was the road built by Agrippa in 22 B.C., connecting Marseille, Arles, and Lyon. This road opened up the north and north-west of Europe to Provençal merchants, for it connected with

[28] On this subject consult the chapter entitled 'Les routes du moyen âge', by J. Hubert, in *Les Routes de France depuis les origines jusqu'à nos jours (Cahiers de Civilisation)* (Paris, 1959); L. Holland, *Traffic Ways about France in the Dark Ages (500–1150)* (University of Pennsylvania, 1919); Y. Renouard, 'Les voies de communication entre pays de la méditerranée et pays d'atlantique au moyen âge', *Mélanges . . . dédiés à Louis Halphen* (Paris, 1951), pp. 587–94.

[29] M. Bertrand Davezac, of Indiana University, informs me that as late as the 1850s wine was shipped down the Dordogne, whose current is far weaker than that of the Rhône, to Bordeaux, and that the barges were always broken up for firewood rather than make the return journey.

[30] For the Roman roads in Provence see L. A. Constans, *Arles antique (Bibliothèque des écoles françaises d'Athènes et de Rome)* (1921).

the network of Roman roads which centred on Lyon. The absence of major towns on the right bank of the Rhône again indicates that it was this road rather than the river which was the major artery of transport.

The efficacy of this transport system depended to some extent upon the existence of regular and reliable methods of crossing the Rhône. The normal method of passage was by small boat, and indeed it was not until the seventeenth century that a bridge of boats was introduced between Beaucaire and Tarascon.[31] The importance and scarcity of bridges at this period is underlined by the construction of the Pont S. Bénézet at Avignon late in the twelfth century. Bénézet's vision, which no doubt reflected actual conditions, was of crowds of pilgrims waiting to cross the Rhône on their way to Rome.[32]

Although communications to the north were exclusively overland, to the south the Roman roads were supplemented by the sea routes.[33] The sea journey from Marseille to the Italian coast was short, safe, and relatively rapid, and probably carried more traffic than the overland routes. When Gelasius II was forced to leave Rome in 1118 he took a boat from Pisa to Marseille; the continuation of his journey to S. Gilles may also have been by water, up the Little Rhône. The sea routes of course also led further afield, to all corners of the Mediterranean and beyond, and the presence of English and Scandinavian vessels in the Mediterranean ports was commonplace.

In short, during the Middle Ages, as in the Roman period, the easiest and most natural lines of communication led to Italy and the south. At the same time the road north was the essential outlet for the dissemination of the traffic which came to Provence from the south. The prosperity of the region therefore depended to a considerable extent upon its role as a commercial clearing-house for Mediterranean trade. During the eleventh and twelfth centuries there was a considerable revival in the indigenous industries, and especially in agriculture, in which the church played a prominent part; but the region never produced enough to constitute a significant export, or even to support itself. Indeed, in 1305 the exportation of food products from Provence was forbidden altogether.[34] Leather goods were produced in several centres, although the raw material was mostly imported, and dyestuffs were also manufactured; but the best-known products were probably wine and oil, together with soap from Marseille.

The two main commercial centres were the great and ancient ports of Arles and Marseille, both with a long history of commercial enterprise, and, to an extent, of rivalry. The former was better placed in relation to the land routes, but the latter was a better and more accessible port.[35] However, Arles still no doubt deserved the description

---

[31] See I. Fournier, 'Le passage du Rhône entre Tarascon et Beaucaire au Moyen Âge et jusqu'à 1670', *Revue des études anciennes*, 9 (1907), 21–6.　　　[32] H. Pigeonneau, *Histoire du commerce de la France* (Paris, 1885), i, 191.

[33] See A. Dupont, *Les Relations commerciales entre les cités maritimes du Languedoc et les cités méditerranéennes de l'Espagne et de l'Italie du xe au xiiie siècles* (Nîmes, 1942).

[34] See R. Brun, *La Ville de Salon au moyen âge* (Publications de la Société d'Études Provençales, vi) (Aix, 1924).

[35] Arles was then much nearer to the sea than it is now. The Italian Franciscan Salimbene de Adam recorded in his chronicle of 1248 that it was five *miles* (about 7·5 km.) from the sea, whereas today it is some 30 km. See *Sur les routes d'Europe au xiiie siècle. Chroniques traduites et commentées par Marie-Thérèse Laureilhe* (Paris, 1959), p. 181.

of it given by Theodulf, bishop of Orléans, at the end of the eighth century, as the place to which all the diverse treasures of the East flowed.[36] Marseille was an equally cosmopolitan city, with its large Jewish community, and Greek, Italian, and north African merchants always present. Much has been made of Marseillais traders in the Latin Kingdom, and although recent studies have shown that the series of charters on which these claims were based are all forgeries, it still seems certain that some Provençal merchants were active in the Holy Land from an early date.[37] The Provençal stake in the first Crusade no doubt paid off well, and on other fronts it is clear that the connection was kept up. Gibelin of Arles became Patriarch of Jerusalem (1110), and Berengar of Orange was legate there, whence we are told he brought back ornaments for his church.[38]

The continual passage of merchants and the presence of foreigners undoubtedly had its effect on the artistic development of the region. The most famous group of foreign merchants passing regularly through Provence were the Jews, the Râdhânyya described by Ibn Khordâdhbeh (in the ninth century) as versatile linguists, whose travels extended between northern Europe and southern China.[39] According to the Arabic chronicler they exported eunuchs, female slaves, boys, deer, beaver skins, sable and other furs, and German swords, and brought back in return various products of the east, including musk, aloes, camphor, and perfumes. Merchants from Provence also travelled abroad, as did artists, who sometimes worked far from home, especially in the Holy Land.[40] It is by no means impossible that foreign artists worked in Provence in the same manner. The famous visit of certain canons of S. Ruf to the marble quarries of Carrara in 1156 gives proof of a continuing artistic connection with Italy.[41] There are numerous artistic links with Spain, especially with the region of Tarragona.[42] To the north too there are artistic connections of a less tangible but more tantalizing nature—the occurrence of column figures in Provençal cloisters, for example, suggests some relationship with the recently reconstituted cloister of Châlons-sur-Marne,[43] and there is of course the more famous problem of the controversial links between the façade of S. Gilles and Chartres.[44]

[36] Theodulfus, 'Versus contra Iudices', *Monumenta Germaniae Historica, Poetae Latini, Aevi Carolini* (Berlin, 1881), vol. i, p. 497.

[37] The traditional view is given by Bourrilly and Busquet, op. cit., pp. 436–8; it is revised by R. Pernoud, *Histoire du commerce de Marseille (Publiée par la Chambre de Commerce de Marseille)*, vol. i, pt. ii, *Le Moyen Âge, jusqu'à 1291* (Paris, 1949), pp. 138–9.

[38] His epitaph reads: 'Illum Legatum Iherusolima sensit et inde Ornamenta sue detulit aecclesie.'

[39] Ibn Khordâdhbeh, *Kitâb al-Masâlik wa'l-Mamâlik (Liber viarum et regnorum)*, ed. M. J. De Goeje (*Bibliotheca Geographorum Arabicorum*, vol. vi) (Leyden, 1889), pp. 114–15. However, for a qualifying view of the Râdhânyya see Cahen, C., 'Y a-t-il eu des Rahdânites?' *Revue des études juives*, 14 ser., iii (July/Dec. 1964), 499–505.

[40] This subject has not been properly studied; the best treatment is still C. Enlart, *Les Monuments des croisés dans le royaume de Jérusalem* (Paris, 1925–8).

[41] V. Mortet and P. Deschamps, *Recueil des textes relatifs à l'histoire de l'architecture, XIIᵉ–XIIIᵉ siècles* (Paris, 1929), no. XXXVII, p. 96.

[42] See V. Lassalle, 'L'influence provençale au cloître et à la cathédrale de Tarragone', *Mélanges offerts à René Crozet* (Poitiers, 1966), ii, 873–9.

[43] The reality of this link was emphasized by the exhibition of Gothic art in Paris in 1968, where the column figure from Avignon was exhibited alongside the Châlons fragments. (Douzième exposition du Conseil de l'Europe, Paris, 1968.)

[44] The most extreme contribution to the argument was that of A. Priest, 'The Masters of the West Façade of Chartres', *Art Studies*, i (1922), 28–44. While Priest's theory that the same master worked at S. Gilles and Chartres must be

There is even a suggestion of an artistic connection with England, and when the extraordinary Gervais of Tilbury arrived in Provence he would have seen buildings decorated with chevron ornament.[45]

In short, Provence was an active and even lively region. The towns were flourishing, and limited communal independence was gained early in the major cities. Despite the feuds and the fighting, the aristocracy flourished too, and a by-product of their prosperity was their patronage, which contributed to the spectacular growth of Provençal poetry.[46] The reformed and consolidated church provided a stabilizing element in this otherwise somewhat amorphous social fabric, giving a sense of unity in lieu of any strong centralized civil authority. It is against this sort of background that one must attempt to place the development of Romanesque art in the region; obviously the building of churches was to a great extent influenced by particular local conditions, and whenever possible these conditions should be taken into consideration. However, in a more general sense, the social, political, and economic development of Provence suggests that artistic growth was possible, and indeed likely, from the middle of the eleventh century onwards.

rejected, there can be no doubt that there are some sort of links between portions of the S. Gilles façade and some early Gothic sculpture. Some discussion of these problems is given in the final chapter.

[45] Gervais of Tilbury became marshal of Arles in 1209, and while there wrote the *Otia Imperilia*. He could have seen chevron in Arles itself, on the doorway of S. Honorat-des-Alyscamps.

[46] At the same time it must be remembered that the troubadours were more prominent in Languedoc than in Provence proper. See A. Jeanroy, *La Poésie lyrique des troubadours* (Toulouse, Paris, 1934).

2 Architectural Decoration in Provence during the Eleventh Century

LITTLE is known of eleventh-century sculpture in Provence. The best-known work is the tombstone of Isarn, abbot of S. Victor, who died in 1048, but this stark and impressive piece has always been something of a puzzle. It appears totally isolated in the region, and it becomes all the more curious if it is compared with the more or less contemporary but entirely dissimilar chip-carved tomb of Count Geoffrey of Provence, from Montmajour (c. 1063), which is decorated with interlace patterns. Neither of these pieces can in fact be regarded as typical of Provençal sculpture, and it is evident that there was no spectacular revival of monumental carving in the region in the eleventh century. On the other hand, there is a considerable amount of eleventh-century sculpture preserved in Provence, in the form of capitals and reliefs. These are little-known, and have been barely studied, but they are essential to an understanding of the development of the Romanesque style in the region.

(a) THE CAPITALS

Any discussion of early Romanesque capitals in Provence is hampered by the almost total lack of firmly dated evidence, and therefore conclusions are largely based upon a formal analysis of decoration.[1] There are a few dates which may be deduced, although none is in any way precise. Firstly, there are the capitals of the chapel of S. Pierre at Montmajour and of the so-called baptistery at Venasque. Montmajour was founded in 949, when a local noblewoman, Teucinda, gave the site to a group of Benedictines.[2] In December 963, Pope Leo VIII placed the new monastery directly under the protection of the Holy See. An undated charter of Pons de Marignane, Archbishop of Arles, who died in 1030, records the dedication of the crypt of Ste Croix, and the granting of indulgences to those aiding the work, then in progress, on the church of Notre-Dame. Neither of these buildings appears to have survived, and the chapel of S. Pierre is not

---

[1] The discussion is also hampered by the lack of a proper inventory. The only published inventory is for the Département of the Basses-Alpes, and is in the enterprising series *Sites et Monuments de Haute-Provence*. Entitled *Les Monuments du haut moyen âge: inventaire* (published by *Les Alpes de Lumière*, no. 34, 1964), this small volume, though not a complete inventory, is invaluable, and points up the lack of similar studies for the other Départements of the region.

[2] On Montmajour see primarily Dom Chantelou, *Histoire de Montmajour* (printed in *Revue historique de Provence*, 1890–1); Labande, *C.A.* (1909), pp. 140–54; F. Benoit, *L'Abbaye de Montmajour* (*Petites monographies*, Paris, 1936); W. Kiess, *Montmajour, Eine Stätte provencalischer Romanik* (*Schriften der Staatsbauschule Stuttgart*, Heft 31, 1965).

mentioned. The present chapel of Ste Croix, which stands some distance to the east of the monastic buildings, is not a crypt, and although its date is open to dispute, it certainly does not appear to be early eleventh century. The chapel of S. Pierre is largely cut into the rock, and it is of course tempting to surmise that the Ste Croix of 1030 subsequently became S. Pierre, perhaps when the new chapel of Ste Croix was built, but there is no evidence to support such a hypothesis. None the less, a date of *c.* 1030 seems eminently reasonable for the capitals of S. Pierre (Pl. 1). This conclusion is based upon the close links between these Montmajour capitals and those of the Venasque baptistery, and the relationship of both to the cloister capitals at Tournus, which are reasonably, though by no means certainly, dated before the death of Abbot Ardain in 1056.[3] The stylistic relationship between these three groups, which P.-A. Fevrier first pointed out,[4] is close, and there is a possibility that they are the work of the same *atelier* (Pls. 2–12). Consequently, provided the Tournus dating is correct, the Provençal work can probably be dated *c.* 1030–50.

Other datable capitals occur in the porch of the church of S. Victor at Marseille, which is one of the surviving sections of the church built by Abbot Isarn and dedicated in 1040.[5] It is perhaps open to question whether the rib-vaulted porch was complete by this date, but, on stylistic grounds, it is reasonable to attribute the capitals to this epoch (Pl. 21).

The third dated monument is the church of Bourg-S. Andéol, which is in the Vivarais, on the right bank of the Rhône, and just beyond the borders of the province of Arles.[6] However, the architecture of the church is related to Provençal work, and its inclusion here is warranted by the fact that it can be dated fairly securely. In 1108 it was ceded to the canons of S. Ruf, Avignon, who are presumed to have undertaken its reconstruction. It was consecrated in 1119 by Pope Calixtus II. This church was subsequently much altered by the addition of a thirteenth-century tower, by the destruction of a western apse in the eighteenth century,[7] by disastrous restorations in the nineteenth, and most recently by bomb damage in 1944.[8] The interior retains none of its original decoration *in situ*, but there are four capitals, stacked upside down against the east wall of the south transept, which almost certainly come from the original blind arcade around the apse.[9] Since these capitals appear to come from the east end of the building, one is justified in dating them shortly after 1108, and certainly before 1119. Thus these

---

[3] See J. Virey, *S. Philibert de Tournus* (*Petites monographies*, Paris, n.d.); J. Vallery-Radot, *S. Philibert de Tournus* (Paris, 1960).

[4] P.-A. Fevrier, *C.A.* (1963), pp. 348–64.

[5] F. Benoit, *L'Abbaye de S. Victor et l'église de la Major à Marseille* (*Petites monographies*, Paris, 1936).

[6] See J. Messié, *Bourg-S. Andéol; Notice historique et guide* (Bourg-S. Andéol, n.d. [*c.* 1965]); M. Aubert, *C.A.* (1923), pp. 185–9; M. Joly, *L'Architecture des églises romanes du Vivarais* (Paris, 1967).

[7] A western apse, which is still preserved, occurs in the parish church of La Garde Adhémar, which lies on the Provençal bank of the Rhône, almost directly opposite Bourg-S. Andéol.

[8] An Allied air-raid on 15 August 1944 was intended to destroy the suspension bridge across the Rhône. The south transept of the church suffered considerable damage, and large numbers of the inhabitants were killed. Despite two further raids, the bridge (which the Germans were not using) remained intact, and, fearing further Allied support, the Bourguésans put it out of action themselves.

[9] The dimensions of the capitals coincide with those in the restored arcade, and at least two of the new arcade capitals appear to be copies of those now in the transept.

four battered capitals take on considerable significance, since they are amongst the small amount of Provençal sculpture which can be securely dated to the first quarter of the twelfth century (Pls. 16–18).

Within this meagre framework of dates, one can attempt to build up a picture of eleventh-century capital sculpture in Provence. The first and most obvious feature is the almost total absence of figured or historiated capitals, and the overwhelming preponderance of foliate types. Figured capitals do occur occasionally—at S. Pierre, Venéjan, at Goudargues,[10]—but they are out of place, handled crudely and without enthusiasm. It is not until one gets further northwards, into the central Rhône valley, that the figured capital comes to life in the eleventh century—as it does, for example, in the crypt at Cruas (Ardèche).[11]

The predominance of the foliage capital in Provence can probably be explained in terms of the Roman inheritance of the region. Despite the political links with Lombardy and with the Empire, the cubic capital does not occur in Provence.[12] Instead, the related form of the chamfered block is used. The difference between these two forms is comparatively slight in terms of manufacture, but in visual terms it is very marked. The cubic capital is formed by rounding off the lower edges of the block, producing a convex surface; in the chamfered block capital the lower edges are cut back to produce a concave surface. The resulting silhouette resembles an embryonic Corinthian shape (Fig. 2*b*); moreover, the shape produced by the cutting of the edge of the block is naturally suggestive of a lanceolate leaf. A rather more sophisticated type also occurs, on which the edges of the block begin to be cut back just below the top of the capital, and the lower part is rounded off instead of being left octagonal (Fig. 2*c*). Thus a proper bell is produced, and the resulting capital comes a stage nearer to Corinthian form. The top of the capital becomes the abacus, and usually carries rose and volutes. A final elaboration of the type is to cut back the edges of the block in two stages, one above the other, producing a two-tiered effect suggestive of two rings of leaves, and a further step towards true Corinthian form (Fig. 2*d*).

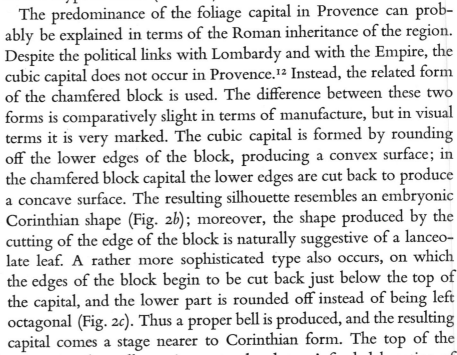

(a)

(b)

(c)

(d)

FIG. 2. Types of eleventh-century capitals

[10] Labande, *Études*, pp. 109–31, has made out a very convincing case for dating the church at Goudargues after 1130, and he regarded the four apse capitals as simply stylistically archaic. It seems to me more probable that the capitals are re-used from the nearby chapel of Notre-Dame-de-Caseneuve, which was restored at the period the parish church was built. It may be noted that the abaci of the capitals in question reveal a curvature which is missing from the (later) imposts above. Despite Labande's excellent study, Goudargues remains sadly little-known and calls out for further investigation, and particularly for excavation.

[11] See M. Joly, *L'Architecture des églises romanes du Vivarais* (Paris, 1967), and *C.A.* (1923), pp. 269–85.

[12] The only true cubic capital from central Provence is re-used as a base in the west gallery of the cloister at Aix-en-Provence (see my M.A. thesis, London University, 1967, 'The Cloister of the Cathedral of S. Sauveur at Aix', unpublished). Cubic capitals do occur in the First Romanesque buildings on the Provençal slopes of the Alps.

In terms of shape, therefore, we have a clear evolution of a type, but it would be a mistake to regard this as a chronological evolution as well. Thus, while the simple chamfered block does not occur at Montmajour and Venasque (*c.* 1030–50), the two more 'evolved' forms are found there. Equally, and not surprisingly, the simple chamfered block occurs most frequently in remote and plain rural chapels, and the reason for this is doubtless that it was the easiest to produce.

The decoration of these capitals is, like their shape, more or less closely related to the Corinthian form. It is possible to divide them into two broad types, geometric and foliate, but this is somewhat misleading, since the geometric forms are, without exception, treated in what may be termed a pseudo-foliate manner. The capital, whose chamfered block is already suggestive of leaf forms, is decorated with abstract linear patterns, which clearly relate to and are arranged as foliage.[13] Once again it is noticeable that the simplest and most schematic treatments come from the most isolated and rural areas, and it would be a mistake to see their simplicity as necessarily very early in date; it seems much more probable that they represent provincial versions of the more accomplished work carried out in the major centres.

The most important traces of such major work occur at Montmajour and Venasque on the one hand, and at S. Victor, Marseille, and Vaison-la-Romaine on the other; these include two distinct types to which the majority of other eleventh-century capitals can be related more or less directly. As has been said, the links between Montmajour and Venasque are close; there is no need to restate these links here, or to undertake a close analysis of either group of capitals, since this has been adequately done by previous writers.[14] However, it will be useful to enumerate the essential features of these capitals, which both groups share, and which also characterize the Tournus work. All these capitals retain the central rose,[15] accompanied in almost all cases by simple scroll volutes (Pls. 2–12). The rose itself is made up either of a schematic flower form or of a whorl. The foliage capitals commonly employ a type of simple acanthus leaf.[16] One group of capitals replaces the acanthus by a series of vertical striations, producing a columnar effect, surmounted by small tri-lobed leaves (Pl. 11). Another variation employs narrow strips of vertical interlace around the bell (Pls. 6, 7, 10). The vertical arrangement of this and the preceding type, together with the retention of the rose and volutes, emphasizes the connections with the purely foliate types. Nevertheless, the interlace itself is definitely an unclassical intrusion, and it appears to be restricted to this particular workshop.[17]

[13] Such treatment may be seen at S. André-de-Rocquepertuis, which Labande (*Études*, p. 177) dated to *c.* 1025–50, in the chapel of S. Pantaléon, near Gordes, and on a single capital in S. Michel l'Observatoire. For the latter see *S. Michel l'Observatoire: Monographie* (*Sites et Monuments de Haute Provence, Les Alpes de Lumière*, 1964), p. 71.

[14] Benoit, *Montmajour*, and Fevrier, *C.A.* (1963).

[15] At Montmajour there is sometimes an additional pair of small leaves replacing the rose.

[16] The leaves are slightly convolute, made up of broad single lobes. They are sometimes pinnate or pinnatifid, and are arranged in one or two rings.

[17] Other types of interlace capital are extremely rare, but a form of foliate interlace does occur on a monolithic colonnette and capital at Montsallier (B.A.) *Les Monuments du haut moyen âge: inventaire*, no. 66.

Capitals which are related in form to the types found at Montmajour and Venasque in fact predominate in Provence, and it is tempting to regard these two centres as the source from which all the related work is derived. This temptation is all the greater because a rough date can be provided for Montmajour and Venasque, whereas the related work is totally undated. However, few of the relationships are of a precise enough kind to allow such a tidy conclusion. For example, two of the apse capitals at S. Pierre, Venéjan, of simple chamfered block type, are decorated solely with an enlarged rose of whorl type. One can postulate some sort of link with the Montmajour–Venasque group, but it is dangerous to go further. In other cases the ground is surer; the three early capitals at S. Pantaléon are all related in a general way to the main group, and in addition one has vertical striations on the bell, relating to the columnar type at Venasque (Pls. 14, 15). A similar form occurs on several of the tower capitals of S. Symphorien at Buoux.[18]

Perhaps the most interesting aspect of the Montmajour–Venasque group is not its relationship with, and presumed influence upon, roughly contemporaneous work, but the survival of this influence into the twelfth century, as witnessed by the four capitals at Bourg-S. Andéol (Pls. 16–18). These are rather squat in appearance, retaining the chamfered block shape, although it is now executed with considerable expertise. All four capitals are foliated, employing broad leaves with thick lobes, surmounted by rose and volutes.[19] They preserve the shape and technique of eleventh-century work, and exhibit a metamorphosis of Corinthian forms which is still a long way from the expert imitation of Roman Corinthian found in later Provençal works. One of the Bourg-S. Andéol capitals is in fact virtually identical with two at Venasque (Pls. 13, 18). The latter do not form part of the three main groups in the baptistery, and may be somewhat later. These, and the Bourg-S. Andéol capital can also be related to certain of the Vaison apse capitals (Pl. 19).[20]

Chamfered block capitals of what may loosely be termed the Montmajour–Venasque type predominate in the eleventh century in Provence, but a second group may be defined, in which the dependence upon antique forms is still more pronounced. The main examples of this group are the porch capitals of S. Victor at Marseille and the apse capitals of the cathedral of Vaison-la-Romaine. The Marseille capitals can be dated

[18] The date and authenticity of the tower at Buoux are open to question, and it is possible that this elegant structure is a post-medieval creation, employing ancient materials. For a brief study of the church see *Sautel*, pp. 101–10. This combination of foliage, rose, and volutes on a chamfered block capital also occurs in the capitals of S. Bonet de Lagoy and S. Gervais, both provincial chapels in which the dependence on pre-existing fashion seems likely. Another capital of the same type is in the private collection of Mme Schley at Grasse.

[19] Two have a double ring of foliage, while the others have a single ring of taller leaves, in one case pinnatifid, in the other spoon-leaved.

[20] Another traditional treatment occurs on a surviving porch capital at Mornas, and this probably also dates from the early years of the twelfth century. The impost of the capital bears the following inscription:

VII.KL.IVNII.(D)EDICA
CIO.ECCLAE.IOHIS.BAPT.

See J. Vallery-Radot, *C.A.* (1963), pp. 257–63.

to *c.* 1040, but the date of the Vaison work is more difficult to establish. For Labande, they and the apse which they adorn were Merovingian,[21] but more recent opinion has tended to advance them into the eleventh century.[22] On the basis of their stylistic connections with the Marseille work, the latter view seems to me correct, and I would date these capitals to the first half of the eleventh century.

The S. Victor capitals consist of carefully executed acanthus leaves, of broad palmette-like formation, with large spiky lobes, arranged in two rings (Pl. 21). The upper ring is surmounted by cauliculi bearing semi-leaves, the outer pairs of which take the place of volutes. It is partly this arrangement of the leaves, and partly the fact that the capitals are roughly bell-shaped, that produces a greater illusion of classicism as compared to the Montmajour–Venasque group. The same tendencies are apparent at Vaison, where the eleventh-century apse capitals are also roughly bell-shaped. They may be divided into two types, the first of which is comparable, in form and arrangement of the leaves, to the Marseille work (Pl. 20).[23]

This brief survey has covered only those capitals for which an eleventh- or early twelfth-century date would probably be widely accepted. We have seen that nearly all these capitals can be considered as versions of the Corinthian, although none is really very close to true antique forms. They exhibit an interest in the antique, but it is still far from the imitative and almost pedantic classicism of some later Provençal work. The Bourg-S. Andéol capitals show that there were still sculptors of this type in Provence in the early part of the twelfth century, and it is just possible that in time this style might have evolved into the elaborate virtuosity of late Romanesque foliage.[24] But such transformation seems unlikely without some form of additional stimulus. The nature of this stimulus and its effect on the evolution of Provençal Romanesque style is one of the concerns of the succeeding pages. In twelfth-century terms, the importance of the eleventh-century capitals is not so much stylistic as formal—they witness how deeply ingrained the Corinthian ideal was. This is ultimately why, as I hope to show, the rather different formal conceptions which were introduced with the nave capitals were never to be wholly accepted.

[21] Labande, *Vaison.*

[22] See J. Hubert, *L'Architecture religieuse du haut moyen âge* (Paris, 1952), pp. 50–1, and Fevrier, *C.A.* (1963).

[23] The actual execution of the leaves is, however, closer to the Montmajour–Venasque type. There is a lower ring of carefully executed acanthus, with clearly marked lobe divisions, surmounted by cauliculi bearing pairs of semi-leaves from which spring helices and scroll volutes. The abacus is markedly concave, and has a small rose at its centre. Below this a striated bell is visible. The second type also employs acanthus leaves, but the execution is flatter and the individual leaves are less clearly delineated. These are arranged in two rows, six below and four above, with the upper leaves placed at the corners and surmounted by volutes. Visible between these upper leaves is a marked bell, decorated with vertical striations or with additional small leaves. The abacus is again cut back, and the rose is replaced by a triplet of vertical bars (Pl. 19). The two capitals in the Venasque baptistery which do not belong with the main group there may be associated with this second type at Vaison, suggesting the possibility of further interconnections between all these main centres. The later development of the S. Victor type is witnessed by the sole surviving apse capital at Pernes-les-Fontaines, dating perhaps from the end of the eleventh century.

[24] On the other hand, I think it can be argued that the decorated portal of Estagel (Gard) is largely dependent on indigenous Provençal traditions. This dates from the second quarter of the twelfth century, and witnesses the static qualities present in these traditions. See M. Aubert, 'La Porte romane d'Estagel au Musée du Louvre', *Mon. Piot.* xxxiii (1933), 135–40.

(*b*) THE RELIEFS AT S. RESTITUT

There seems little doubt that the foliage capital, in its various forms, was the commonest type of architectural decoration in the eleventh century in Provence. The only other form of embellishment of which significant traces remain is the frieze, made up of individual panels bearing figural subjects. Fragments of such friezes can be found at L'Escale, at Valréas, and at Notre-Dame-de-Salagon,[25] but the most considerable evidence occurs on the so-called funerary tower at S. Restitut and on the south transept of the cathedral of S. Paul-Trois-Châteaux. The present discussion will be limited to these last two examples.

The western tower of the small church of S. Restitut, just to the south of S. Paul-Trois-Châteaux, bears a continuous frieze, composed of a series of small rectangular reliefs (Pls. 22–7). These are set on the four sides of the square tower, at a height of some six metres above the ground. A cursory inspection immediately reveals two facts: firstly, the tower itself is not a uniform structure, and secondly, the single-aisle church which adjoins the east face of the tower was conceived and constructed when the tower, at least in some form, was already standing. Above the frieze on the tower is a projecting cornice, decorated with carefully executed floral motifs, and above this the upper part of the tower is constructed of the well-cut ashlar which is characteristic of Provençal Romanesque in general, and of the adjoining church in particular. The lower parts of the tower include at least three distinct types of masonry construction—*petit appareil*, courses of larger but roughly dressed stone, and ashlar of the same quality as the upper part of the tower.

The relief panels vary in length, but are of uniform height (0·40 m.) and are placed end to end to produce a continuous frieze. The only panel to break with this arrangement is on the centre of the west face of the tower, where the rectangular block, containing a figure of Christ enthroned, is placed on end (Pl. 23). The subjects of the panels are clearly in part religious; besides the enthroned Christ, one can distinguish Adam and Eve, the Adoration of the Magi, a Lamb of God, and (on separate panels) the symbols of the Evangelists (Pl. 25). In addition there are panels showing groups of figures (never more than three) holding palms, staves, and (?) dishes, which can be interpreted as elements in an iconographic scheme. There are also panels depicting mounted soldiers, but the majority of the remaining reliefs are given over to animals and birds, both real and imaginary. Attempts have been made to interpret all the reliefs in symbolic and iconographic terms, but this is clearly unwarranted. The most objective treatment of the subject-matter of the frieze was made by Émile Bonnet.[26] He rejected any overall 'symbolic' interpretation, but was puzzled by the fact that those scenes which clearly do have religious connotations are distributed around the tower

---

[25] L'Escale (B.A.) possesses a frieze which originally decorated the (destroyed) chapel of Ste Consorce, and which is now in the possession of the mayor. The frieze is no. 72 in the *Inventaire* published by *Les Alpes de Lumière* (see above, n. 1). The Valréas fragments, on the gable of the west front and on the south porch, are unpublished. For Salagon see R. Collier, *Monuments et art de Haute-Provence* (Digne, 1966).

[26] E. Bonnet, 'Les bas-reliefs de la tour de S. Restitut', *C.A.* (1909), ii, 251–74.

haphazardly. He therefore suggested that the reliefs are not in their original positions but have been reset. This is certainly a possibility, but to my mind an unlikely one. It is probable that the reliefs were always intended to form a frieze, but even if this were not the case it is difficult to arrange them in a way that makes any real iconographic sense. In addition, the enthroned Christ at the centre of the west face seems to be in its original position. However, it is impossible to speak with complete certainty on this point, since portions of the frieze are hidden by the church which adjoins the tower.

Nineteenth-century scholars dated these reliefs variously between the sixth and the eleventh centuries, but these opinions were based almost exclusively upon their 'primitive' appearance. The first (and only) serious attempts to date them were made by Labande[27] and Bonnet, who concluded that this 'primitive' aspect was misleading, and that they in fact dated from the twelfth century. Labande's dating rested on the following observations:

1. Only small parts of the masonry of the tower, on the lower north face, were in *petit appareil*, and could be considered ancient.
2. All the upper parts of the tower, above the frieze, and several portions below, were constructed in good twelfth-century ashlar.
3. The cupola inside the tower was clearly twelfth century.
4. The floral design of the cornice was close to that found on many twelfth-century monuments.
5. The relief panels were very close in style to those on the south transept at S. Paul-Trois-Châteaux.
6. The *opus reticulatum* which borders the frieze recurs on the *maison romane* at S. Gilles and on the chapel of Beaucaire castle.

On the basis of these observations Labande concluded that although the tower might date back to the eleventh century in a few places, the major part of it, including the frieze, was mid-twelfth century. Bonnet, noting previous opinions, accepted these points and attempted to find confirmation in the costumes of the figures. However, he concluded that the only significant feature was the occurrence of pointed shields, which only appeared in the eleventh century and were much used in the twelfth. He then, somewhat arbitrarily, dated the reliefs to the very end of the eleventh century or the beginning of the twelfth, ignoring the mid-twelfth-century implications of Labande's evidence. Presumably he was also influenced by the supposed primitiveness of the work, and by his belief that the panels had been reset.

Labande's arguments were, as always, weighty and deserve serious consideration. However, in this instance, his observation was less than usually penetrating. In regard to the dating of the frieze, his two strongest arguments were the twelfth-century usage of *opus reticulatum* in Provence, and the relationship between the reliefs at S. Restitut and those at S. Paul-Trois-Châteaux. Thus, while he admitted parts of the lower tower

---

[27] Labande, *C.A.* (1909), pp. 121-7.

to be earlier, the frieze itself was twelfth century. A closer examination of the *opus reticulatum* which flanks the frieze above and below reveals a curious fact: the majority of this masonry is indeed *opus reticulatum*—i.e., small squared stones set diagonally. However, in places, notably on the south face of the tower, this is replaced by a course of rectangular blocks on which an *opus reticulatum* pattern has been incised (Pls. 25, 26). Now Labande's parallels for the *opus reticulatum* at S. Restitut are at S. Gilles and Beaucaire, where we find not the authentic use of small squared stones, but the imitation form described above. It is highly unlikely that at S. Restitut the real and the false *opus reticulatum* date from the same period; the natural explanation is that the tower was altered and restored at some point, when sections of genuine but damaged *opus reticulatum* were replaced by the imitation. Since this imitation form occurs in twelfth-century monuments, this restoration may well have taken place then. Such a conclusion is strengthened by the evidence of the masonry of the lower parts of the tower, containing sections of twelfth-century patching, and by the twelfth-century character of the upper part of the tower.

Since the *opus reticulatum*, in both its forms, flanks the reliefs above and below, it establishes a *prima facie* case for a remodelling of the tower in the twelfth century, rather than a rebuilding of it, and also strongly suggests that the reliefs should be dated with the genuine rather than the imitation work. However, Labande's second major argument—the relationship with the reliefs at S. Paul-Trois-Châteaux—seems to pose a formidable objection. These reliefs occur on the exterior of the west wall of the south transept, and they appear to be an integral and original part of the courses of the wall (Pl. 28). Labande dated the eastern parts of S. Paul to the mid-twelfth century, and although this dating is challenged in a later chapter,[28] I would not propose that this part of the building dates from the eleventh century. At the same time, the connection between the reliefs at S. Paul and those at S. Restitut is undeniably very close.

Once again, however, closer examination reveals a curious factor which Labande ignored; the majority of the S. Paul panels are formed in precisely the same manner as those at S. Restitut. The surface of the rectangular block is cut back to a depth of about 1 in., leaving the figures standing in relief; the edges of the block are not cut back, and so form a narrow rectangular frame for the scene. The style of these blocks is also very close to that of the S. Restitut frieze (questions of style will be discussed shortly). There are in addition five other reliefs on the interior of the south transept, which are different in conception. The relief is shallower, and the frame does not follow the rectangular shape of the block but rather the shape of the figure in relief (Pl. 29). This is particularly apparent on the block with the figure of a horseman. There is also an evident difference in quality. Despite their supposed 'primitiveness', the reliefs in the rectangular frames, as at S. Restitut, are cut firmly and clearly. The second group, on the other hand, are crudely conceived and executed, and when they are compared to the first group readily reveal themselves as nothing more than ~~rather inept~~ copies.

[28] See below, Ch. 8; Labande's discussion of the church is in *C.A.* (1909), pp. 112–21.

This is particularly clear in the case of the Sagittarius, which occurs in both groups (Pls. 28, 29). Although this is an extremely common motif, the two representations here are so close in conception that there can be no doubt that one is copied from the other. It is also, I think, abundantly clear that the inferior version, in the irregular frame, is the copy. The other subjects in the second group at S. Paul (horseman, standing figure with staff, bird, and a standing soldier) do not occur in the first group of seven, but they do occur in the closely related work at S. Restitut, which is only some two kilometres distant.

The most plausible explanation for the two groups of reliefs at S. Paul would seem to be that the first group is re-used. This would explain their arbitrary positioning on the west wall of the transept, where they are practically out of sight, as well as the fact that they are not all placed together, but are set in groups of 3, 3, and 1, in different courses. The reliefs of the second group are clearly copies, executed by masons who were not expert sculptors. The major difficulty in this interpretation is that although the relief blocks vary in length, they are of uniform height and fit exactly with the courses of the wall. This can, however, be explained as the coincidence which prompted their re-use—i.e. the stones were re-used precisely because they happened to be the right size.

In sum, the evidence which Labande produced for dating the reliefs to the twelfth century is not convincing; on the contrary, the two forms of *opus reticulatum* at S. Restitut, and the two groups of reliefs at S. Paul, suggest that they are earlier than the reconstruction of the tower at the former and the construction of the transept at the latter.[29] This suggests that, whatever their date, they are pre-twelfth century, or at least earlier than the twelfth-century restoration of the tower. It is perfectly possible to accept Labande's contention that the cornice which surmounts the frieze is twelfth century, since this clearly goes with the upper parts of the tower and not with the frieze. In the absence of any more secure form of dating, we therefore have to turn to the style of the reliefs. They are badly worn and the surface detail is somewhat erased, but the general characteristics of the sculpture are readily apparent. The relief is comparatively low and the figures are simply but firmly constructed. All the reliefs are essentially linear and there is no apparent relationship of figure to ground or of figure to frame. Human figures are rigid, seen either in profile or frontally. They have large heads and eyes, and are dressed either in tunics which reach the knees or in long robes which cover the feet. There is no attempt to articulate the figures or the drapery, and while the outline is created by the relief itself, further details are only suggested by lightly incised lines. To call these reliefs crude or primitive is misleading; accepted on their own terms,

[29] None of Bonnet's iconographical evidence really reflected on the date of the reliefs, apart from his view that the shields carried by the mounted soldiers were pointed at their base, and that this form did not evolve until the eleventh century and was widely used in the twelfth. In fact the form of the shields seen on the reliefs is more nearly oval, and they closely resemble Roman shields, as depicted, for example, on the mausoleum at S. Rémy. The S. Restitut shields are certainly not the marked kite shape seen on the Bayeux tapestry, and they seem to represent a transitional type, which had not yet evolved into the elongated form used in the later eleventh and twelfth centuries.

and not judged in terms of the Provençal Proto-Renaissance,[30] they appear as strong and effective. This is particularly clear if they are compared with what can more justly be seen as the 'crude' twelfth-century works in the region, such as the tympana of Salon-de-Provence and of S. Gabriel, near Tarascon. The central figure of Christ on the former exhibits a much greater interest in, but also a misunderstanding of, drapery folds, and there is a serious attempt to extend into three dimensions (Pl. 30). S. Gabriel is perhaps closer to the S. Restitut tradition, but the figures are characterized and articulated in a quite different manner.[31]

The stylistic links of the S. Restitut frieze lie not with twelfth-century Provence but with an earlier phase of European art, which is broadly speaking pre-Romanesque and in this case corresponds to the styles termed Lombardic, Merovingian, and Visigothic. These terms denote an international style loosely by its regional and ethnic distribution, and although there are many significant regional characteristics, they share essentially the same stylistic basis. This basis is late Roman and sub-Antique art overlaid with the essentially linear art of the barbarian invaders. In all regions this style has a long and comparatively static history; it does not undergo any very rapid internal evolution (in the way that, for example, twelfth-century Romanesque art does) and consequently works in this style can seldom be dated accurately on the basis of purely stylistic criteria. Thus, if we consider Lombardic works alongside the S. Restitut reliefs we can find a series of fairly striking parallels which span several centuries. Using stylistic criteria alone, a case could be made out for an eighth-century dating of the S. Restitut reliefs. However, since this style persists through the ninth, tenth, and eleventh centuries, and since very few works in this style are preserved in Provence itself, such comparisons are not very helpful.[32]

In order to try and date the S. Restitut reliefs more closely we must consider not only their style but also their form and function—that is as framed rectangular panels set as a continuous frieze on a free-standing tower. A clear parallel for this type and arrangement is provided by the frieze panels of the old bell-tower at S. Hilaire, Poitiers. This tower, like the one at S. Restitut, was originally free-standing. The reliefs, set between corbels and beneath a foliated cornice, are constructed in exactly the same manner as those at S. Restitut, and the subjects isolated within a rectangular frame. The subjects themselves are closely comparable, including a *Sagittarius*, various types of dragon, and one can even see an exotic camel as complementing the equally exotic elephant at S. Restitut.[33]

Unfortunately, the reliefs at S. Hilaire are not themselves certainly dated. Professor

30 The term Proto-Renaissance was applied to Provençal sculpture by Hamann (*Deutsche und französische Kunst im Mittelalter*, vol. i (Marburg, 1922)), although it seems to have been invented by Burckhardt, who used it to characterize north Italian Romanesque.   31 For a fuller consideration of the S. Gabriel sculpture, see below, Ch. 8.

32 For Lombardic stone sculpture see E. Schaffran, *Die Kunst der Langobarden in Italien* (Jena, 1941); also P. Toesca, *Storia dell'arte italiana; il medioevo*, vol. 2, 2nd edition (Turin, 1965). For Merovingian and Visigothic sculpture see J. Baum, *La Sculpture figurale en Europe à l'époque mérovingienne* (Paris, 1937); J. Puig y Cadafalch, *L'Art Wisigothique et ses survivances* (Paris, 1961).

33 M. Thibout, 'L'éléphant dans la sculpture romane française', *B.M.* (1947), pp. 178–89.

Crozet classified them as pre-Romanesque, and it is probable that they were executed at the time the bell-tower was built.[34] This was almost certainly by the time of the consecration of the church in 1049, and the tower was most probably erected during the time that Fulbert, later Archbishop of Chartres, was treasurer of S. Hilaire, that is between 1020 and 1029. This evidence for the S. Hilaire reliefs does not of course establish any sort of certain date for those at S. Restitut, but it does suggest that a dating in the first half of the eleventh century is entirely possible.

Over and above the problem of their date, the S. Restitut reliefs should, I think, be seen as one of the key points in any discussion of Provençal sculpture. If the present view is accepted, and they are seen as stylistically coherent pieces, not simply as inexpert work nor as rustic and *retardataire*, then they immediately suggest a stylistic milieu which is apparently incompatible with what is supposedly typical of Provençal Romanesque style—e.g. the north gallery of the cloister at Arles. The difficulty of the situation becomes even more apparent if, for example, we accept the date, often proposed,[35] in the 1130s for the Arles work. Indeed, any notion of coherent stylistic development becomes impossible if at the same time we accept Labande's date of *c.* 1150 for the S. Restitut reliefs. Viewed in these terms, it is easy to understand why the reliefs have been generally discarded as insignificant and crude, for it is only in this way that Provençal developments can be made wholly explicit.

For these reasons, one of the major aims of this essay is to attempt a reconciliation, or at least a feasible transition between these two seeming polarities of style. I begin from the conviction that S. Restitut witnesses the existence of a valid artistic tradition of figural sculpture in eleventh-century Provence; in this context, the twelfth-century copying of the very similar panels at S. Paul would support such a contention—presumably the panels were only copied because someone thought they were worth copying. Secondly, the stylistic tradition which the reliefs represent was by no means exhausted, and its development and gradual transmutation can be traced up to the end of the twelfth century and beyond. It is the strength of this tradition, and its influence upon both the form and the style of architectural sculpture, which determined much of the course of Provençal development.

It is also of course apparent that the stylistic tradition which I have outlined at S. Restitut was in essence dissimilar to that which I attempted to define in the eleventh-century capitals. I have argued that the latter retained the Antique Corinthian form as their base, while the forerunners of the relief style lie in the sub-Antique. In actual terms the contrast is not so marked, because the extant capitals reveal a dissolution of classical forms, but it is not perhaps entirely coincidental that none of the main centres of surviving capital sculpture give any evidence of ever having possessed some form of frieze decoration. The two traditions were not to merge until the twelfth century, and even then neither one completely absorbed the other.

---

[34] R. Crozet, 'La corniche du clocher de l'église St. Hilaire de Poitiers', *B.M.* (1934), pp. 341–5.
[35] Notably by Hamann, *Deutsche und französische Kunst*, and von Stockhausen, *Die Kreuzgänge*.

3   *The Nave Capitals: Notre-Dame-des-Doms, Avignon*

THE design of Provençal churches is almost invariably extremely simple. Such complexities as ambulatories and radiating chapels or three- or four-storey elevations are almost totally unknown. The churches are, for the most part, simple in plan, design, and execution. The nave, with or without aisles, is succeeded by a bay covered by a cupola on squinches, which in turn gives on to the apse. Where aisles are present they normally terminate in eastern absidioles. Transepts are infrequent.[1] The elevation of the nave is equally simple; massive compound piers support a main arcade and a broken barrel vault with transverse arches. Direct lighting is infrequent, and the whole effect is one of massive solidity and sombre darkness—frequently enhanced by coats of post-medieval paint. Churches of this type do not lend themselves readily to much interior decoration, and for the most part such decoration is restricted to a blind arcade round the apse, supported by colonnettes and capitals, and by the placement of the symbols of the Evangelists in the squinches of the cupola. On the other hand the exterior, illuminated by the bright Provençal sun, is a more promising field for sculptural embellishment, and cornices and corbels as well as elaborate porches and gables abound. Within this framework of somewhat plain interiors balanced by rather more elaborate exteriors, one group of churches stands out, on account of their more elaborate and, it must be admitted, slightly incongruous embellishment of the interior. This is the group with nave capitals.

The term nave capitals, as it is used here, itself requires some explanation, for these are not nave capitals in the sense in which we meet them, say, in Burgundy. Two features distinguish them; in the first place they are almost exclusively foliated, and secondly they and the colonnettes which support them are placed in a somewhat odd position. The dosserets flanking the central pilaster of the standard Provençal pier are cut back at a point normally some two metres below the springing of the vault, and the colonnette and capital inserted just below the transverse rib of the barrel.[2] Their

---

[1] The best summary of Provençal Romanesque building is still probably R. de Lasteyrie, *L'Architecture religieuse à l'époque romane* (Paris, 1929), i, 410–22.

[2] There does not appear to be any generally accepted terminology for the various elements of a multi-angular

ostensible function is therefore to support the transverse rib itself, although they can hardly be termed active architectural members. In fact their purpose is clearly decorative, although they are placed high up in buildings which are habitually poorly lit, and so tend to be largely invisible from the ground.[3] Some speculations as to the origins of this rather bizarre form of decoration will be offered later; here it may simply be noted that the nave capitals are in all cases accompanied by another elaboration of the decoration, a foliated cornice which runs the length of the building above the capitals themselves, at the point of the springing of the vault.

Nave capitals occur in the following buildings: Notre-Dame-des-Doms, Avignon; S. Trophime, Arles; S. Sauveur, Aix-en-Provence; Notre-Dame, Cavaillon; S. Restitut; S. Siffrein, Carpentras; S. André-de-Rosans; and, in a restricted way, Notre-Dame, Vaison-la-Romaine, and S. André-du-Gard, Conneaux.[4] A version of the system, in which the central pilaster of the compound pier gives way, at approximately half its height, to a column and capital, occurs in the cathedral of S. Paul-Trois-Châteaux.

NOTRE-DAME-DES-DOMS, AVIGNON

Notre-Dame-des-Doms is often considered as one of the most typical products of 'l'école romane de Provence'. It is a simple and dignified building which retains much of its original character, despite the fact that it was badly disfigured in the seventeenth and nineteenth centuries. At the end of the twelfth century it consisted of an aisle-less nave of five bays, the easternmost bay covered by a cupola, the other four by a broken barrel vault (Pls. 31, 32, and Fig. 3). To the west, the façade is surmounted by a bell-tower, enclosing a low narthex at ground level. The west door to the church is set in an imposing porch. The present east end consists of a choir bay giving on to a polygonal apse; however, these were erected in the seventeenth century, when more space was required, and the original east end, consisting of an apse opening directly from the cupola bay, was destroyed.[5] The elevation of the nave consists of a main arcade, carried

compound pier. Here the following system is adopted: assuming the core of the pier to be cruciform, the terminals of the cross are termed pilasters. The subsidiary elements are termed dosserets:

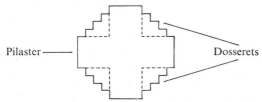

Pilaster ———   ——— Dosserets

---

[3] Nave capitals are best seen at Aix, where the floor level has been raised and the adjoining gothic nave is fairly well lit, and at S. Restitut, which is smaller and lower than the rest of the group. The height of S. Trophime at Arles makes the capitals difficult to see clearly, and Cavaillon and Avignon are so dark that they are almost invisible. However, in the latter the baroque gallery affords a unique opportunity of examining the nave capitals at relatively close quarters.

[4] Despite considerable efforts, I failed to visit the chapel of S. André. None of the inhabitants of Connaux knew where it was, and it is not marked on maps. I have therefore had to make do with the drawings of these capitals made by Léon Allègre, and published by Labande, *Études*, pp. 97–9. Fortunately, the monument appears to be of comparatively minor importance, and in addition it is not of course in Provence.

[5] See *C.A.* (1963), p. 45.

by compound piers, supporting a broken barrel vault with transverse ribs. In the eastern-most bay, above the arcade, a series of four lateral arches are stepped out, to convert the rectangular bay into a square on which a cupola on squinches is mounted. The cupola itself is preceded by a lantern. At the west end, above the low narthex, is a square chamber, opening on to the nave, and also vaulted by a cupola on squinches. The western porch has only a single storey. The decoration of the building is comparatively modest, consisting, on the interior, of the colonnettes and capitals of the lantern and nave, the foliated cornice which runs the length of the nave, and the Symbols of the Evangelists in the squinches of the western cupola. The exterior of the lantern also bears colonnettes and capitals, and there are truncated colonnettes on the four faces of the bell-tower, the vestiges of its original decoration. The corbels of the nave roof appear to be for the most part modern replacements. On the south side of the building the lateral walls and the buttresses bear a blind arcading. Curiously, there is no trace of such arcading on the north side of the church.[6] The most lavishly decorated part of the exterior is the west porch. This small edifice is flanked by fluted half-columns, with Corinthian capitals, surmounted by an entablature and gable.[7] During the nineteenth century the date of this porch was the subject of much controversy, and its 'classical' appearance led many to regard it as a late-Antique monument, and therefore pre-dating the church which it adjoins. All that need be said here on this point is that Labande demonstrated beyond doubt, on the basis of purely architectural observation, that the porch was an addition to the church and therefore later in date.[8]

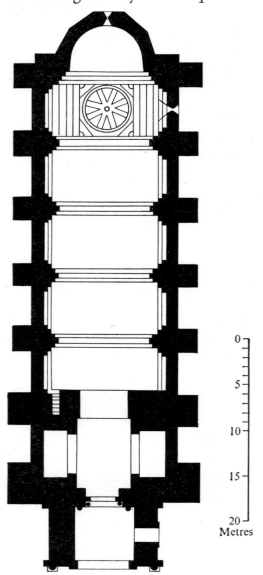

FIG. 3. Notre-Dame-des-Doms, Avignon. Plan,
c. 1200

---

[6] On the north side of the church the nave walls have largely been pierced and obscured by the addition of lateral chapels. However, if arcading had existed on this side, one would have expected it to be visible at the west end of the nave and on the westernmost buttress.

[7] I here exclude the capitals inside the porch flanking the door, since these appear to have been renewed, perhaps in the seventeenth century.

[8] Labande, *Avignon*, pp. 335–9.

Before considering this decoration in detail, one or two general points about the building may be noted. In the first place, the occurrence of a western tower is extremely unusual in Provence.[9] The tower is normally placed over the last bay of the nave, that is the bay normally covered by the cupola. At Avignon the nave cupola has a developed lantern and, according to Labande's interpretation, this made the erection of a tower impossible, so one was built at the west instead. A second odd feature arises from this disposition, namely the occurrence of two cupolas, one under the tower and one in the nave. This arrangement is unique in Provence, and the oddity is increased by a further factor. The cupola under the bell-tower is almost totally invisible, and one can easily visit the church and remain unaware of its existence. This is because the roof of the narthex largely obscures the view into the chamber above, and although the latter opens on to the nave through a sort of triumphal arch, it is only possible to gain a glimpse of the base of the cupola by standing in a carefully chosen spot in the nave. The chamber can, however, be reached by a staircase cut in the thickness of the north wall of the tower. A curious fact is that the squinches of the cupola are decorated with the symbols of the Evangelists; in itself this is not surprising, for this form of decoration is monotonously common in Provence, but it seems odd that at Avignon they should be placed where no-one can see them, while the visible cupola over the nave has plain squinches but for a simple scallop-shell ornament.

The manner in which this nave cupola is constructed is again puzzling. The reduction of the rectangular bay to a square by the use of stepped arches does occur elsewhere,[10] though it is rare, and it may be noted that at Avignon the arches rest, most unusually, on corbels. But perhaps the most unusual feature of all at Notre-Dame-des-Doms is the lantern tower, for which there are no parallels at all in Provence.

Thus Avignon's reputation as a typical example of Provençal Romanesque does not appear to be too well-founded. Yet it is still possible, as Labande maintained and as has since been universally accepted, that (with the exception of the porch) it is a unified structure dating from the middle years of the twelfth century.[11] Nevertheless, ignoring for the present the documentary evidence, the accepted interpretation must stand up to two tests: firstly, the building must show no signs of (medieval) remodelling, and, secondly, the decoration must be stylistically unified.

The nave capitals form the most obvious element of the interior decoration. There are twenty-four in all, but the four in the choir bay can of course be excluded since they are contemporary with the reconstruction of the east end. The remaining twenty are all *in situ* and, although the majority are in an excellent state of preservation, they do not appear to have been restored (Pls. 35-40). The capitals and colonnettes are

---

[9] There is a western tower at Ste Marthe, Tarascon, and a further example (now destroyed) at Mollèges (see *Revoil*, vol. iii, Pl. XLII). At S. Restitut the tower is an earlier construction, and for that reason not really comparable with Avignon.

[10] At Noves, S. Étienne-des-Sorts, S. Laurent-des-Arbres, S. Honorat-des-Alyscamps, and La Major, Marseille. The latter is the most closely comparable with Avignon, for it is a building of similar size and also employs a series of four lateral stepped arches.

[11] Labande, *Avignon*. The date was accepted without question as recently as the 1963 *C.A.*

monolithic, which is unusual in Provence. The decoration of all twenty monoliths is very similar and they form a coherent group which must be attributed to a single workshop. The capitals are all bipartite and two main types can be distinguished.

Type (a): Pls. 35, 36

The colonnette is plain. The capital is square at the base and the astragal, if present, is also square. Indeed, the transition from round to square is made not in the capital, but below it in the colonnette, and, as if to emphasize this point, the top of the colonnette is sometimes embellished at its four corners with a small ternate leaf. The lower part of the capital proper is decorated with a horizontal strip of egg-and-dart surmounted by bead-and-reel, both very competently executed. The upper part, which retains the square shape, is much more extensive and is also more elaborately treated. Thick acanthus leaves, soft in appearance, rise to almost the full height of the capital. They are markedly convolute, with a thick main rib and three main lobes, which are themselves subdivided. On some capitals small subsidiary leaves, of the same pattern, are placed between the main leaves, at the centre of the face.

While these leaves and their arrangement are on the whole symmetrical, the top of the capital is treated much more idiosyncratically. The position of the capital means that two of its faces are obscured by walls, and only one angle of the square block projects. The projecting angle usually carries, above the main acanthus, a pair of scroll volutes. However, these volutes are not matched, as one would expect, by others on the un-exposed corners of the capital. Instead, where the capital meets the wall, there is a large cluster of what appear to be caespitose buds or leaflets.[12] The size of this cluster appears out of proportion to the rest of the capital and gives it a somewhat top-heavy look. In addition, the missing scroll volutes emerge illogically from behind the main acanthus leaves, at the centre of the face.

Type (b): Pls. 37, 38

The colonnette, which normally has spiral fluting, remains circular to its full height, where it is crowned by a marked astragal. The lower part of the capital is cubic and decorated either with flat, but ill-defined, leaves of acanthus type or with egg-and-dart. The upper part bears acanthus leaves, as on type (a), although in some cases the leaves are executed in a crisper fashion. The treatment of the top of the capital differs slightly from that found in the preceding type, although it is equally incongruous. The projecting angle has, instead of volutes, curving semi-leaves with lobes facing down. This semi-leaf springs from the centre of the face and curves down over the main acanthus to form a sort of pseudo-volute. Springing from the same point, but curving in the opposite direction, it is matched by an actual scroll volute. The complexity is increased

---

[12] I am very grateful to the staff of the Herbarium, the Royal Botanic Gardens, Kew, who examined the photographs of these capitals for me. They concluded that it was impossible to determine with certainty what (if any) botanical form these clusters represent. The individual elements resemble pomegranate flowers, but these occur singly, not in clusters. In my own view, they most closely resemble artichokes.

by the fact that this scroll volute is surmounted by strands of foliage which appear to spring from within the capital. Occasionally these strands are replaced by a caespitose cluster, familiar from type (a).

These capitals are surmounted by a plain block, of the same dimensions as the pier element which the colonnette and capital have replaced. Above this runs the foliated cornice, made up of convoluted acanthus which is closely related to the form found on the capitals.

It is obvious that in form and treatment these capitals are quite unlike any of the eleventh-century work considered in the previous chapter. Undoubtedly their most curious feature is what might be termed their anti-classical tendency. In other words, although they employ classical elements (acanthus, egg-and-dart, etc.), the form of the capitals and the treatment of the upper parts, with its marked asymmetry, is deliberately contrary to classical principles. This anti-classicism, which is present at Avignon, persists in some subsequent examples of nave capitals, and at Aix and Cavaillon becomes a dominating factor. The feature distinguishes the capitals from those of the eleventh century considered in Chapter 2, and also from those normally considered typical of the twelfth century in Provence. The nave capitals at Avignon are not versions of the Corinthian, executed by men who were insufficiently familiar with the original; they are subtle and technically accomplished mutations of Corinthian form.

When we turn to the colonnettes and capitals of the lantern we find a different, and more orthodox treatment (Pls. 41–3). The colonnettes are round to their full height and fluted. As far as one can tell, they do not form monoliths with the capitals.[13] The capitals abandon the elaborate, two-tiered effect of the nave. They are foliated, employing acanthus leaves, central rosettes, and scroll volutes, arranged in a more or less orthodox Corinthian fashion. On the majority of the capitals there is only a single ring of leaves, surmounted by the rose and volutes. There are, however, two variants of this type. On these there are two rings of decoration; the lower ring has either a series of stiff vertical bars or vertical strips of interlace (Pl. 43). The upper part of the capital reverts to Corinthian form. The formal links between these types and the capitals of the Montmajour–Venasque group, dating from the first half of the eleventh century, are obvious. Finally, one capital on the exterior of the lantern bears a species of wind-blown acanthus, made up of curving semi-leaves.

The last group of capitals to be considered is that of the porch. Here one is struck not simply by the usage of classical elements but by the classical feeling of the whole. It is evident that the architect was seeking to achieve a Roman effect, and this serves to point up the fact that the builders of the church were not in the same way concerned with 'authentic' classicism. The authenticity of the capitals flanking the porch is indeed remarkable; the left-hand capital is even cut from two separate blocks, as antique capitals frequently were. The acanthus leaf used here is quite different—no longer the

---

[13] As they cannot be seen at close quarters certainty is difficult. However, on the exterior of the lantern, the capitals and colonnettes can occasionally be seen not to have precisely the same axis.

undisciplined growth of the nave, but beautifully executed, dry, and brittle foliage. The lower ring of leaves is surmounted by cauliculi bearing semi-leaves. The top of the bell has a ring of egg-and-dart. This motif also figures prominently in the cornice, surmounted by acanthus, beading, and key pattern.

We have therefore three groups of capitals; the nave, the lantern, and the porch. The first two groups can be distinguished by the shape of the capitals, the anti-classicism of the nave, and the use of a somewhat flatter acanthus leaf in the lantern. Nevertheless, this is not in itself evidence that they are widely separated in date, or even that they are not contemporary work by different *ateliers*. However, the difference in the treatment of the nave capitals, together with the oddities in the layout of the building mentioned above, increases the suspicion that the church is not after all a unified structure.

For Labande there was no question about the fact that the building was unified (always excepting the porch), although he was a little bothered by the way in which the cupola was mounted. It is none the less surprising that he dismissed so lightly the assertion of abbé Pougnet that the cupola was a later addition, and that the traces of the vault which the cupola replaced could still be clearly seen.[14] Unfortunately, Pougnet did not specify what these traces were, but it is still surprising that Labande did not notice them. They do exist, although they are not as readily apparent as abbé Pougnet claimed. On the north side of the cupola bay (interior) the wall is completely hidden by the organ casing; however, on the south it is visible, although it is covered by layers of paint and the actual masonry cannot be seen. Nevertheless, this wall does reveal a very curious feature. Above the foliated cornice the surface can be seen to be slightly concave, and this curvature persists to a point roughly one metre above the cornice, before the wall becomes vertical (Pl. 34). The feature is not very marked and can only be easily spotted by following the arris produced by the splay of the window cut in the wall. However, its presence strongly suggests that the bay was originally covered by a barrel vault, and the degree of curvature matches that which occurs above the cornice in the other nave bays.

There is another piece of evidence which points in the same direction. The nave capitals occur in each bay of the nave, including the cupola bay. This arrangement is unique, and nowhere else can nave capitals be found in a cupola bay. The reason for this is that these elements were conceived as (visual rather than actual) supports for the transverse rib of the vault, and they appear out of place as supports for an arch which carries an elaborate superstructure, including a high lantern. In short, this feature, together with the curvature of the wall, and the differences between the nave and lantern capitals, make it, in my opinion, certain that the cupola was a later addition.

It is now possible to attempt a reconstruction of the original appearance of the building. It consisted of a five-bay aisle-less nave, covered by a barrel vault, opening directly into an apse. At the west end was a tower, covered by a cupola; the barrel-vaulted narthex which today obscures the cupola was probably not originally planned. On the

---

[14] Abbé Pougnet, *Étude analytique sur l'architecture religieuse de la Provence au moyen âge* (Aix, 1867).

exterior there was of course no porch, and the tower was probably somewhat lower than it is today. The two staircase towers which flank the central massif are, as Labande observed, medieval, but they do not belong to the original scheme. This is apparent from fragments of cornice on the central tower which run into the flanking towers, and by the fact that these side towers break into the now fragmentary arcade of the second storey of the main tower. However, it is probable that the tower was flanked by smaller buttresses, similar to those of the nave.

The second stage was occasioned by the reconstruction of the last bay of the nave. There are several possible reasons for this; the vault may have fallen, or perhaps it was simply decided to improve the lighting of the building, hence the uncharacteristic lantern. At the same time it was perhaps felt that two cupolas, one at either end, produced an unbalanced effect, and so the tower was turned into a narthex by the construction of the low barrel vault which today obscures the view of the cupola.[15]

The third stage comprised the construction of the porch, and at the same time the tower was heightened and the side massifs added, to act as buttresses, and also to balance the façade, which would have looked curious with the porch alone, since the latter is the same width as the tower.

DOCUMENTARY EVIDENCE RELATING TO NOTRE-DAME-DES-DOMS

The documentary evidence relating to Notre-Dame is fairly well known and much of it is fortunately readily available as a result of the publication of the Cartulary. However, it deserves to be reconsidered here, since it is usually set aside, on the assumption that it does not relate to the present building.

During the tenth and early eleventh centuries the church in Avignon, as in the rest of Provence, lacked both strength and prosperity. The local aristocracy recovered more quickly than the church from the incursions of the Saracens, and for a time the clergy must have felt that William the Liberator had merely replaced one antagonist by another. However, as mentioned in the first chapter, the reform of the church, and more particularly the rise of canonical organization, brought an improvement in the position. This improvement, marked by a spectacular enlargement of the territorial domain, can be dated in Avignon from the third decade of the eleventh century, and more specifically from a charter of 1027 in which a priest named Randulfus gave property to the canons of Notre-Dame, St. Stephen's, and St. John the Baptist.[16] This was the first of a long series of donations to the canons of Notre-Dame which continued throughout the eleventh century. Moreover, the document makes it clear that the canons had already adopted a common life (*ea in commune teneant et possideant et eorum*

[15] I do not wish to stress this argument about the insertion of the narthex. It is possible that it was part of the original plan, and that the upper chamber was intended as the pew of the Count. The point to be stressed is rather that the eastern cupola is an addition to the original building.

[16] *Duprat*, no. XXXI. The churches of S. Etienne and St. John were situated close to Notre-Dame on the rock. See Labande, *Avignon*, pp. 283–5.

fructus in communi cellario recondant). However, the establishment of the regular chapter is first officially mentioned some eleven years later, when it is laid down that Benedict, Bishop of Avignon, and Berengar, proconsul of the same town, should choose men of good repute to live in the cloister of Notre-Dame. The canons are given the right to elect their dean, and are also accorded several properties. One of these donations provides us with the first mention of a church building; they receive the houses to the west of the church for use as the infirmary, so that the sick may continue to attend Mass.[17]

It was shortly after this, in 1039, that four canons of Notre-Dame obtained permission to establish a new community at the ruined abbey of S. Ruf, outside the city walls.[18] In the course of the next hundred years the order of S. Ruf was to become both rich and influential, and one may suspect that jealousy underlay some of the quarrels which the canons of Notre-Dame picked with those of S. Ruf in subsequent years, one of which is mentioned below.

In 1059 the chapter received a house 'ante portam canonicalem ad rocha',[19] which indicates that some form of claustral building existed at this date. It is usually stated that it was ten years after this, in 1069, that a new church was consecrated. I shall return to this point shortly.

Somewhat strangely, it is not until 1096 that there was papal confirmation of the establishment of regular canons. A bull of Urban II, dated 15 September of that year, confirms the arrangement, and ratifies the donations which the chapter has received.[20] During the episcopate of Albert (1109–18) a dispute arose over the appointment of the dean,[21] and this marks the beginning of a series of disputes between the bishop and the chapter. In or about 1123 a group of canons gave notice of their refusal to recognize one Peter Berengar, or anyone else appointed uncanonically, as bishop, provost, dean, or sacristan. Moreover, they threatened to walk out if Berengar appeared 'in choro ecclesie beate Marie, nec in capitulo, vel refectorio claustri nostri'.[22] Another quarrel is recorded in the 1150s, between Bishop Geoffrey and the chapter, again over the appointment of the dean and other offices. In 1153 the Archbishop of Aix was called in to arbitrate, and in 1157 there was a committee of inquiry including the Bishops of Arles and Carpentras, the abbot of S. André, and the sacristan of S. Paul-de-Mausole.[23] The 1153 settlement was made 'in capitulo Avinionensi, in maximo ecclesie'.

Two other references to the church can be found in the twelfth century. Between 1125–9 Bishop Leodegar transferred a quarter of the tithe of the church of Entraigues to the chapter, reserving for himself 'sextareum olei de Baiolis ad accendendum lumen ante altare Salvatoris, in ecclesia beatae Marie'.[24] Then, between 1130 and 1150,[25] a

---

[17] *Duprat*, no. XXXIII. 'Ad hutilitatem sive necessitatem infirmorum, concedimus eis mansiones contiguas ipsi ecclesie, scilicet ad occidentalem plagam, quatenus ipsis infirmis non desit cotidiani misterii sacra celebratio.'

[18] *Duprat*, no. CIV.   [19] *Duprat*, no. XXX.   [20] *Duprat*, no. XXVI.

[21] *Duprat*, no. LXI.   [22] *Duprat*, no. LXXVII.   [23] *Duprat*, nos. CXXII, CXXV.

[24] *Duprat*, no. LXXXIV.

[25] Labande, *Avignon*, p. 334 gives the date as 1146, but does not specify the reason for this.

certain viscount Geoffrey, following a dispute with this same Bishop Leodegar, swears an oath of fidelity to the church of Avignon and promises not to harm 'ecclesiam tuam vel clocarium et episcopales domos'.[26]

During the second half of the twelfth century I have found no references to this church, although several acts are signed 'in claustro canonicorum', and one (in 1213) 'in claustro, ante ostium capituli'. Finally, a document of 1215 records the necessity of carrying out restoration work to the cloister, the dormitory, and the refectory.[27]

We may now go back to the record of the consecration of the cathedral. This occurs in an eleventh-century Martyrology, preserved in the municipal library of the city (MS. 98, fo. 144*v*.). Here, under the date 8 October, the following words have been added, in a darker ink (Pl. 44):

Apud avennicā urbē dedicatio eccle beate virginis mariae.

In the margin of this same page, and in the same hand as the above, is a curious verse of ten lines. It is perhaps a copy of an inscription, and the fact that there seems to be a syllable missing in the last line (before 'quod') may well mean that the scribe could not read or did not copy correctly his exemplar:

Somno plasma datur; capit os Deus, Eva creatur.
Parte pius patitur, duo fert latus; aula politur.
Fusca sed alba rubet; virgo manet, est quoque mater.
Cujus floretum lac, panem, mel, dat acetum.
Huic docet exemplo tanto sita formula templo,
Ut petra murorum fuit humo dempta duorum,
Quod cum trigenis sacrarant quinque gerarchis,
Cum jubar archelis undena luce recessit,
Anno milleno bis trigenoque noveno
Prefuerat Verbum quod gustaret acerbum.

The precise meaning of some of these lines is not at all clear, but it is certain that the first six lines describe, in symbolic terms, the building of a new church, while the last four tell of its consecration.[28] It is equally clear from the last two lines that this consecration did not take place in 1069, as is normally stated, but in the 1,069th year of the Passion of Christ. This immediately gives a date some thirty years later, depending upon what date was accepted for the Passion in Avignon. Fortunately, we can calculate the precise year, since the Martyrology records the consecration under 8 October, and the verse tells us that it was the eleventh day of the moon. In the period in question the only possible year is 1101, when there was a new moon on 27 September thus making 8 October the eleventh day. Final proof of this interpretation is that in 1069 the new

[26] *Duprat*, no. cxix.

[27] *Duprat*, no. clviii. I would here agree with Labande that this document does not refer to a restoration of the church itself, although it can be read this way. However, the references to the church are of a general nature, whereas those parts in need of attention are clearly specified.

[28] The text was first published by A. Deloye, 'Note relative à la date de la dédicace de la cathédrale d'Avignon', *Bulletin archéologique du Comité des traveaux historiques* (1891), pp. 292–301. When Labande published the verse (*Avignon*, p. 312) the last line read 'pistaret' for 'gustaret'. 'Pistaret' is meaningless, and since Labande was certainly familiar with the manuscript, and since the reading is perfectly clear, I assume this to be a printer's error.

moon occurred on 21 September, making 8 October the seventeenth rather than the eleventh day.[29]

There remains to consider one of the most interesting of all documents relating to the church at Avignon. It can, I believe, be dated to the late 1190s.[30] The document relates to disputes between the canons of Notre-Dame and those of S. Ruf, and it begins with a sort of historical *résumé*. The founding of S. Ruf in 1039 is retold, and it is pointed out that the new house was given a considerable amount of property as well. The tone is clearly and intentionally that of a reasonable parent scolding a rebellious child. To begin with, Pons Baldus, provost of the cathedral, was rector of the new order, and in the early days relations between the two chapters were excellent. One demonstration of this accord was the fact that the canons of S. Ruf sent their artists to help in the construction of the major church, during Lent and whenever they were needed.[31] Soon, however, the canons of S. Ruf began to claim their independence, and assumed the right to elect their rector from amongst their own number. The disputes date from this time. There follows a list of complaints, and the one which has caused the most ill-feeling is given in considerable detail. The canons of Notre-Dame charge that those of S. Ruf have abducted a young artist. This young man had been taken in, fed, and taught the art of painting by one of the canons ('quem ille suscipiens, diligenter nutrivit, et artem suam pictoriam edocuit'). He at first faithfully served Notre-Dame, and was even allowed to eat in the cloister with the brothers. However, after three years he was induced to defect to S. Ruf.

Fortunately the outcome of this dramatic affair is known to us, for the whole dispute was adjudged by the bishops of Lyon and Grenoble, in consultation with those of Canterbury and Die, and the painter was returned to Notre-Dame. This act is traditionally dated between 1096 and 1119, but it can almost certainly be more closely dated between May 1099 and May 1105.[32] This suggests that the complaint itself dates from the same period, or shortly before, and one may further speculate that a certain

---

[29] Deloye, op. cit., correctly stated that the eleventh day of the moon in 1069 was 1 October but claimed, incorrectly, that this was the 'new style' dating, and corresponded to 8 October.

[30] See below, n. 32.

[31] *Duprat*, no. XLIII. The key passage reads as follows: 'De inobentia autem domni Pontii rectori substituti vel subiectorum eius quamdiu domnus ille prepositus apud nos fuit querimoniam nullam audivimus, imo tante obedientie tunc temporis extitisse ab his qui viderunt asseruntur quod illi qui lignorum artifices vel lapidum culptores [*sic*] vel scriptoria arte valentes inter eos abebantur, per totum quadragesimam vel quolibet tempore quo opus erat maioris ecclesie structure operam dabant.

[32] The document is *Duprat*, no. XXVII, where it is dated between 1096 and 1119. However, it is reasonable to assume that the Archbishop of Canterbury was only called in because he happened to be on the scene, since a dispute of this local nature can hardly have been referred to England just for the archbishop's advice (*cum consilio Cantariensis archiepiscopi*). During the period in question the archbishops of Canterbury were Anselm (1093–1109) and Ralph d'Escures (1114–22). The latter was at Lyon during Christmas of 1116, recovering from gout and a carbuncle on the face, which he had contracted at La Ferté. Apart from this he does not seem to have spent any length of time in the Kingdom of Burgundy. However, Anselm, wandering in exile, was a frequent visitor, and Archbishop Hugh of Lyon was an old friend. He visited the city several times, and there were two protracted stays—from May 1099 to August 1100 and from December 1103 to May 1105. Moreover, Eadmer records that during these times Anselm played a very active rôle in the ecclesiastical affairs of the region. It is therefore more than likely that it was during one of these sojourns that Hugh asked Anselm for his opinion of the S. Ruf case. See *The Life of St. Anselm, Archbishop of Canterbury, by Eadmer*, ed. R. W. Southern (Nelson Medieval Texts, London, 1963), especially p. 116.

Constantine the Painter (*Constantius Pictor*), mentioned in an act of 1095, was the man at the centre of the dispute.[33]

To summarize the information gleaned from the documents, a church existed in 1037, and the infirmary was established to the west of it. Subsequently work was started on a new church, but this was not consecrated in 1069 as has been assumed, but thirty-two years later, in 1101. The absence of a clear time-scale in the complaint of Notre-Dame against S. Ruf is unfortunate, but bearing in mind the foundation date of 1039 for S. Ruf, and the fact that the first concern of the new house must have been to establish itself and construct its own buildings, it seems unlikely that its members could have co-operated in the work on the cathedral before the 1060s or 70s. The subsequent references to a church in the first half of the twelfth century include the 'choro ecclesie' of 1123, the altar of the Saviour in 1125–9, the church and bell-tower of 1130–50, and the 'maximo ecclesie' of 1153.

So far the evidence is clear enough, but we now have to consider Labande's proposed date of 1140–60 for the whole church, excluding the porch. Not only is there no documentary evidence of such a re-building, but there is, I believe, evidence to the contrary. Assuming that the references to a church in the twelfth century mean what they say, they prove the existence of a church in 1123 and in 1153, with a third reference falling somewhere between these dates. This hardly allows enough time for Labande's reconstruction. In addition there were the disputes between the bishop and the chapter, recorded between 1109–23 and again in the 1150s. Such disputes would probably have hindered any building enterprise, which would in itself probably have provided an additional source of controversy. However, the quarrels do not refer to any building programme or to any attendant financial problems. Finally, it is revealing to analyse the gifts to the chapter recorded in the Cartulary. Considering only outright gifts, and not sales and exchanges, we find that between 1027 and 1110 there were a total of twenty-five. After 1110 there are a total of five, and none at all after 1150. The majority of transactions in the twelfth century were either sales or exchanges. This is of course because in the eleventh century the canons were in the process of building up their domain while in the twelfth their position was established. None the less one might think that an expensive operation like building a cathedral would be the occasion for an appeal for funds, and would result in various donations.[34] Also, it is revealing to analyse the pattern of donations in the eleventh century. There are three peak periods when donations were most numerous: firstly between 1027 and 1041, and this coincides with the establishment of canonical organization. The 1040s and 50s are lean years, but from 1059 to 1073 there is a sudden upsurge in donations, and this may well relate to the start of work on the new cathedral. The final, and largest, group occurs between

---

[33] *Duprat*, no. LXXXIII. Teubaldus gives Constantius certain property, to be held under the protection of the canons of Notre-Dame.

[34] Compare, for example, no. LXXXIX in the Apt cartulary, where a certain Henry specifically lays down that the revenues of his gift of houses and a vineyard are to be used for the reconstruction of the cathedral. See N. Didier (ed.), *Cartulaire de l'église d'Apt (835–1130?)* (Paris, 1967), pp. 237–8.

1094 and 1110, and this may be related to the completion and consecration of the cathedral in 1101, and to the papal ratification of the chapter in 1096.

Thus on the basis of documentary evidence there can be no suggestion that the building consecrated in 1101 was rebuilt in the middle of the twelfth century. Of course, Labande's case for dating the present building *c.* 1140–60 was based not upon documents, which he regarded as relating to an earlier building, but upon the similarity of Notre-Dame to other Provençal buildings which he dated to the twelfth century. However, having decided upon the date of Notre-Dame, he then proceeded to date other buildings by reference to it.[35] In short, his whole system of interrelationships, while largely valid in itself, is based upon questionable premises. I here suggest that Notre-Dame dates, for the most part, some fifty years earlier than Labande maintained. To a large extent his case, and of course mine also, depends upon the date which we assign to the related buildings, and this will be one of the main concerns of the subsequent pages. Here one further point against Labande's theory may be noted; the church which undoubtedly existed in the first half of the twelfth century, with its choir, its bell-tower, and altar of the Saviour, disappeared in its entirety in Labande's rebuilding of 1140–60. Although I have argued that the nave and cupola are of different date, it is not possible to fragment the building further than this. There are no traces of earlier walls or of earlier masonry to be found. We must make the unlikely assumption that the eleventh-century church, the existence of which Labande never denied, was annihilated completely.[36]

The church constructed in the eleventh century was subsequently altered by the introduction of the cupola over the eastern bay of the nave, and by the addition of the western porch. In the capitals of the lantern the improved technique of the nave capitals has survived, but the anti-classical tendency has not. The obvious relationship with the Montmajour–Venasque group has been pointed out, but the Avignon capitals have been transmuted by technique. Similar capitals can be found elsewhere in Provence,[37] but the most important group of related material occurs in a major building to be discussed shortly, S. Trophime at Arles. The date of the Avignon lantern capitals has to be considered in the light of this connection, but the internal evidence can be given at this point. The proposed first stage of the building was finished by 1101, and the porch was added in the second half of the twelfth century. The capitals of the lantern fall

[35] e.g. Labande, *Aix*, pp. 339–44.

[36] I am of course here using an argument which can be turned against my own hypothesis, since I have argued that the church which existed in 1037 was not that consecrated in 1101. However, it is more likely that a building extant in 1037, probably already ancient and weakened by long periods of inattention, could have disappeared without trace in a re-building. The complete disappearance of a modern building, not yet a hundred years old, is more mysterious.

[37] The apse capitals in the parish church at Noves, just south of Avignon, employ similar foliage types, and it is here also that there is another example of a cupola mounted on stepped arches. The building may well be a copy of Stage II of Notre-Dame, built shortly afterwards, and adopting the system which had resulted from accidental necessity at Avignon. In *C.A.* (1963), pp. 442–59, Sigros argues that the church was built in two stages, the east end *c.* 1140–50, together with two nave bays, the remainder of the nave and cupola *c.* 1180. Also related to the Avignon lantern are two capitals at Valréas, encased in the masonry of the south piers of the nave, and perhaps surviving from an original porch. See *C.A.* (1923), pp. 319–27.

stylistically between those of the nave and those of the porch, and therefore should date from the first half of the twelfth century. The quarrels between the bishop and the chapter between 1109 and 1123 and again in the 1150s suggest a climate in which building operations would have been difficult, and consequently the building of the lantern would fall most readily into the 1130s or 1140s.

The suggestion that the main body of the present church was built by 1101 is at variance with the accepted interpretation of Provençal Romanesque. It is also seemingly incompatible with the view of eleventh-century development given in Chapter 2 (although, as pointed out in that chapter, I was there concerned only to establish some sort of broad picture of the material which could be placed in the eleventh century without too much controversy). However, assuming for the moment that my conclusions about Avignon are valid, it is clear that the church has to be explained as something of an intrusion, a break with the normal pattern of development. Shortly after the middle of the eleventh century a new church began to be built; it was constructed by expert masons, whose techniques, particularly in the field of stone cutting, were in advance of the best work hitherto produced in Provence. Sculptural techniques were also in advance at Avignon, although the sort of decoration produced, using monoliths and with capitals which I have termed anti-classical, is not out of place in the context of the late eleventh-century experiments which characterized Romanesque sculpture of the period throughout Europe. But before discussing these wider implications, we must consider Avignon in relation to the other nave capital churches of the region.

4 *Aix-en-Provence: the Corpus Domini*

THE south aisle of the cathedral of S. Sauveur at Aix is the second nave capital church to be considered. This aisle, now known as the Corpus Domini, has all the characteristics of an independent church, despite the fact that it is surrounded by a complex of structures, both earlier and later. However, it is difficult to disentangle all the various elements and to visualize the original appearance of the building, and the problems are compounded by the nature of the documentary sources concerning the cathedral. Once again the standard monograph on the Romanesque parts of the structure is by Labande.[1] More recently a major study, with conflicting interpretations, was made by Jean Pourrière, but this invaluable volume does not deal with the art-historical evidence, although it bears directly upon the problems.[2]

The cathedral of S. Sauveur presents a highly irregular plan, but it can be seen to consist essentially of a nave of four bays, flanked by aisles and succeeded by a transept (Fig. 4). At the east end the apse is flanked by single chapels on either side. The main body of the church is an important example of Provençal Gothic, and owes its inception to Archbishop Rostan de Noves, *c.* 1285. Work proceeded slowly from east to west, including the main apse, transepts, and nave, and it was not until 1473 that the westernmost bay was finally erected, while the façade was not completed until 1513.[3] The new building was consecrated, together with all the altars it contained, in 1534 and 1535.[4]

The lateral walls of the first three bays of the nave from the west retain clear traces of an earlier building (Pl. 45). These traces are most apparent on the south wall, and can be seen to consist of a main arcade, of blind round-headed arches, extending for five bays, surmounted by a simply moulded cornice. Two of these bays correspond to one bay of the Gothic nave.

The north aisle is made up of a series of chapels, the earliest of which dates from the second quarter of the fourteenth century; these chapels were converted into an aisle in

---

[1] Labande, *Aix*, pp. 289–344.

[2] *Recherches sur la première cathédrale d'Aix-en-Provence* (Paris, 1939), hereafter cited as *Pourrière*.

[3] On the later parts of the cathedral see especially N. Coste, *Les Architectes, sculpteurs, et maîtres d'œuvre de l'église Saint-Sauveur d'Aix au XVᵉ siècle* (Paris, 1894), and J. Pourrière, *L'Achèvement de Saint-Sauveur d'Aix-en-Provence* (Aix, 1949).

[4] G.C.N., i, no. 40, cols. 97–9.

1697, by piercing their lateral walls. In this north aisle there is no trace of any pre-fourteenth-century masonry.

The corresponding south aisle, known as the Corpus Domini and the part of the building which immediately concerns us, consists of a five-bay nave giving on to the

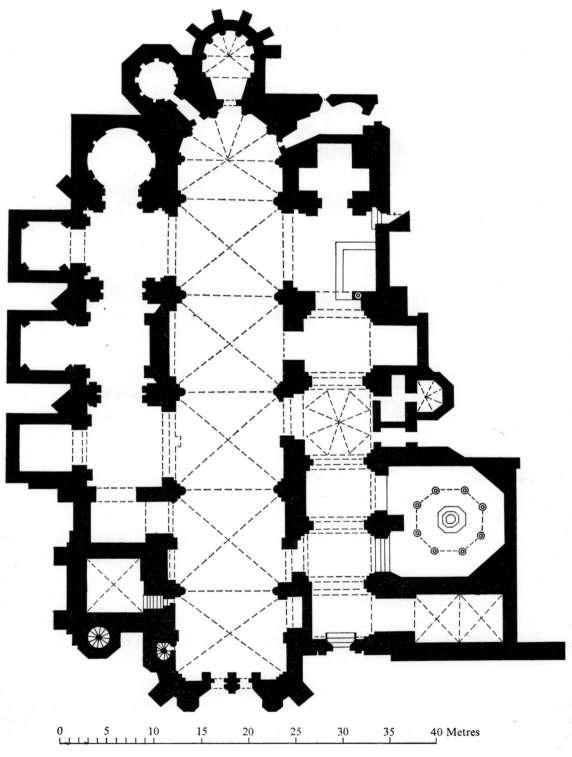

0   5   10   15   20   25   30   35   40 Metres

FIG. 4. S. Sauveur, Aix. Plan

Gothic transept. It is covered by a broken barrel vault, with the exception of the fourth bay which bears a cupola. Opening off the south side of this nave, in the second and third bays, is an octagonal baptistery, whose floor level is 0·90 m. below the present level of the church. This is undoubtedly the earliest extant section of the cathedral, dating probably from the fifth century.[5] To the south-east of the baptistery is the cloister, which may be attributed to *c.* 1190.[6]

A small chapel, no longer extant, was situated in the south-west corner of the south transept. Known as the oratory of S. Sauveur, this ancient building was destroyed in 1808 by Archbishop Champion de Cicé, on the grounds that it did not harmonize with the architectural lines of the cathedral. Although it disappeared relatively recently almost nothing is known of its appearance, and there are unfortunately no drawings and no real descriptions of it. Its position is known; the entrance was at the west, adjoining the south-east terminal pier of the Corpus Domini (Pl. 46). The floor of the chapel, which was covered with a mosaic, was lower than that of the main church, and the interior was barrel-vaulted.[7]

It is clear that the south aisle (the Corpus Domini) was erected after the building which originally occupied the site of the Gothic nave, the traces of which are still visible. The builders of the Corpus Domini utilized the existing church, constructing the piers of their arcade directly against its southern wall.[8]

The interior decoration of the Corpus Domini consists primarily of the nave capitals and cornice. The squinches of the cupola bear the symbols of the Evangelists, and there are two figured imposts in the second bay of the nave. There is a total of twelve nave capitals; they do not occur in the cupola bay or at the ends of the bays immediately flanking the cupola. Both the capitals and colonnettes which support them are treated in an extremely elaborate fashion; the latter have a variety of decoration, including spiral and vertical fluting, and scale patterns. The capitals, which are foliated, are large and bipartite (Pls. 49–52). They are superbly executed, and are clearly the work of master-craftsmen. All twelve capitals are closely similar, but each exhibits minor individual variations. The shape, however, is constant, and consists of a lower part which is cubic, and an extended upper part, which retains a basically rectangular form. This shape immediately recalls the capitals of the Avignon nave, but at Aix the lower cubic section receives greater emphasis, occupying at least one-third of the total height of the capital, and is decorated with great care. This decoration consists of acanthus-type leaves, arranged in varying ways, surmounted by a narrow strip of bead-and-reel. The extensive upper part of the capital bears large convolute acanthus leaves whose spines run along the edges of the block. Thus the capital would normally have four

---

[5] *C.A.* (1932), pp. 277–90.

[6] See my unpublished M.A. thesis, 'The Cloister of the Cathedral of St. Sauveur, Aix-en-Provence'.

[7] See *Pourrière*, pp. 70–1. Traditionally, the oratory was built by S. Maximin himself, but it is difficult to discover the actual age of the building; Labande believed that it dated from the same period as the baptistery, but there appears to be no firm evidence for his assertion that the floor levels of the two buildings were the same. With regard to the size of the building, the circular of Rostan de Fos (discussed below, p. 52) states that it could only hold ten people.

[8] Labande, *Aix*, p. 296.

such leaves, but in several cases four additional smaller leaves are placed at the centre of each face.

As at Avignon, it is at the very top of the capital that the most unorthodox treatment occurs. A pair of semi-leaves, or one semi-leaf and one scroll volute, spring from the centre of the face and curve over the main acanthus leaves. On several capitals behind these semi-leaves one can discern the edge of a marked bell, on an otherwise rectangular capital. The caespitose clusters, which occurred on the Avignon capitals on the sides adjacent to the wall, recur at Aix. However, they are treated rather more soberly, and in several cases abandoned in favour of an even more extraordinary form—a floral rosette, of the type which one would expect to find at the centre of the face of a capital, but which here seems to protrude from the wall (Pl. 52).

It is clear, therefore, that in decoration as well as in shape the Aix capitals closely resemble those of the Avignon nave. The chief difference lies in the execution; whereas the Avignon work has a luxuriant, overflowing appearance, the treatment of the foliage at Aix is much more restrained. The acanthus at Aix is multi-lobed and rather flat. A great deal of use is made of the juxtaposition of smooth and spiky lobe edges to produce triangles of shadow, but the patterns produced appear linear, and the leaves lack the almost rubbery quality of the Avignon work. In short, while the actual form and arrangement of the capitals is close to that of the Avignon nave, the handling of the individual leaves is more assured. The result is an increase in visual clarity, which serves to point up the 'anti-classical' tendency already noted at Avignon.

The cornice on the north side of the nave of the Corpus Domini is made up of convolute acanthus leaves, comparable to those found on the capitals. On the south side this is replaced by an egg-and-dart moulding, surmounted by stiff vertical bars. A similar cornice occurs in the south aisle of the cathedral of Apt,[9] and an inversion of the motif will be noted on one of the capitals of the Arles nave.

On the basis of the chronology proposed for Avignon in the preceding chapter, one would conclude that the Aix capitals, as more developed versions of those in Notre-Dame-des-Doms, probably date from the early years of the twelfth century. Such an opinion would of course conflict with the conclusion of Labande, since universally accepted, that the Corpus Domini 'par sa construction et son décor, rentre exactement dans la catégorie des monuments édifiés de 1150–1180'.[10] Before testing these conclusions against the documentary evidence, we may consider the remaining decoration of the Corpus Domini.

Two imposts of the main arcade, in the second bay from the west, are decorated with

---

[9] The cathedral of Apt is a very complex building, and I do not propose to study it here in detail. Suffice to say that there is good evidence that the Romanesque cathedral was constructed between 1056 and *c.* 1100, and there is no evidence to suggest that it was then reconstructed in the second half of the twelfth century, as is usually stated. R. Doré (*C.A.* (1932), p. 69) was of the opinion that the south aisle was an addition to the original plan; in my view there was no long break in construction, and this aisle may be dated *c.* 1110–20. For the history of the cathedral see A. Roux, *La Cathédrale d'Apt d'après des documents inédits* (Apt, 1949); J. Barruol, *Sainte-Anne d'Apt d'après une documentation nouvelle* (Apt, 1964); N. Didier (ed.), *Cartulaire de l'église d'Apt.*

[10] Labande, *Aix*, p. 343.

figured compositions (Pls. 55, 56). On the north side is the figure of a man, placed horizontally, though clearly intended to appear standing, who is grasping the stem of a stylized vine in his left hand. The figure is stiff and stylized, dressed in a plain robe, the drapery of which is merely indicated by a series of parallel lines. Opposite, on the south side of the nave, the impost bears a pair of griffins, flanking a chalice which is surmounted by a human mask. These are treated in a similarly flat stylized manner. It would, however, be wrong to consider these imposts as crude or unskilled work; the stiffness and stylization is clearly intentional, and the execution is crisp and competent. There is no reason to doubt that they are the work of the capital sculptors, and they witness the fact that the latter's taste for neatness and clarity was carried over into their figure work. Moreover, the flat and precise aspect of the sculpture links it clearly on the one hand with the eleventh-century tradition (see Chapter 2) and on the other distinguishes it from the figural work in the neighbouring cloister, which is largely derived from the cloister and façade of Arles.[11]

The decoration of the fourth bay, covered by the cupola, presents more of a problem. As Labande observed, the lateral walls of this bay show obvious signs of re-working, and in this section of the building the number of masons' marks increases, especially on the cupola itself.[12] It is therefore possible that this bay was reconstructed at some period. However, the foliated cornice at the base of the cupola shows hardly any variation from the nave cornice. The four symbols of the Evangelists in the squinches of the cupola are shown as frontal half-figures holding books (Pls. 53, 54). They bear inscriptions from the *Carmen Paschale* of Sedulius.[13] These figures have a greater plastic quality and are more three-dimensional than the nave imposts, but they share the same type of stylization. The drapery of St. Matthew's robe is treated as a series of parallel folds, and the bull of Luke is decorated in a similar manner. It is therefore possible that these figures were produced along with the nave capitals.[14]

The cupola itself is decorated with flat pilaster ribs, surmounted by capitals at the apex (Pl. 48). These are less carefully executed than the other foliage work in the church, and the leaves appear thicker and more fleshy. This leads me to suspect that the reconstruction of this bay was limited to the cupola itself, which was perhaps renewed some time after its initial construction. However, this is far from certain, and, as will be seen shortly, the reconstruction of the first plan for the church which I give here is most successful if we assume that the cupola bay was not part of the original scheme. A final observation on the question is that the nave capitals do not occur at the east end of the third bay, immediately before the cupola. This is unusual, and visually unsatisfying (Pl. 47). However, if the cupola were not planned to begin with,

---

[11] See n. 6 above.

[12] Labande, *Aix*, pp. 308–9.

[13] The texts are given by Labande, *Aix*, pp. 302–4.

[14] The Aix figures may be linked stylistically to the famous altar frontal in La Major, Marseille, which Kingsley Porter dated to 1122. The documentary basis for this dating is not very satisfactory, but the style provides reason for accepting it. The frontal shares the pattern-like stylization of the Aix figures, achieved by the repetition of parallel folds. See A. K. Porter, *Romanesque Sculpture of the Pilgrimage Roads* (Boston, Mass., 1924).

capitals could have existed at this point, but it would have then been necessary to remove them when the transverse arches supporting the cupola were constructed.[15] But the evidence is unclear, and the matter must be left open.

THE GROWTH OF THE CATHEDRAL COMPLEX

We may now turn to the problems involved in the identification and dating of the various parts of the cathedral on the basis of the documentary evidence. However, before entering into detail, it is apposite to recall Labande's remarks concerning the central piece of documentary evidence, the record of the consecration of a church of S. Sauveur in 1103. Interpreting the text of this document to mean that the church was complete in that year, Labande acknowledged that, if this S. Sauveur turned out to be the Corpus Domini, then all the dates which he himself had proposed for Provençal buildings were incorrect, and the whole school would have to be dated some half a century earlier.[16] Not surprisingly therefore he concluded that the 1103 document was of doubtful authenticity and anyway did not refer to the Corpus Domini. However, the whole question must now be re-examined in the light of Pourrière's detailed researches.

There is a long-standing tradition that the medieval cathedral of Aix was not on the site of the present building, but some 700 m. distant, in the Ville des Tours, on the site of the church of Notre-Dame-de-la-Seds. It is known that the medieval cathedral was a church of Notre-Dame, and therefore it was readily assumed that Notre-Dame-de-la-Seds had preserved a memory of its former status in its name. The major part of Pourrière's book is devoted to proving, beyond any shadow of doubt, that this assumption is incorrect, and that the cathedral of Notre-Dame occupied part of the site of the

---

[15] In this discussion of the decoration I have excluded all reference to the west door. This is flanked by columns and half-columns, and the whole is, most unusually, set back into the façade. However, the four capitals involved are totally unlike those inside the church, nor do they resemble the cloister capitals. I think that they were renewed at some point, and that the present capitals are post-medieval.

[16] It is worth quoting the actual text (Labande, *Aix*, pp. 323–4). 'A notre point de vue spécial, il faut accepter comme réelle la consécration en 1103 d'un édifice de Saint-Sauveur nouvellement fondé entre une église Notre-Dame au Nord, l'oratoire du Sauveur à l'Est, le baptistère au Sud. S'il est prouvé que cet édifice est le collatéral sud de la cathédrale actuelle, l'église Notre-Dame s'identifie avec le monument dont on a reconnu les vestiges dans la nef principale, l'oratoire serait devenu la Sainte-Chapelle. Consacrée en 1103, l'église Saint-Sauveur aurait été commencée dans le troisième quart du XIe siècle par l'archevêque Rostan de Fos, le prévôt Benoît et les chanoines: le témoignage formel en est donné par leur circulaire; il se déduit aussi de la charte de l'archevêque Pierre Geoffroy. Mais elle a été conçue dès le début sur le plan qu'elle présente, par conséquent avec les piédroits des doubleaux de sa voûte, des grands arcs de sa coupole, de ses arcades latérales. Donc ce mode de construction remonterait au moins à la seconde moitié du XIe siècle. Les cathédrales d'Avignon, de Carpentras, de Cavaillon, les églises de Saint-Restitut, de Pernes, du Thor, ressemblent étrangement en tout ou en partie à la nef du *Corpus*; elles seraient par conséquent du même temps, c'est-à-dire du XIe siècle. La nef de Saint-Trophime est moins avancée dans sa décoration; elle devrait donc plutôt appartenir à la première moitié du XIe siècle. Ainsi tout s'enchaîne; si les textes présentés doivent être accueillis, s'il faut les interpréter comme on l'a fait, à la fin du XIe siècle les légendes saintes de Provence avaient déjà cours, l'architecture et la décoration des édifices romans de Provence étaient déjà parvenues au degré le plus élevé et le plus artistique de leur évolution. La question vaut la peine qu'on l'examine de beaucoup plus près qu'on ne l'a fait jusqu'ici, car c'est non seulement la critique de la tradition relative à sainte Madeleine, c'est surtout l'histoire entière de l'art après l'an mille qu'il faudrait reviser.' It should be pointed out that I would not accept all the conclusions which Labande draws from his premise; my own views are given in the course of this book. Some observations on the last sentence quoted are given in the final chapter.

present church of S. Sauveur.[17] There is no need to rehearse the long and extremely detailed arguments which confirm this view; it can be accepted that *Beata Maria de Sede ville Turrium Aquensium* was not the same as *Beata Maria Sedis Aquensis*, and that the title of the former related to the existence of extensive possessions, and at times also the residence of the archbishop, in its vicinity. The original cathedral must have been close to the still extant baptistery, and documents of the late eleventh and twelfth centuries prove that it remained there at this period.

The question of the position of the church of S. Sauveur, which Pourrière also investigates, must be considered here more thoroughly. The first documentary reference to this building occurs in an encyclical addressed to all Christians by Rostan de Fos, Archbishop of Aix (1056–82), which relates that a new church is in the course of construction, because the ancient oratory, founded by S. Maximin, is too small.[18] The authenticity of this document has frequently been challenged, notably by Manteyer and Labande,[19] whose criticisms carry a great deal of conviction. Pourrière also rejects this document, but it seems possible that, though itself a forgery, the circular contains elements of fact. In view of the evidence which follows, it seems more than possible that Rostan did indeed at least make plans for a major building operation. A document of 1092 (?), recording a donation to the chapter by Archbishop Peter II, is undoubtedly authentic, and this contains a great deal of valuable information.[20] It states that the cathedral of Aix ('sedem Aquensis ecclesie in honore sancte Marie') has for years remained in solitude, together with the oratory of S. Sauveur and the baptistery of St. John.[21] Because of the love and respect in which the oratory was held ('ob amorem et reverentiam illius venerabilis oratorii'), it had come to be served by a group of religious, the most notable of whom was the provost Benedict. Benedict had requested a donation for the restoration of the place ('ad restaurationem loci'), and in response the archbishop conceded various properties to the chapter. A second donation is recorded in 1103, when Archbishop Peter III confirmed the terms of the previous act.[22]

In the same year (1103) the consecration of a church of S. Sauveur took place. The text which records this important event must be given in full:[23]

Anno Domini Nostri Jhesu Xpisti millesimo C.III., domnus Petrus, Aquensis archiepiscopus, congregatis quibusdam comprovincialibus episcopis apud Aquis, videlicet, domno Gibilino, Arelatensi archiepiscopo, et Petro, Cavallicensi episcopo, et Berengario, Forojuliensi episcopo, et Augerio, Regensi episcopo, una cum consilio clericorum suorum, videlicet, Fulconis prepositi et Hugonis archidiaconi et Bermundi sacriste et archipresbiterorum Gaufredi et Petri, et chanonicorum Norberti, Petri, Hugonis, Willelmi, Giraldi, et aliorum, quorum nomina, timendo moras, non

---

[17] *Pourrière*, especially Pt. I, Chs. 1 and 2, and Pt. II, Ch. 1.

[18] *G.C.N.*, i, no. 1, cols. 1–3.

[19] See M. G. de Manteyer, 'Les Légendes saintes de Provence et le martyrologe d'Arles-Toulon', in *Mélanges d'archéologie et d'histoire*, XVII (Rome, 1897), pp. 467–89, and Labande, *Aix*, pp. 324–5.

[20] *G.C.N.*, i, no. 2, cols. 3–5.

[21] At the risk of increasing the confusion, I normally refer to the oratory and to the 1103 church by their French name, S. Sauveur, since this is familiar as the present designation of the cathedral. However, it seems perverse to refer to the baptistery as S. Jean, so I have adopted the English equivalent.

[22] *G.C.N.*, i, no. 2, cols. 3–5.   [23] *G.C.N.*, i, no. 4, cols. 6–7.

ennumeramus, statuit consecrare aecclesiam Domini Salvatoris, noviter fundatam inter duas aecclesias, videlicet versus septemtrionem aecclesiam Dei Genitricis sitam, versus meridem vero aecclesiam beati Johannis Babtiste positam; oratorio quoque ejusdem Domini Nostri Salvatoris versus orientem constructo. Hanc denique consecrationem domnus Petrus archiepiscopus, tantorum religiosorum virorum, quorum superius nomina ennumeravimus, auctoritate muniri voluit, quatenus venerabilis aecclesia gloriosi Salvatoris, a venerabilibus viris consecrata, in posterum per infinitum venerabilius veneraretur. Sed quoniam earumdem aecclesiarum quas superius exaruimus Beatus Maximinus et Beata Maria Magdalena primi fundatores extiterunt, in eadem aecclesia Salvatoris a supradictis religiosissimis viris in honore Beati Maximini et Beatae Mariae Magdalenae altare dedicatum est. Cujus consecrationis diem in hac presenti pagina describimus, videlicet VII. idus augusti, quatenus futuris temporibus, absque ulla dubitatione, in aecclesia illa dies ista caelebris annuatim caelebretur.

The authenticity of this text was questioned by Manteyer and Labande, but in this case their objections were not well-based, and they are convincingly rejected by Pourrière.[24] The text may therefore be accepted without reservation.

Considering the habitual vagueness of medieval documents when referring to buildings, the information given here is extremely precise. We are told that the new church of S. Sauveur had the church of St. John to the south, the oratory of S. Sauveur to the east, and the church of Notre-Dame to the north. The first two of these can be identified with absolute certainty as the baptistery which still exists, and the oratory destroyed in 1808. Thus even if we ignore the location of the church of Notre-Dame, there is only one site for the church of S. Sauveur which would conform with these directions—namely the site of the Corpus Domini. Furthermore, it is then easy to identify the church of Notre-Dame as the building which occupied the site of the Gothic nave, the traces of which are still visible. Labande, however, argued that this interpretation was incorrect; the Corpus Domini dated from *c.* 1150–80, and so could not be the building consecrated in 1103. Also we must remember the fact that he accepted the view that the cathedral of this period was Notre-Dame-de-la-Seds in the Ville des Tours. He therefore proposed the following interpretation: the S. Sauveur of 1103 was on the site of the Gothic nave; the church of Notre-Dame would have been on the site of the present north aisle, while the south aisle, the Corpus Domini, is the church of S. Maximin, built in the second half of the twelfth century, and first mentioned in 1175. This church of S. Maximin, which complicates the picture considerably, will be considered shortly. For the present we may concentrate on the theory that S. Sauveur was on the site of the Gothic nave. Two factors make this impossible. Firstly, it would not accord with the text, for the oratory would have been to the south-east of the new church, and not to the east as stated. Secondly, there is absolutely no trace or record of the church of Notre-Dame on the site of the north aisle. This argument could be dismissed if Notre-Dame was, as Labande believed, merely some small chapel, but, as Pourrière has proved, it was in fact the cathedral. On the other hand, the literal

---

[24] See Manteyer, *Les Légendes saintes*, and Labande, *Aix*, pp. 322–3. The most serious objection raised by Labande was the usage of the word *comprovincialis* to include the Archbishop of Arles. *Pourrière*, p. 201, shows that this word was used simply to denote fellow Provençals.

interpretation of the document accords perfectly with the known layout of the cathedral, and there can no longer be any real doubt that the building consecrated in 1103 occupied the site of the Corpus Domini. However, the position is not as simple as this, and there are other complicating factors to be considered.

Seven years after the consecration of S. Sauveur, in 1110, Archbishop Peter III 'consecravit altare fundatum secus oratorio Sancti Salvatoris, in honorem gloriose Resurrectionis Domini Nostri Jhesu Xpisti'.[25] Labande, following Albanès, assumed that this altar was inside the oratory, and was therefore puzzled by the term 'secus', which appeared to be an error.[26] Pourrière has skilfully sorted out the confusing terminology involved, and has shown that the chapel of the Resurrection was distinct from that of the Saviour, and that this notice relates to the consecration of the former chapel. He has further suggested that the chapel of the Resurrection may be identified with a chapel of the Trinity, the destruction of which is recorded in 1316. This is a point to which I shall return.[27]

The final series of documents with which we are concerned is three papal bulls, dating from 1175, 1186, and 1191, all of which are confirmations of the possessions of the chapter of Aix.[28] All three list the possessions of the chapter in the same order, so it is easy to compare them.[29] The following table sets out the first group of buildings as listed in each bull:[30]

Bull of 1175

Ecclesiam Sancti Salvatoris
Ecclesiam Sancte Marie
Ecclesiam Sancte Resurrectionis
Ecclesiam Sancti Maximini
Ecclesiam Sancti Johannis

Bull of 1186

Ecclesiam Sancti Salvatoris
Sancte Marie Aquensis Sedis
Ecclesiam Sancte Resurrectionis
Ecclesiam Sancti Maximini
Ecclesiam Sancti Johannis

[25] *G.C.N.*, i, no. 5, col. 7.   [26] Labande, *Aix*, p. 334.

[27] See *Pourrière*, p. 204. He quotes the following passage from the Martyrology of S. Sauveur (Aix, Bibliothèque Méjanes, MS. 14, fo. 78, marginal note): 'Anno Domini MCCCXVI eodem die fuit disruta capella Sancte Trinitatis que erat et est infra ecclesiam Sancti Salvatoris Aquensis et fuerunt invente in muro dicte capelle diverse relique sanctorum quorum nomina apud homines ignorantur.' He further quotes a text of the early sixteenth century (p. 204, note 31) which refers to 'capellam Trinitatis que olim erat conjuncta capelle Sancti Salvatoris'. It is surely extraordinary that a chapel destroyed some two hundred years previously should be remembered in this way, and it is possible that this text refers to a later chapel. Whether or not the Trinity and Resurrection chapels were the same, the position of the latter remains a puzzle. It cannot have been to the west of the oratory, blocking its door, or to the south outside the walls of the church. The reconstruction of the church of S. Sauveur, proposed later in this chapter, makes it unlikely that the chapel was to the north of the oratory, and its most likely position was to the south of the fifth bay of the Corpus Domini, where there is now a fifteenth-century chapel.

[28] The texts are given in *G.C.N.*, i, no. 12, cols. 13–15; no. 14, cols. 16–19; no. 15, cols. 19–20.

[29] Detailed comparison has been made by *Pourrière*, Pt. I, Ch. 3.

[30] The full lists are compared in this fashion in *Pourrière*, p. 68.

Bull of 1191
Ecclesiam Sancte Resurrectionis
Ecclesiam Sancti Maximini
Ecclesiam Sancti Johannis

The identification of these buildings is for the most part comparatively simple; the sole new title is that of S. Maximin, which occurs in all three bulls. Also it will be noted that S. Sauveur and Notre-Dame are missing from the 1191 list.

It was mentioned above that this church of S. Maximin was identified by Labande as the present Corpus Domini. Since it is first mentioned in 1175, this would coincide nicely with his dating of the building *c.* 1150–80. He based his identification on a very late reference, the re-dedication of the cathedral in 1534 and 1535.[31] More recently Pourrière has brought forward a great deal of evidence which makes Labande's hypothesis a certainty.[32] However, we have seen that the concomitant part of Labande's theory, that the S. Sauveur of 1103 occupied the site of the present main nave, is not correct. Consequently the only possible conclusion is that S. Sauveur and S. Maximin were one and the same building, or at least occupied one and the same site. Further investigation suggests that the title of the church was changed from S. Sauveur to S. Maximin some time between 1150 and 1175.[33] This change may be connected with another which occurred in the second half of the twelfth century, when the cathedral, till then known as Notre-Dame, adopted the title of S. Sauveur.[34] Although this second change no doubt took place gradually, a key to the development can be found in the bulls of 1186 and 1191. In 1186 the first two foundations listed are *Sancti Salvatoris*, i.e. the oratory,[35] and *Sancte Marie Aquensis Sedis*; in 1191 both have disappeared. Instead the only reference to the cathedral is in the vague formula 'locum ipsum in quo prefata ecclesia sita est cum pertinentiis suis'.[36] Thus it is probable that between these dates the cathedral was in the process of adopting the title of S. Sauveur, and this is confirmed by references in 1204 and 1211 to 'ecclesiae Sancti Salvatoris Aquensis et Beate Marie', and 'ecclesie nomine Sancti Salvatoris et Beate Marie Aquensis Sedis'.[37]

We may now sum up Pourrière's argument. The cathedral of Notre-Dame was on the site of the present main nave. By the construction of the Corpus Domini, Notre-Dame was indirectly linked with the oratory of S. Sauveur, the most sacred place in the complex, and therefore it was natural that the cathedral should adopt the same title. To avoid confusion, the Corpus Domini became known as S. Maximin. Pourrière

---

[31] *G.C.N.*, i, no. 40, cols. 97–9. The south aisle of the cathedral is here qualified 'et hec pars vocatur chorus Sancti Maximini'.

[32] *Pourrière*, p. 128.

[33] The church of S. Sauveur is not cited after 1150. *Pourrière*, p. 221.

[34] The date at which the title of the cathedral changed from Notre-Dame to S. Sauveur has been disputed. Again it is *Pourrière*, pp. 229–32, who provides the most convincing solution.

[35] 'Sancti Salvatoris' cannot in this instance refer to the church of 1103, since this is now listed under the title of S. Maximin.

[36] *G.C.N.*, i, no. 15, col. 19.

[37] *Pourrière*, p. 231.

further suggests that, also for reasons of clarity, the oratory of S. Sauveur became known as the chapel of the Resurrection, and the latter adopted the title of the Trinity.[38] While the latter suggestion is not impossible, the former seems highly unlikely. There is no evidence that the oratory was ever known as anything but S. Sauveur, and indeed this was the one edifice which one would expect not to change its title. In addition the Trinity chapel is not mentioned in the 1191 bull, so it can hardly have been the former chapel of the Resurrection (which is listed—though Pourrière suggests it is the oratory) at this date.

There is, however, a more serious problem in Pourrière's theory of the development of the complex: why was the Corpus Domini consecrated to the Saviour in the first place, and why did the change in the title of the cathedral only take place some ninety years later? Pourrière resolved this difficulty by rejecting Labande's assertion that the text of the 1103 document implies that the church of S. Sauveur was complete at this date. Instead he argued that only the foundations were laid at this point, and the building was not finished until the second half of the century.[39] Pourrière therefore accepted Labande's dating of the existing Corpus Domini. Once the building was complete, its original title was abandoned and it became the church of S. Maximin. The reason for this was that the new church indirectly linked the oratory of the Saviour with the cathedral of Notre-Dame; thus on its completion the process whereby the cathedral adopted the title of S. Sauveur began.

This is inherently unlikely. It is not perhaps necessary to regard the 1103 building as totally complete, and we can agree with Pourrière that the phrase 'statuit consecrare' has an impromptu, 'spur of the moment' air about it, suggesting that the archbishop's action was taken simply because four other high-ranking prelates happened to be in Aix. But at the same time the Corpus Domini certainly does not show any signs of prolonged or interrupted building, except in the cupola bay. Nevertheless we can here accept the other main points of Pourrière's thesis; they may be listed as follows:

(a) The cathedral of Notre-Dame was on the site of the present main nave.
(b) The S. Sauveur of 1103 was on the site of the Corpus Domini.
(c) By 1175 this S. Sauveur had become S. Maximin.
(d) Between 1186 and 1191 the title of the cathedral was changing from Notre-Dame to S. Sauveur.

On the basis of these points, we may now offer a fresh hypothesis, taking into account what the actual arrangement of the buildings must have been.

According to the donation of 1092, the cathedral of Notre-Dame, the baptistery, and the oratory of S. Sauveur had originally stood in isolation.[40] Thus we can reconstruct

---

[38] *Pourrière*, p. 222.

[39] *Pourrière*, p. 214.

[40] 'Ad noticiam cunctorum fidelium pervenire volumus sedem Aquensis ecclesie in honore sancte Marie consecratam cum oratorio sancti Salvatoris et baptisterio beati Johannis destructione gentilium cum eadem Aquensi civitate per multa curricula annorum in solitudine permanisse.'

the plan easily enough.[41] The only doubtful features are the length of the cathedral and the form of its east end. It is possible that the surviving traces of five bays represent the full length of the original cathedral nave, since five-bay naves are standard in the region.[42] The form of the east end is entirely unknown, but we may surmise that the building was terminated by a single semicircular apse. The church appears to have been wooden-roofed, yet even so its width was extraordinary; it is perhaps possible that the surviving traces represent aisle rather than nave walls, but their height and articulation argues against this.

The second stage was the construction of S. Sauveur, consecrated in 1103. The main problem here is the form of the east end of the building. The fifth bay of the nave gives directly on to the gothic transept, where, until 1808, stood the oratory of S. Sauveur. According to Labande, the church (for him, S. Maximin) was terminated by a flat wall, in which there was no doubt a door leading to the oratory. It is very difficult to visualize such an arrangement—which would have been unique in Provence—and the possibility of such a solution is greatly lessened by an architectural feature which Labande ignored. The two terminal piers of the Corpus Domini are much larger than the other nave piers, and the southern terminal pier in particular is of vast dimensions. On the exterior of the building this pier can be seen to project some distance above the roof, to form a square turret which today is functionless. If the church had terminated in a flat wall there would have been no need for this great mass of masonry. It seems much more likely that there was some form of tower at this point, and the piers were enlarged to provide buttressing. In other words, the 1103 church, instead of being cut off from the oratory, in fact enclosed it, as the later Gothic church did. This interpretation would explain a puzzling factor in the 1103 text—namely how a church could be consecrated to the Saviour, and at the same time have its altar consecrated to S. Maximin. Clearly the altar of the Saviour already existed in the oratory, and therefore a new altar was consecrated in the body of the church. The building of a tower over the oratory would be consonant with all we know of the place, which was regarded as the most sacred spot in the city, and was served by a special body of canons. The erection of a tower would confirm the oratory as, in effect, a relic; a building consecrated to Christ by one of his immediate disciples, S. Maximin.[43]

[41] I am not concerned here with the age of the church of Notre-Dame, and the surviving traces visible in the present main nave are not especially easy to date. The masonry is of excellent quality, and it is at least clear that this cannot be the original cathedral building—i.e., dating from the same period as the baptistery. My own view is that the building was probably erected in the tenth or early eleventh century.

[42] e.g.—S. Trophime, Arles; Notre-Dame, Avignon; Cavaillon; Carpentras; and of course the Corpus Domini itself.

[43] There are numerous examples of sacred buildings being enclosed in larger structures, and of the construction of towers over such 'relics'. For the twelfth century pertinent examples are obviously the Holy Sepulchre in Jerusalem and the tomb of St. James at Compostela. The dedications to the Saviour and to the Resurrection at Aix do suggest a connection with, or at least some knowledge of buildings in the Holy Land, and such connections become the more possible when we recall that the dating proposed here places the Corpus Domini only shortly after the First Crusade. Also it may be mentioned that the *confessio* chapel at S. Gilles was enclosed by both the crypt and the upper church. The evolution and chronology of S. Gilles is discussed briefly in the final chapter of this essay.

The exact form of this tower must remain speculation, since only the terminal piers of the nave survived the Gothic rebuilding. It may well have enclosed a cupola, according both with Provençal habits and with the veneration of relics.[44] Whether or not there was an eastern apse is even more uncertain; it may indeed have been in such an apse that the altar of the Resurrection was consecrated in 1110. This, however, is not at all likely, since the three bulls of the end of the century list 'ecclesiam sancte Resurrectionis', implying that it was an independent building.

Thus the situation by *c.* 1110 was that the old cathedral of Notre-Dame, though a much wider building than the church of S. Sauveur, was shorter and remained unvaulted. It was flanked by a narrower but longer modern building, vaulted throughout, and enclosing the most revered object in the city, the oratory of S. Sauveur. The general change around in the titles of these buildings, which occurred in the second half of the century, resulted, I believe, not from a reconstruction or changes to the Corpus Domini, but from changes to this old cathedral.

Unfortunately the details of this stage rest upon pure hypothesis, for there are no apparent traces of earlier work in the eastern parts of the Gothic cathedral. However, this is easily explained. The Gothic reconstruction began in 1285, at the east end, and work was in progress on the transepts in 1316.[45] We can conclude that the final bay of the nave, adjoining the transept, was built by 1329–48, for during this period Archbishop Armand de Narcès constructed a chapel, of the same height and dimensions as this bay, immediately to the north of it. Today this chapel forms the easternmost bay of the north aisle. However, the subsequent work on the church was hampered by frequent financial disputes, and the nave was not completed for over a hundred and fifty years. The original intention was no doubt to replace all the old church by a completely new construction, but by *c.* 1330 the initial enthusiasm and the initial funds had gone, and work stopped with only one bay of the nave completed. Consequently in the western three bays of the nave sections of the old walls were retained, in order to simplify construction and reduce the cost of building.[46] Thus the presumed lack of physical evidence of a reconstruction of the east end of Notre-Dame is not, to my mind, particularly significant. Furthermore, even if such evidence existed, it would be impossible to see it, since the walls of the easternmost bay of the nave are completely obscured on both sides by the massive organ casing and choir stalls.

The facts to be explained by this hypothetical reconstruction are as follows:

(a) Why did the title of the cathedral change from Notre-Dame to S. Sauveur?
(b) Why did the S. Sauveur of 1103 become S. Maximin by 1175?
(c) Why does the oratory of S. Sauveur figure in the bulls of 1175 and 1186, but not in that of 1191?

---

[44] It may also be significant that Archbishop Peter II of Aix (1082–1101) was a frequent visitor to Italy, especially to Rome, and consequently the idea of building a church around a shrine would have been directly familiar to him. See *G.C.N.*, i, cols. 52–3.

[45] This may be deduced from the destruction of the chapel of the Trinity in that year. See above, n. 27.

[46] See above, n. 3.

As mentioned above, Pourrière's suggestion that the oratory adopted the title of the Resurrection seems unacceptable. There is, I think, only one possible explanation for the disappearance of the oratory from the 1191 list *and* for the change in title of the cathedral—namely that the oratory had become incorporated directly into the body of the cathedral. The indirect link which had existed ever since the construction of the 1103 church was not sufficient to cause the transfer in the title of the cathedral, and naturally enough only the building linked directly to the oratory (i.e., the Corpus Domini) received the title of S. Sauveur. However, if the cathedral of Notre-Dame were extended eastwards it in turn could be directly linked to the oratory, and the original east end of the church of S. Sauveur would become the south transept of the cathedral. This was no doubt matched by the construction of a north transept; in other words the building took on the dimensions, and very roughly the plan, of the present cathedral. The resulting building would have had a tower on the south transept, and this disposition is not unknown in Provence. There is a tower over the south transept at S. Paul-Trois-Châteaux, and there is one over the north transept at Vaison-la-Romaine.

At the same time the original S. Sauveur of 1103 adopted the title of S. Maximin, and this transition could be made naturally enough, since the building had always contained an altar dedicated to this saint. It is of course true that this last transformation had taken place by 1175, while the cathedral continued to be known as Notre-Dame until 1186–91; however, this may be explained on the assumption that the reconstruction of Notre-Dame had been undertaken by 1175, but that it was not completed until *c.* 1191.

An alternative explanation for the development of the cathedral complex derives from the fact that in the second half of the eleventh century there were two separate bodies of canons in existence,[47] one serving the cathedral of Notre-Dame and the other serving the oratory of S. Sauveur. Given the small size of the oratory, it is likely that the canons of S. Sauveur would have felt the need to have their own church, and this would explain the S. Sauveur of 1103. However, Pourrière has argued, with considerable reason, that this double arrangement only lasted up to 1103, since after this there are no clear references to two separate organizations. Equally to the point is that there are in fact very few explicit references to the canons at all in the first half of the twelfth century, and if we therefore assume that the fusion of the two bodies did not in fact take place until the second half of the century, then the general change around in the titles which we have noted can be seen as a natural consequence of this development.[48]

This is an attractive theory, but it must be treated with caution. Even if we discard Pourrière's arguments for the unification of the chapter by 1103, such a solution would not really affect any of the architectural problems involved, except perhaps to complicate things still further. It would seem probable that a church for the canons of S. Sauveur in 1103 would have terminated in a simple apse, and would not have enclosed

[47] See *Pourrière*, Pt. II, Ch. 2.
[48] I am grateful to Mr. C. Hohler for suggesting this interpretation to me.

the oratory. In this case the cupola bay and the easternmost bay of the Corpus Domini would be reconstructions of, presumably, the mid-twelfth century. However, we have seen that there is no strong evidence for this; on the contrary, the eastern bay includes two nave capitals which cannot be separated from the rest of the group. Thus, unless these two capitals have been moved (and they could of course have come from the eastern end of the third bay, adjoining the cupola), we are stuck with a five-bay nave and the enlarged terminal piers, i.e. the tower theory. It might still be possible to discard my hypothetical twelfth-century reconstruction of Notre-Dame, if it could be proved that the fusion of the two bodies of canons did not take place until the mid-twelfth century, and that that was the occasion for the various changes in title, but I do not think that such an argument can alter or explain the architectural oddities of the S. Sauveur of 1103.

It is extremely important to arrive at a comprehensible solution to the problems of the ecclesiastical complex which is now the cathedral of S. Sauveur. Parts of the above hypotheses may well prove unacceptable, and the proposed third stage could only be confirmed by excavation, but certain clear facts can now be stated. The Corpus Domini is undoubtedly the church of S. Sauveur under construction in 1103. There is every reason to believe that it was completed within a few years, and probably by the time of the consecration of the altar of the Resurrection in 1110. There is no evidence that it was reconstructed or rebuilt when it became the church of S. Maximin. The decoration of the building is very closely linked with that of Notre-Dame-des-Doms at Avignon, which I have dated independently to the late eleventh century. Thus the documentary and the stylistic evidence can be seen as entirely complementary. Labande's proposed date of *c.* 1150–80 contradicts his own interpretation of the 1103 consecration notice (which he believed did not apply to the Corpus Domini). However, it is no exaggeration to say, as Labande himself admitted, that the late dating of the Corpus Domini was the cornerstone of his whole interpretation of the Provençal school; if this is removed, the whole system is in danger of collapse. The evidence brought forward by Pourrière, together with the more specifically art-historical arguments given here, suffice to disprove Labande's dating. In contrast, I would submit that the late dating of the Corpus Domini is unjustified, that it was built in the early years of the twelfth century, and that it can in fact be regarded as one of the most securely dated monuments in Provence.

5

S. Trophime at Arles

IN 1903 and 1904 Labande published a lengthy study of S. Trophime at Arles.[1] It was the first of his major studies of individual Provençal buildings, and it is, to my mind, the best of them. Combining immaculate and wide-ranging scholarship with detailed archaeological observation, this study remains a model of what such a monograph should be. However, it is now almost three-quarters of a century since Labande's study was published, and since that time the church proper, as distinct from the cloister and the façade, has received almost no serious attention.[2] The following remarks are not in any sense a replacement for Labande, but rather a reconsideration and expansion of the one aspect which he somewhat neglected, the decorative embellishment of the building.

Like Notre-Dame-des-Doms, S. Trophime has lost its original east end, and now possesses an apse and ambulatory dating from the mid-fifteenth century.[3] Apart from this, the two buildings are largely different (Pl. 57). S. Trophime has a five-bay aisled nave, giving on to a projecting transept (Fig. 5). Originally there were single absidioles in each transept, flanking the main apse.[4] The nave and transept arms are covered by a broken barrel vault, the aisles have half-barrels, and the crossing supports a cupola on squinches. The building shows obvious signs of frequent alterations, and, unlike Notre-Dame-des-Doms, at least four different types of masonry construction can be found. The lower parts of the aisle walls and the façade are constructed in *petit appareil*; the transepts are built of rectangular blocks, larger than the normal *moyen appareil* of Provence, and these are set in thick beds of mortar (Pl. 58). The easternmost bay of the nave shows considerable traces of a similar type of construction, but this is distinguished from the transept by the occurrence of several masons' marks. By studying the disposition of this masonry, and by reference to the irregular shape of the piers, it

---

[1] Labande, *Arles*.

[2] In this sense it was perhaps unfortunate that the volume in the series of *Petites monographies* was entrusted to Labande (*L'Église S. Trophime d'Arles* (Paris, 1930)). It is of course an excellent volume, but it does not contain any new or revised opinions.

[3] The work was inaugurated by Archbishop Louis Allemand, who died in 1450. The reconstruction appears to have been completed shortly after this; see Labande, *Arles*, ii, 13.

[4] The excavations of 1870 did not cover the transepts, and consequently no physical evidence of the existence of these chapels was discovered. However, their existence is certain, since they contained altars, which are frequently referred to in documentary sources. Labande, *Arles*, ii, 13.

becomes apparent that as originally constructed the bay possessed cruciform piers.[5] However, these were subsequently altered, becoming multi-angular compound piers. The new construction is excellent ashlar work, typical of the best Provençal masonry, in which the stones are regularly and beautifully cut and set, in very thin beds of mortar. This type of masonry occurs in all the remaining bays of the nave, which show no sign of remodelling.

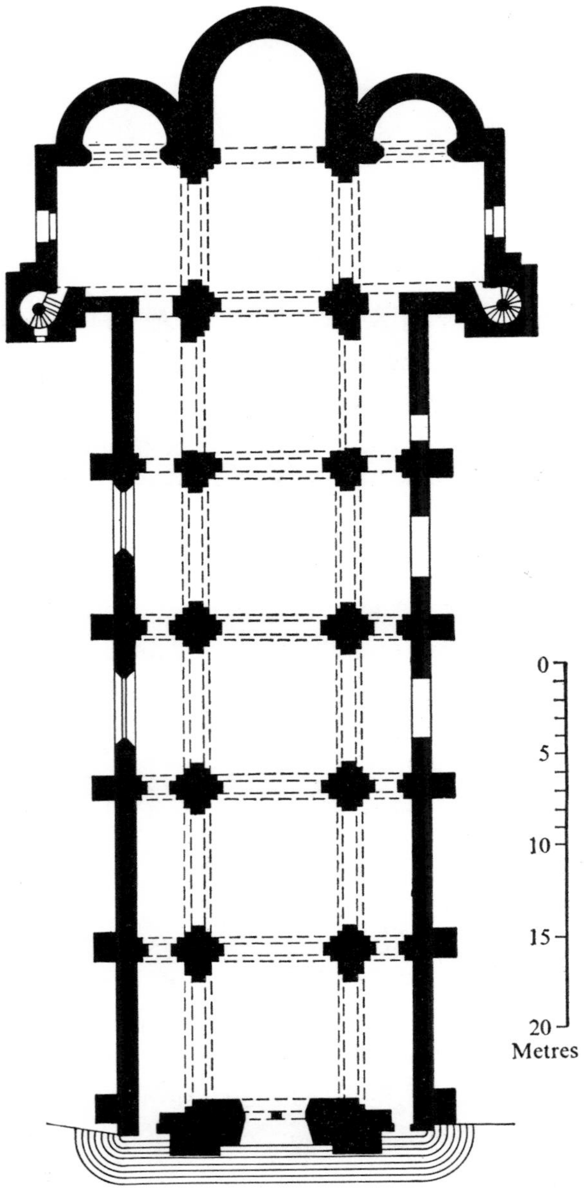

It is apparent that the first stage of the present church, represented by the *petit appareil*, was a basilican structure having the same dimensions as the present nave. This building was subsequently altered by the addition of a transept. Shortly after this it was decided to reconstruct the nave, and the easternmost bay was built.[6] However, for some reason, perhaps lack of money, this project was rapidly abandoned. It was taken up again a considerable time later, when a much more ambitious plan was undertaken. This involved heightening and vaulting the nave, and in the process the eastern bay, which had previously been altered, was again remodelled to harmonize with the remaining bays.[7]

The last of these stages is the important one for the decoration of the building, since the interior is entirely plain but for the nave capitals and the accompanying cornice (Pls. 59–64). As at Avignon, there are twenty of these nave capitals, similarly inserted into the dosserets of the pier, flanking the central pilaster, just below the springing of the vault. The building

FIG. 5. S. Trophime, Arles. Plan, *c.* 1200

---

[5] The irregular shape of these piers is immediately obvious from the plan, and one can deduce that they were originally cruciform on the basis of observation alone. However, this was confirmed by the excavations of 1870. See *Revoil*, ii, 33–47.

[6] I am here following Labande, *Arles*. An alternative, or rather a complementary explanation for the reconstruction of the eastern bay is given below, p. 66.

[7] This was not the last campaign of building; the belltower was added in the late twelfth century. See Labande, *Arles*, ii, 39–40.

itself is considerably higher than Avignon, or indeed than any other Romanesque building in Provence, except the cathedral of S. Paul-Trois-Châteaux. However, the single-storey elevation is retained, and above the main arcade the wall rises vertically for a considerable distance, before giving way to the vault.[8] This means that the nave capitals are correspondingly higher than those at Avignon or Aix, and are therefore more difficult to see clearly. This is a point of some significance, since a system of decoration which was odd at Avignon and Aix becomes rather ludicrous at Arles. For this reason alone it is difficult to envisage the construction and decoration of Arles without the prior knowledge of the nave capital system as it is employed in Notre-Dame-des-Doms and the Corpus Domini.

The nave colonnettes are all, with one plain exception, fluted either vertically or spirally. They are round to their full height, and crowned by astragals. The capitals are all foliated, and all one-tier; the bipartite form of Avignon and Aix does not occur, and instead they appear somewhat squat. All twenty capitals bear a very strong family relationship, and are undoubtedly the work of a single *atelier*. In several instances exactly identical capitals occur three or four times, and it is impossible to tell them apart. Elsewhere, minor differences in the handling of the leaves point to individual hands within the *atelier*. The design of the capitals is simple, again contrasting with the complexity of the two groups previously studied. The bell carries a single ring of convolute acanthus, treated in a flat and stylized fashion. The four main leaves are separated by smaller leaves, whose spiky lobes press up against the smooth-edged main lobes of the larger leaves, creating triangles of shadow. The upper part of the capital bears a large floral rosette, and normally a pair of scroll volutes at the angles. Sometimes the central rosette is replaced by a pair of helices.

This accounts for sixteen of the twenty capitals; the remaining four each have individual variations. One has tall acanthus leaves alone, rising to the full height, without rosette or volutes. The second has a lower ring of acanthus, surmounted by cauliculi bearing semi-leaves. The third replaces the central rosette by a wreath bearing a cross (Pl. 63), and the fourth has a lower ring of stiff vertical bars, surmounted by egg-and-dart; the upper part has a central rose, and acanthus leaves replacing the volutes (Pl. 64). The lower ring of this capital is an inversion of the motif which forms the southern cornice of the Corpus Domini.

The foliate cornice is made up of convolute acanthus. The formation of the leaves varies at several points in the nave, and these variations correspond to the individual hands discernible on the capitals.

These nave capitals are clearly distinct from those previously considered. The treatment is more restrained, the bipartite form does not occur, and the anti-classical tendency is missing. They are in fact much closer to the eleventh-century tradition of capital sculpture, as it was defined in Chapter 2. A comparison with the capitals of S. Pierre,

---

[8] This elevation, out of place in the southern part of Provence, does occur in several churches in the Tricasin and Vivarais, e.g. La Garde Adhémar and Bourg-S. Andéol.

WITHDRAWN-UNL

Montmajour, immediately reveals the nature of this link. The arrangement of the leaves is very similar, the nature of the adherence to Corinthian forms is the same, and a characteristic enlargement of the central rosette occurs on both. The difference lies for the most part in the purely technical superiority of the Arles work.

There is, however, another element present at Arles; the capitals have a distant but distinct Byzantine feeling, arising largely from the characteristic treatment of the foliage. The leaves are treated flatly, as stylized, almost abstract patterns, executed carefully and cleanly, recalling late antique and early Byzantine capital sculpture. This feeling is emphasized by the one capital which replaces the central rosette by a wreath bearing a cross (Pl. 63). There is no need to press this Byzantine analogy too far, nor is it necessary to seek any very distant parallels, since a Byzantine ram's head capital, now in the *Musée de l'Art Chrétien* at Arles and which was found in the city, has been convincingly attributed by Fernand Benoit to the basilica of St. Virgilius, which was on the site of the present church of S. Trophime.[9] It is therefore possible that the sculptors of the nave capitals were influenced by Byzantine work already in Provence, and even perhaps still remaining in the ancient church which was being replaced by the new nave.

These two elements—allegiance to the eleventh-century tradition, together with an echo of Byzantine forms—are also characteristic of the Avignon lantern capitals. The former aspect has already been noted;[10] the latter may be traced in the unusual occurrence of a wind-blown acanthus capital on the exterior of the lantern, and in the replacement of the central rosette on another capital by the Christian monogram (Pl. 33).[11] These facts alone serve to link the Arles nave with the Avignon lantern, and there are other, more definite, stylistic links. In both groups the capitals are treated in a similar manner, with a single ring of leaves, surmounted by rosette and volutes. The rather spiky and flat acanthus found at Arles is closely matched on several of the Avignon capitals. The most striking parallel is the one capital at Arles which employs a lower ring of stiff vertical bars, and which is very similar to one of the interior lantern capitals (Pls. 43, 64). The use of the central monogram in place of the rosette at Avignon may be compared to the central wreath and cross at Arles (Pls. 33, 63).

Because of the height and inaccessibility of both groups of capitals, it is only possible to state that the links between them exist, and that in all probability they were executed within a few years of one another. Without examining the capitals in close proximity, one cannot state that they are the work of the same *atelier*, although this is certainly a possibility.

9 F. Benoit, 'Chapiteau byzantin à têtes de belier du musée d'Arles', *B.M.* (1938), pp. 137–44.

10 See above, p. 37.

11 This is the only occurrence known to me of the monogram on a capital in Provence. It occurs frequently on pre-Romanesque objects, such as altar tables, and in the Romanesque period it is sometimes used as a form of mason's mark. However, where this happens (Aix, cupola, S. Paul-Trois-Châteaux), the form is not identical with that used at Avignon. See Labande, *Aix*, p. 308.

THE DATE OF THE ARLES GROUP

The documentary and historical evidence relating to S. Trophime is less rich than it is for Notre-Dame-des-Doms or for S. Sauveur at Aix. There do not appear to be any references to the building of the church, or to consecrations or dedications. All the surviving evidence is somewhat indirect, and therefore open to interpretation, and this is made more difficult by the fairly complex development of the building in at least four campaigns.

Since it is only the last phase of this development which is relevant for the decoration, the dating of the earlier stages may be summed up rapidly, on the basis of Labande's conclusions. The earliest extant church, represented by the *petit appareil*, is probably Carolingian of the ninth century. This judgment is based solely on the character and quality of the masonry. The remaining traces appear to represent a large basilican structure, and were not, in Labande's view, consonant with a church dating from the time of St. Virgilius in the sixth century.

The first alteration to this Carolingian structure was the addition of transepts, involving presumably a total reconstruction of the east end of the building. In order to try and date this and subsequent alterations, we have to turn to the medieval wanderings of the body of St. Trophimus around the city of Arles. Before the invasions of the Saracens the body of the Saint rested in the ancient cemetery of the Alyscamps.[12] At this time, the church now known as S. Trophime had no connection with this Saint, and was in fact dedicated to St. Stephen. However, by the year 972 the relics of Trophimus had been deposited in the church of St. Stephen.[13] How and when they got there is not clear. It is almost certain that the body would have been removed from the Alyscamps, which is outside the city walls, as soon as the Saracen threat materialized. However, it is unlikely that it would have gone straight to St. Stephen's, where it would have been only marginally safer. More probably it was taken, like the relics of St. Genesius, to the safest possible place, the arena fortress.[14] At any rate, there is no mention of its presence in St. Stephen's before 972, while after this date it is recorded on several occasions.[15] At the same time Trophimus begins to challenge Stephen for the titular of the church. At first the church is referred to jointly as St. Trophimus and St. Stephen, but, after a brief challenge from St. Caesarius,[16] Trophimus is left in sole command by the beginning of the twelfth century.

It therefore seems reasonable to suggest that the body of Trophimus arrived in the church shortly before 972, at the time when the city was beginning to recover from over

---

[12] *G.C.N.*, iii, 9.   [13] *G.C.N.*, iii, 275.

[14] The church of S. Genès-aux-Arènes was destroyed in 1826. Regarding the use of arenas and other Roman monuments as fortresses, see R. André-Michel, 'Les Chevaliers du château des arènes de Nîmes', *Mélanges d'histoire et d'archéologie* (Paris, 1926).

[15] *G.C.N.*, iii, 293, 294, 315, 327, 354, 386, 414, 431, 434. The phrase normally used is 'ecclesie Sancti Stephani sedis Arelatensis, ubi corpus beati Trophimi confessoris quiescit', or 'in qua requiescit Trophimus apostolus almus'.

[16] The occasional designation of the church as *Sancti Stephani vel Sancti Caesarii* would suggest that the relics of Caesarius were brought to the church along with those of Trophimus. The whole development is studied by Labande, *Arles*, ii, 6–10.

a century of disasters, both real and imaginary, resulting from the Saracen invasions. It is also probable that this event may be connected with the construction of the transept. Labande argues that the transept was probably finished before the relics were deposited, but this need not have been the case.[17] The form of the construction is close, as Labande pointed out, to that of the choir of the cathedral of Vaison, for which a date in the first half of the eleventh century now seems most likely. At the same time, the occurrence at Arles of a cupola on squinches, although of comparatively primitive construction, reveals how deeply rooted this form of vaulting was in the region. Indeed, if Labande's dating of the transept is correct, it indirectly weakens the accepted view that nearly all eleventh-century buildings were replaced some hundred years later by new ones. If major eleventh-century churches were anything like as solid and well-constructed as this transept, then they surely would have left more traces (Pl. 58).

The easternmost bay of the nave, as initially reconstructed with cruciform piers, reveals a group of masons' marks, which distinguishes it from the transept, where no marks occur. For this reason Labande suggested that it was slightly later than the transept, and dated from the first half of the eleventh century. Since in my view the transept itself is of the early eleventh century, I would rather date this bay to the 1020s or 1030s. This can be seen as the first stage in a reconstruction of the nave, which was then abandoned, but its real function was to buttress an octagonal tower, mounted on the cupola. Whether or not this tower was ever completed, the traces of its base are still clearly visible inside the first storey of the present square twelfth-century tower (Pl. 65).

The next stage was the total reconstruction of the nave. This phase, which includes the nave capitals, has to be dated on the basis of rather indirect and ambiguous evidence. The key again lies in the movements of the body of St. Trophimus. It will be recalled that this had rested in the church from about 972 onwards. It is mentioned there in 1078, but then there is no further reference to it until 29 September 1152, when it was translated from the church of S. Honorat-des-Alyscamps back to S. Trophime. The transference of the body back to its old home in the Alyscamps has always been connected with the undertaking of a major building operation in the church of S. Trophime.[18] This campaign had two main results; in the first place the reconstruction of the nave, including the alteration of the eastern bay, and in the second, the construction of a raised crypt at the east end of the building. This crypt was unfortunately destroyed in 1450–1, when the new Gothic choir was undertaken, but its foundations were excavated

---

[17] The subsequent argument that the reconstruction of the church was finished at the time of the second translation of 1152 (see below) is based upon the existence of the crypt. As far as we know, there was no special site allotted to the relics in 972.

[18] It is normally assumed that the relics were deposited in the Alyscamps throughout this period, i.e. 1078–1152. However, this is extremely unlikely. The canons of the cathedral would have thought twice about handing over their relics to another corporation for seventy years. In this connection, it is interesting to note that the *Pilgrim's Guide* of c. 1140, although somewhat confused, does not state that the relics of Trophimus were then in the Alyscamps; rather it implies the reverse (see J. Vielliard, *Le Guide du pèlerin de Saint-Jacques de Compostelle* (Mâcon, 1963), pp. 34–6). It seems more probable that they were deposited only overnight in the Alyscamps, on 28 September 1152, in preparation for the major procession to the refurbished church of S. Trophime on the next day, and that for the rest of the time they were kept in one of the direct dependencies of the canons.

by Revoil in 1870.[19] There seems little doubt that this crypt was built to receive the relics of the Saint, and that it was therefore complete by 1152. It consisted of a series of rib-vaulted chambers, extending through the last bay of the nave, the transepts, and the apse. These were constructed directly on the floor of the church, with no attempt to excavate below it. Consequently the floor level of the whole east end had to be raised about four metres above the rest of the church. A flight of eighteen steps in the penultimate bay of the nave led up to the new level; a central corridor through these steps led into the crypt itself.[20] In 1870 Revoil partially uncovered the remains of the crypt, and made the significant discovery that the colonnettes which supported the vault of the first crypt chamber had been attached to the piers of the easternmost bay of the nave after those piers had been remodelled. It will be recalled that, when the pier was first erected, probably in the early eleventh century, it was cruciform, but that its original shape was disguised when the remainder of the nave was reconstructed. Consequently Revoil's evidence proves beyond doubt that the reconstruction of the nave had been undertaken, and had in all probability been finished before the crypt was built. The whole process may be dated between 1078–1152, but it is difficult to be more specific. We may probably assume that the crypt was finished before the translation of 1152; also that the reconstruction of the nave began after 1078, and that this appears to have been finished before the crypt was undertaken. Yet, even if these assumptions are correct, there is no indication of the length of time which elapsed between the two campaigns. The body of St. Trophimus is mentioned in the church in 1078, but it may not have been moved until some years later. Despite all these unknown factors, Labande, somewhat arbitrarily, dated the nave between 1100 and 1140. This seems an excessively long period, and the nave itself does not show signs of interrupted work. His guess (and unfortunately it can be no more than a guess) that the body of Trophimus had been moved by 1100 is reasonable, but to extend the campaign for forty years requires some explanation.

It was in 1060 that the chapter of Arles was organized on a regular basis.[21] We have seen that at Avignon the organization of the chapter in 1038 was followed by the construction of a new cathedral in the second half of the eleventh century, and it is probably legitimate to see some sort of connection between the two events. Similarly the formation of the regular chapter at Arles in 1060 lends credence to the belief that the relics of Trophimus were moved shortly after 1078, so that a major rebuilding could take place.[22]

---

[19] There is a considerable amount of information about this excavation in *Revoil*, ii, 33–47. There is no mention of this work in the Arles *dossier* of the *Monuments Historiques* in Paris, and I do not know the whereabouts of the excavation reports (assuming that such reports were made).

[20] Subsequently the floor of the nave was raised by about one metre, so that one descended into the crypt. The porch was built to coincide with this higher floor level, which proves conclusively that it was not built, or even envisaged, in 1152. Labande, *Arles*, ii, 21–2.   [21] *G.C.N.*, iii, 407.

[22] Clearly the first concern of the newly organized chapter must have been the construction of claustral buildings, such as the refectory and the dormitory. Considerable sections of the canonical buildings survive at Arles, although they mostly appear to date from the twelfth century. They have never been studied.

In contrast with Avignon, the Bishop and chapter of Arles appear to have maintained friendly relations, and there is no evidence of disputes. However, in 1110, Archbishop Gibelin was elected Patriarch of Jerusalem, a post which he held for two years, until his death in Jerusalem in 1112.[23] It is not clear when Gibelin went to the Holy Land, but he appears to have been still in Arles early in 1107.[24] He went to Jerusalem first as papal legate, with instructions to reform the church there, and was shortly after elected Patriarch. From Jerusalem he wrote a letter to his suffragans, and to the chapter and people of Arles, urging them to choose a successor.[25] This they apparently failed to do, for the next archbishop was Atton, who was not elected until 1115, five years after Gibelin's election as patriarch, and three years after his death. All this in itself proves nothing, since the chapter were presumably perfectly capable of organizing and carrying out a building campaign without a bishop; nevertheless, it is perhaps somewhat unlikely that work should have gone ahead on the cathedral during a five-year vacancy in the see.[26]

It has been suggested above that the use of nave capitals in S. Trophime is only explicable on the assumption that the builders were acquainted with the system from elsewhere. It is not only the height of S. Trophime, and the consequent semi-visibility of the capitals, which leads to this conclusion. In other ways too the building stands outside the remainder of the group. It is the only one with aisles, and the only one with transepts,[27] even though these features were inherited from earlier phases of the building. In addition, the capitals themselves are not bipartite, but are versions of the standard Corinthian form. This distinguishes them not only from Avignon, but also from Aix, Cavaillon, and S. Restitut. In short, it is difficult to avoid the impression that the usage of nave capitals at Arles represents a concession to fashion, a desire to be smart.

If this is correct, then there are two possible sources of inspiration. The first is Avignon. The relationship between the lantern capitals of Notre-Dame and the nave capitals of S. Trophime is close, even though one cannot assert definitely that they are the work of the same *atelier*. Equally, it is not possible to state in what order they were produced. However, it is virtually certain that the builders of Arles would at least have been familiar with Avignon.[28] The other source of possible influence is Aix, where the church of S. Sauveur was consecrated in 1103, and the building was in all probability completed shortly after this.[29] As we have seen, this employs the nave capital system and is closely related to Avignon. It may therefore be significant that one of those present at the 1103 consecration was the future patriarch of Jerusalem, Gibelin of Arles.

---

[23] *G.C.N.*, iii, 470, 471, 479.

[24] *G.C.N.*, iii, 468.

[25] *Duprat*, no. LX. See also no. LIX, in which the pope (Paschal II) also urges that the Arlésiens choose a successor rapidly.

[26] We do not know what happened to the revenues of the see during this vacancy. It is most likely that the Emperor was unable to get them, and it would probably have caused a scandal if the Count had seized them. On the other hand, if the chapter got them they could have used them for building.

[27] S. Paul-Trois-Châteaux has both aisles and a transept, but it does not have true nave capitals; see below, Ch. 8.

[28] Arles is some 40 km. from Avignon.

[29] See above, Ch. 4.

In short, the nave of S. Trophime fits nicely into the early part of the twelfth century. Work was probably begun shortly after 1100, was possibly halted or slowed down during the vacancy in the see,[30] and completed in the 1120s. It is from this period that the nave capitals date. Then, in the 1140s, the crypt was built, and finished for the translation of the relics in 1152.

These conclusions tally for the most part with those of Labande, but, having dated the nave to *c.* 1100–40, he then suggested, admittedly without a great deal of conviction, that the nave capitals were a later addition, probably dating from the last quarter of the century and the work of the *ateliers* which produced the cloister and the façade. The reasons for this claim are fairly obvious. In the first place, Labande had accepted and reinforced Lasteyrie's dates for the cloister and façade sculpture at Arles.[31] He then assumed, rather too readily, that the work in the nave was similar to this. Secondly, and more compellingly, he had already formed his opinion of the date of the major Provençal churches, notably Avignon and Aix, and he no doubt felt it impossible that Arles could be the first of the series with nave capitals, for the reasons set out above.

It is readily apparent that Labande's suggestion is inherently unlikely. On purely technical grounds the operation would have been extraordinarily difficult. A high scaffold would have to have been erected, and moved to at least twelve different points in the nave, in order to insert a series of colonnettes and capitals which are hardly visible from the ground. The operation would also have involved the insertion of the cornice. However, all this was done so skilfully that no traces at all were left. This is surely impossible, and in fact it is quite clear that the dosserets have not been cut back at all, but were built with the inset prepared to receive the colonnette. The only exception to this is at the east end of the nave, immediately before the cupola bay, where the impost above the capital can be seen to be inserted into the central pilaster. However, this is just as one would expect, since this eastern bay is the one which was rebuilt early in the eleventh century and then remodelled in the major campaign in the nave.

But perhaps an even stronger argument against this theory of insertion is that the nave capitals simply do not look like any of the later work done at Arles. The capitals of the cloister and the façade, which stretch over a period of perhaps twenty years,[32] employ thick and fleshy acanthus leaves, habitually placed in two rings around the bell. The flat, stylized leaf types of the nave are nowhere to be found. Conversely, the characteristics of the cloister capitals, notably the foliated collar forming an astragal, and the use of human masks to replace the volutes or the central rose, do not occur in the nave. The comparison may be simply made by studying the corbels of the gable of the nave and those of the gable of the porch. The former bear leaves of the nave capital

[30] See above, n. 26.

[31] R. de Lasteyrie, 'Études sur la sculpture française au moyen âge', *Mon. Piot.*, viii, 1 (1902).

[32] Some authorities have argued that the north and east galleries of the Arles cloister are widely separated in date, e.g. Stockhausen, *Die Kreuzgänge*. However, in my view, the two galleries are in fact quite close in date; see below, Ch. 8.

type, flat and stylized, the latter bear the fleshy leaves typical of the late Arles style (Pls. 66, 67).

There can in fact be no doubt that the nave capitals date with the reconstruction of the nave. They gave the building a smart, up-to-date appearance, but at the same time they marked the beginning of a movement which was to reject the exaggerated forms and anti-classical tendencies of Avignon and Aix, and which was ultimately to lead to the triumph of that Romanesque classicism which characterizes later Provençal sculpture.

6

Cavaillon, S. Restitut and Pernes

THE three buildings which have been considered in some detail in the preceding chapters are those for which there is the most abundant documentary and historical evidence. I have shown that, taken individually or as a group, there is no reason to set aside this evidence, as is normally done. By contrast, the majority of related buildings with which we are concerned are almost totally undocumented, and they must be dated primarily on the basis of stylistic comparisons.[1] This is particularly true of the former cathedral of Notre-Dame at Cavaillon, and the parish churches of S. Restitut and Pernes. However, as Labande and others have recognized, they are closely linked with both Notre-Dame-des-Doms at Avignon and with the Corpus Domini at Aix, and consequently it is comparatively easy to date them on the basis of this stylistic relationship. By the same token of course the dates which we assign to Avignon and Aix take on an increased significance, since these are ultimately going to form the basis for our whole interpretation of the school.

Notre-Dame at Cavaillon has been largely ignored by scholars in the past. The architectural and decorative aspects of the building have never been properly analysed, and little consideration has been given to the problem of the position of Cavaillon in the development of Provençal Romanesque.[2] However, it is certainly one of the key monuments, and it is also one of the most beautiful, despite the fact that alterations have greatly mutilated it (Pl. 68).

In the twelfth century the building consisted of a nave of five bays, covered by a broken barrel vault with transverse arches. The main arcade is supported by compound piers, with nave capitals, while the lateral walls are set back behind the buttresses, producing a series of chapels flanking the nave itself (Fig. 6). Chapels were of course constructed between the buttresses at Avignon, but they were not originally envisaged, whereas at Cavaillon they appear to have been an original feature (although they have

---

[1] There are of course certain other Provençal buildings which are dated more or less precisely, such as Le Thor, Tarascon, and the Cistercian abbeys; some consideration of these is included in the final chapter. However, one of the major premisses of this study is that such buildings are not in fact at all closely related to the Aix–Avignon group, and that in this context their dates are irrelevant.

[2] The only serious studies of the church are Labande, *C.A.* (1909), pp. 173–9; J. Zwaab, *La Cathédrale de Cavaillon* (Cavaillon, 1949); and J. Thirion, *C.A.* (1963), pp. 394–406.

subsequently been altered and enlarged). Thus the building can be seen as architecturally a step ahead of its predecessors.

The nave is succeeded by a square bay, vaulted by a cupola on squinches, and this gives directly on to the apse, which is polygonal on the exterior but semicircular on the interior. The decoration of the building consists of the nave capitals and colonnettes, surmounted by a cornice. There are Evangelist symbols in the squinches of the cupola, and four corbels supporting retaining arches in the same bay. The internal decoration of the apse cannot be seen, but it consisted of a blind arcading supported by colonnettes and capitals. Now hidden by seventeenth-century screens, it is said to exist in an extremely mutilated condition.[3]

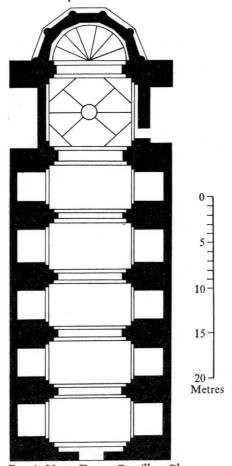

Fig. 6. Notre-Dame, Cavaillon. Plan, *c.* 1200

0
5
10
15
20
Metres

Much of this decoration is extremely difficult to see, and some of it is virtually invisible (e.g., the Evangelists in the cupola squinches). In common with other Provençal churches, the building is naturally dark, and in this case the obscurity is greatly increased by the fact that every available surface is adorned with sombre nineteenth-century paint. The result is unbelievably tasteless, and it succeeds in making any form of art-historical observation very difficult.

The façade was rebuilt in the eighteenth century, and the original portal is lost. In addition, the conglomeration of surrounding buildings makes it difficult to study the exterior of the church closely, especially on the north side. The decoration of the upper parts of the walls can only be seen clearly on the south, where a beautiful *rinceau* frieze runs the length of the nave. On the north, the frieze is largely destroyed, but the surviving fragments reveal that it consisted of a series of panels, bearing a variety of motifs, including a man playing a pipe, Eve and the serpent, an Agnus Dei, pairs of dragons, assorted animals, wheels, palmettes, and other foliage forms (Pls. 70, 71).[4] The buttresses, visible only on the south side, are decorated with pairs of blind arches, some of which bear a foliate design. This immediately suggests a relationship with Avignon, where similar arcading occurs on the buttresses; curiously enough, it occurs, as far as one can tell, only on the south side of

---

[3] Zwaab, op. cit., pp. 13–14.

[4] No photographs of this frieze have previously been published, but a short section of it was drawn and published by *Revoil*, ii, Pl. xxvi. This drawing is not at all accurate, as may be seen by comparing it with the photographs given here. The frieze can only be seen from the upper floors of the houses adjoining the north side of the church.

both churches.[5] The octagonal tower over the cupola is embellished with simple foliage capitals, several of which appear to have been renewed. The apse bears a blind arcade, supported by fluted half-columns and capitals (Pl. 76). The central window, which is blocked, has a moulded and decorated hood, and there is a series of corbels below the roof.

There are twenty nave capitals, inserted as always into the dosserets of the pier, flanking the central pilaster (Pls. 78–81). However, it is known that seven of the capitals were replaced in the nineteenth century, in the course of restoration, by a M. Laffite, sculptor of Avignon.[6] This was in 1863, and now, under the layers of paint, it is by no means easy to tell which seven they are, for M. Laffite was adept at his trade. I have attempted to exclude all the replacements, but it seems highly possible that all the capitals have been more or less re-cut, and they must be treated with caution. However, they retain their original form, and this in itself is sufficiently revealing. The colonnettes which support the capitals are fluted, either vertically or spirally, but the more elaborate treatment noted at Aix does not occur.[7] The capitals are all bipartite and all foliated. The lower part is normally cubic, treated as at Aix, although occasionally the cubic form is replaced by a lower ring, forming a sort of enlarged astragal, decorated with foliage or with egg-and-dart. A similar variation occurs at Avignon. The extended upper part is rectangular, and decorated in a fashion similar to those in the Corpus Domini at Aix, with four large leaves, whose spines run along the edge of the block.[8] These are surmounted by a pair of volutes, or one volute and one semi-leaf, behind which a bell is sometimes visible. A half-rosette occurs at the top of the capital, on the side adjacent to the wall.

Even allowing for restorations, these capitals are clearly very closely related to those at Aix. These links are reinforced by the cornice, which on the north side is made up of convolute acanthus, but on the south consists of egg-and-dart surmounted by stiff vertical bars; not only is this form found at Aix, but the disposition of the two cornices is the same.

It is only when we take into account the external decoration of the Cavaillon nave that a new element appears to enrich the decorative scheme established at Avignon and Aix. This is the frieze at the summit of the nave walls, fragmentary on the north, but complete on the south. These are the first such friezes which we have come across, but they are a major element in the decoration of Provençal churches, and an important group of buildings decorated in this manner will be considered shortly. There is good reason to believe that the builders of Cavaillon were the instigators of the fashion.

[5] It is characteristic of Provençal buildings that the south side, in the sun and sheltered from the Mistral, is more lavishly decorated than the north. The most exaggerated example, considered in detail in a later chapter, is the cathedral of S. Paul-Trois-Châteaux. There are, however, several exceptions to this rule, equally decorated on both north and south, and of these Vaison cathedral is perhaps the most notable.   [6] Zwaab, op. cit., p. 43.

[7] Three of the colonnettes were also renewed by M. Laffite.

[8] This description treats the capitals as though they were free-standing. However, at Cavaillon, as at Avignon and Aix, the capitals are only visible on two of the sides. In all cases they appear to have been carved for the positions they occupy, and consequently they are only worked on two sides.

On the north side of Cavaillon the frieze is for the most part lost, except for several panels which survive at the eastern end (Pls. 70, 71). These show a variety of motifs, described above, and are executed in a formalized style which recalls the figured imposts at Aix. The relief is, however, somewhat higher, and the panels may not unjustly be termed rather more expert versions of the eleventh-century figural tradition found on the funerary tower at S. Restitut. At Cavaillon we also find that the human figures are treated rather awkwardly and without conviction, whereas the strictly decorative motifs, such as confronted dragons, are handled much more confidently. The beginnings of this trait are already apparent on the imposts at Aix, and, in the group of buildings to be considered below, this tendency becomes even more strongly marked. It is in fact clear that this school of sculptors were highly specialized but at the same time extremely limited in their capabilities. The man who could carve the most sumptuous and beautiful *rinceau* scroll could not, or perhaps more accurately would not, produce anything more than a rudimentary human figure. The prejudice against 'realistic' figure sculpture was eventually to be overcome, but this northern frieze at Cavaillon represents an important link in a developing chain, and it will be necessary to return to it later.

The frieze on the south side consists of a *rinceau* scroll (Pls. 72–4). As on the north, this is made up from short blocks, each bearing between one and two turns of the scroll. The excellent quality of the carving, and the fact that occasionally the scroll does not run quite smoothly between blocks, implies that the work was executed in the shop, and only erected when it was complete—again a point of some significance for future developments. One curious factor is that the scroll is not uniform for its full length; at the east end it is composed of a full leaf, which is somewhat spiky, and the divisions between the lobes are drilled out. However, after only a few feet this form is replaced by a *rinceau* formed of semi-leaves, with ribs outermost, in very low relief and treated with extreme flatness. This difference does not seem to be very significant, and both sections should be attributed to the same date. Both share the linear, pattern-like quality which characterizes the rest of the work at Cavaillon, and which derives from Aix. This frieze is of startlingly good quality, and witnesses a highly developed sculptural technique. Both in form and in quality it is obviously inspired by a classical prototype, and fortunately one such prototype is still preserved in Cavaillon itself. The city was a flourishing Roman community, although today there is only one extant Roman monument, the so-called arch of Marius, fragments of which stand in the market-place (Pl. 75). This was obviously an elaborate monument, with lavish and rather unusual decoration. The supports of the arch itself bear a beautiful *rinceau* scroll, and it has been suggested that the top of the monument also bore a frieze decoration.[9] The *rinceau* which survives

9 See G. Bourges, 'Le Monument triomphal de Cavaillon', *Mémoires de l'Académie de Vaucluse* (1897), pp. 199–223. The only Roman arch known to me which closely resembles the decoration of that at Cavaillon is the third-century arch of the Argentarii in Rome. This too has vertical *rinceau* scrolls, and significantly this is surmounted by another horizontal *rinceau* frieze. In addition several of the extant Roman monuments in southern France possess *rinceau* friezes which could have inspired the Romanesque fashion—for example, the Maison Carrée at Nîmes or the bridge at S. Chamas. The whole question of Roman influence on Provençal Romanesque has now been studied by

on the arch is close in form to that on the cathedral and it very probably provided the source for it.

The introduction of the frieze at Cavaillon, and especially of the classicizing *rinceau*, is of great importance. It marks the beginning of the rejection of that 'anti-classical' tendency which was observed at both Avignon and Aix.[10] At Cavaillon the internal decoration of the nave still shares this quality, with the now familiar bipartite and asymmetrical nave capitals, but the external frieze shows that the attraction of actual classical works was now exerting a strong influence. This influence was as yet limited to the decorative motifs, and the Cavaillon sculptors chose to ignore the Roman figure sculpture which they saw (the arch still preserves a pair of Victories and no doubt there was an amount of other figural sculpture on it), and instead reverted to the eleventh-century S. Restitut tradition of formalized representation.

The relative date of the Cavaillon nave is now fairly easy to establish; its décor is in several respects close to that of the Corpus Domini at Aix, but the friezes represent a new element, and architecturally the building, designed from the start with lateral chapels, represents a development of the scheme found at Avignon. It has previously been established that the Corpus Domini dates from the early years of the twelfth century, and that it was probably completed by *c.* 1110. It seems very likely that some of those who worked at Aix also worked at Cavaillon, and therefore the nave there may be dated to *c.* 1115–25.

So far I have not discussed the decoration of the easternmost bay, bearing the cupola, and the apse. The building is normally assumed to be a unity, but this is manifestly incorrect. Even a cursory examination of the decoration convinces that the eastern parts represent a subsequent modification.[11] The capitals on the exterior of the apse are of quite different type from those in the nave, and they employ entirely dissimilar leaf forms (Pls. 77, 78). Their date may be established on stylistic grounds as after the middle of the twelfth century.[12] To this evidence may be added purely architectural observation; the eastern parts of the building make extensive use of roll mouldings on the arches, and the cupola itself possesses true ribs, whereas roll mouldings are nowhere to be found in the nave. There is also the generally ungainly and unbalanced aspect of the east end, which is apparent even from the plan, and there are two masonry breaks, between the nave and the cupola bay and the cupola bay and the apse.

The original form of the east end was almost certainly a low apse opening directly from the last bay of the nave—that is, the same disposition as that assumed for Notre-

V. Lassalle, *L'Influence Antique dans l'Art Roman Provençal* (*Revue Archéologique de Narbonnaise, Supplement 2*), Paris, 1970, which appeared while the present volume was in press.

[10] A rather different form of this rejection has already been observed in the nave capitals of S. Trophime at Arles.

[11] The assertion of Thirion, *C.A.* (1963), that the acanthus cornice at the base of the cupola is of the same form as that in the nave is incorrect. They are similar, but then so is every other acanthus cornice in Provence, and consequently valid connections based upon foliage motifs must rely upon precise observation.

[12] The capitals of the apse at Cavaillon can be related to some of those in the cloister at Vaison, which may be dated to the 1150s (see below, pp. 90–91 ff.). The Cavaillon work appears to be somewhat more advanced, and probably dates from the 1160s.

Dame-des-Doms, Avignon. This is supported by the fact that the *rinceau* frieze can be seen to turn the corner at the east end of the nave and run directly into the massif of the cupola tower, which suggests that the frieze originally ran uninterrupted across the east end of the building, above the apse.

As has been stated, there is no helpful documentary evidence relating to the building of the cathedral. There was a tradition, recorded in the thirteenth century, that a cathedral was built by S. Véran in the sixth century, and that this building could only be consecrated by a pope. Indeed, almost the only sure fact we know is that there was a consecration by Pope Innocent IV in 1251.[13] This consecration must have been of the present building, but it can hardly have been newly erected. However, assuming that the tradition of papal consecration was real, it is equally significant that when Urban II passed through Cavaillon in 1096 there was no consecration, and we may assume that work had not been started on the new cathedral at that date. Between these two extremes we have to rely solely on stylistic relationships with other, better-dated monuments, and, as we have seen, this gives a date in the first quarter of the twelfth century for the nave. We should not ignore the fact that the Bishop of Cavaillon, like the Archbishop of Arles, attended the 1103 consecration in Aix, and it may well have been after this that the idea for the new cathedral was conceived. On the other hand, the east end dates from the second half of the century, most probably from the third quarter, and it was this that received a belated consecration in 1251.

There are two other buildings which are closely connected with Cavaillon, and which appear to be the work of the same *atelier*. These are the parish churches of S. Restitut and Pernes-les-Fontaines. One curious fact, shared by these two buildings, together with the majority of those related buildings which are studied in the next chapter, is that they represent restorations rather than complete rebuildings. In this sudden outburst of restoration work in the middle years of the twelfth century one may perhaps see a connection with the political and economic climate of the age. It was in these years that the Les Baux wars reached their climax, and the long struggle must inevitably have had an effect upon the economic situation and upon people's attitudes. The increasing difficulty of the times appears to be reflected in the numerous decisions to restore rather than rebuild churches.

The parish church of S. Restitut consists of an aisle-less nave of three bays, succeeded by an apse. At the west end is the so-called funerary tower, which was discussed in Chapter 2. Although a small building, it is treated as a miniature version of the major cathedrals, with the same single-storey elevation, broken barrel vault and transverse ribs (Pls. 82, 83). The apse (internally semicircular, externally polygonal) bears a blind arcade, supported by six columns and capitals, while the nave is embellished with six nave capitals, placed in the westernmost bay and at the western end of the adjoining bay. A foliated string course runs the length of the nave and continues round the apse. On the exterior, in addition to the tower frieze, there is a gabled entrance porch on the

[13] A. Potthast, *Regesta Pontificium Romanorum* (Berlin, 1875), ii, no. 14299.

south side, between the westernmost buttresses of the nave (Pl. 22). The apse is decorated with pilasters and capitals, surmounted by a series of grotesque corbels (Pl. 91).

The six nave capitals need not detain us; they reproduce exactly the form and pattern of those at Cavaillon (Pls. 82–5). The only noticeable difference is in what might be termed an increasing looseness in the treatment of the individual leaves. The acanthus is formed in the same way, but it is not so tightly controlled; the convolutions are not so firm and the whole effect is slightly softer and more plastic. It none the less seems highly probable that they are the work of the same *atelier*, and they are certainly close in date.[14] The only other feature distinguishing those at S. Restitut from Cavaillon is the occurrence of a colonnette bearing scale pattern, of the type found at Aix. However, reinforcing the link with Cavaillon is a fragment of *rinceau* frieze, placed internally on the south side of the western bay of the nave (Pls. 86, 87). It is inserted above the nave capital but below the foliate cornice, and it serves to bind these two features together. The fragment is very short, continuing for less than half the length of the bay, but it is beautifully executed, consisting of a semi-leaf *rinceau* in very light relief, and reminiscent of the form found at Cavaillon. The centre of each turn of the scroll is here occupied by a small human or animal figure, instead of the flower form found at Cavaillon. Close observation reveals that this short length of frieze was almost certainly executed *in situ*, for the final block is unfinished but there are signs that it was meant to continue on the adjoining block. The experiment, if that is what it was, was discontinued, perhaps because of the difficulty of doing this sort of work outside the workshop. If so, the lesson was quickly learned, and an improved system was employed at Pernes. However, the transference of the *rinceau* frieze from the exterior to the interior was a significant step, which was to have a fruitful development in the region.

Apart from the difficulty of execution, there is another possible explanation for the discontinuance of the frieze. S. Restitut, despite its small size, is one of the most highly complex buildings in Provence, for there are several visible breaks in the decoration and in the masonry. The cornice which runs the length of the nave is made up of convolute acanthus at the west end; however, this breaks in mid-leaf, immediately after the first pier from the west on the south side, where it is replaced by a much flatter, non-convolute form. This might not be thought very significant but for the fact that it is also at this point that the nave capitals are abandoned. However, there is absolutely no indication of any break in the masonry, and since the cornice varies again on the north side of the nave, the break could be interpreted as no more than a different, but contemporary hand. The abandonment of the nave capitals is more significant, and taken in conjunction with the cornice break it can perhaps be interpreted as evidence of a change in the leadership of the *atelier*. As it was started, the S. Restitut nave was very much in the Aix–Cavaillon tradition, and one might even hazard that the *atelier* was

---

[14] The relationship is so close that one is entitled to question Labande's reasons for dating Cavaillon to 1160–80 and S. Restitut to the extreme end of the twelfth century or the beginning of the thirteenth. See *C.A.* (1909), pp. 114, 173.

led by a veteran of the Corpus Domini, who still adhered to the nave capital form. On his departure (or, more likely, his death) a new man, trained at Cavaillon, took over and promptly abandoned the nave capital scheme. The new leader of the *atelier* (which probably comprised only two or three sculptors) did not impose his new ideas at S. Restitut, but merely finished off the remaining two bays of the nave in a simple fashion, with just the cornice for decoration.

This hypothesis depends on the assumption that the nave was built from west to east, but this is a virtual certainty since the new construction must have taken the existing work, namely the funerary tower, as its starting-point.

If this were the sum total of the decoration at S. Restitut the church would not present very serious problems; closely allied to the nave of Cavaillon, but probably a little later, it could be dated *c.* 1130–5. But this is to exclude the capitals of the apse and of the porch. These are smart, well-executed, and largely orthodox Corinthians (Pl. 89), and, together with the apse imposts and corbels, are the work of one of the most distinctive Provençal *ateliers*, whose major decorative achievement was the nave of the neighbouring cathedral of S. Paul-Trois-Châteaux. This *atelier*, which will be considered in detail in a later chapter,[15] was active in the second half of the twelfth century. However, observation of both architectural and decorative features make it clear that the apse and porch are not contemporary with the nave. A comparison of the type and formation of the foliage on the nave and apse capitals immediately reveals their total dissimilarity (Pls. 85, 89, 91). There is an equally marked difference between the nave and apse cornices (even allowing for the variations in the former). The porch, inserted between two western buttresses on the south side, clearly goes with the apse.

In addition to the clear evidence of the decoration, the building provides one of the few obvious and unambiguous masonry breaks visible in this whole group of Provençal churches, occurring at the point at which the apse springs from the north-east pier of the nave (Pl. 90). The whole apse is also slightly off-axis,[16] and both the apse and the porch are mounted on a slight plinth, which does not occur in the other parts of the building.

Thus there can be no doubt that the nave and the apse are of different periods, and the various stages in the development of the building can be reconstructed. The first stage was the tower in isolation, while the final stage is the present church; the appearance of the intermediate stage(s) is more puzzling. The most likely possibility seems that the whole orientation of the building has been reversed. Notwithstanding the theory previously formed, the position of the six nave capitals in the building, at the west end, is decidedly odd, and decoratively unsatisfactory. Standing in the nave looking into the apse they are invisible; only if we stand in the apse and look west, that is into the tower, can the capitals be properly seen. The tower itself has a cupola built into it, but a low second storey has been added, cutting off the view of the cupola, very much

---

[15] See below, Ch. 8.
[16] This is not apparent on the plan by Chauliat, *C.A.* (1909), p. 109.

as under the western tower at Avignon. Thus, if we imagine the church without the present western apse, and without the low storey in the tower, and reverse the orientation, we have a standard Provençal church, in which the decorative layout makes sense. All that is missing from this scheme is a terminal apse, that is at the west end opening off the tower. Yet when we examine the exterior of the tower we find that the base of it on the western side projects quite markedly (Pl. 88); not only does this thickening not occur on the northern and southern faces, but also the western face, above this projection, is the only one to contain no traces of early masonry at all. For some reason the whole of this face has been rebuilt, instead of merely being restored as the other faces were. Thus there is a strong supposition that there was some form of construction, presumably an apse, to the west of the tower. This was removed when the tower was again restored.

An explanation for the proposed arrangement may be found by reference to the Corpus Domini at Aix and in the geography of the site of S. Restitut. The funerary tower was clearly a valued edifice, hence its careful preservation and restoration. It seems very possible that the original intention was to preserve it, like the oratory of S. Sauveur at Aix, as the focal point of a new church. This could only be done by abandoning a correct orientation, since the ground rises steeply to the west of the tower, and consequently the nave had to be constructed to the east. In this case, the original entrance would have been to the east as well, while an apse was opened on the west face of the tower. The reasons for the subsequent alterations, and the ultimate adoption of the correct orientation, can only be guessed, but it is possible that the tower was in need of further repair and that this was made the occasion for more general changes.

Whether or not this hypothesis is correct—and I do not wish to insist upon it unduly here—the starting-point for it, namely that the present apse and porch are of later date than the nave, seems certain. It is a point of some importance, especially since the unity of the building (excluding the tower) has never been questioned. As mentioned above, the *atelier* which produced the apse capitals was certainly active in the second half of the twelfth century; it is worth pointing out that the other work of this *atelier* nowhere includes nave capitals, or the types of foliage found in the S. Restitut nave. Conversely, if the buildings are unified, it is surely surprising that the links between the naves of Cavaillon and S. Restitut should be so very close, while the decoration of their apses is totally different. Indeed, a comparison of the apsidal capitals shows that there is no direct link between them at all (Pls. 77, 91). On this basis one could perhaps argue that one of the two buildings was unified, but it is not possible to argue that both are. The arguments drawn from each building individually support the conclusion that both have been the subject of considerable medieval alteration, comprising in both cases the reconstruction of the east end of the church. At the same time the decoration of the two naves is consonant with the forms seen at Aix and Avignon, and, to a lesser extent, Arles, and therefore these naves must be dated on the basis of the chronology which we accept for the major cathedrals.

The third building in this group is the church of Notre-Dame-de-Nazareth at Pernes-les-Fontaines. This is another case of the restoration of a pre-existing building, and the single surviving apse capital, from the earliest extant part of the building, was mentioned in Chapter 2.[17] As so often, the restoration with which we are concerned was by no means the last to take place, and the twelfth-century appearance of the building has since been altered considerably, by the reconstruction of the lateral chapels, the building of a belltower, and a reconstruction of the façade. The earliest parts of the building are the apse and sections of the lateral walls of the nave, between the buttresses. It appears that the original church was of the same dimensions as the present building, with aisles, and covered by a wooden roof.[18] The restoration consisted of heightening and vaulting the nave, and replacing the aisles with lateral chapels between the buttresses. The resulting nave consists of five bays, divided by compound piers and transverse arches; it therefore resembles the nave of Cavaillon, with the single-storey elevation, broken barrel vault, and lateral chapels (Pls. 92, 93). The main difference lies in the decoration and the complete abandonment of the nave capital scheme. Instead the decoration consists of an interior frieze, surmounted by a foliate cornice. The frieze itself is made up of a variety of forms of *rinceau*, while the central pilaster and some of the dosserets of the compound piers bear figured panels. The height and obscurity of the building make it difficult to study these low relief panels, but they can be seen to include a variety of both secular and religious subjects, arranged in no apparently significant order.[19] The only certainly religious subjects are Adam and Eve (Pl. 94), and an Orans figure between two lions, which must be Daniel (Pl. 97). It is also possible to identify two fighting men as (?)David and Goliath, and another panel as the (?)Sacrifice of Isaac. Other panels include an ox pulling a plough (Pl. 95), a horseman with drawn sword, soldiers, dragons, and purely ornamental motifs, including a draped curtain (Pl. 96). In between the piers the frieze is composed of lengths of *rinceau* scroll, the form of which varies in each bay (Pls. 98–9). The frieze was originally continuous on both sides of the nave in all except the easternmost bay. In this bay the compound piers are still ornamented, and the cornice is continuous, but the connecting *rinceau* frieze does not occur. I can offer no explanation for this arrangement. On the north side the frieze has been lost in the first three bays from the west, owing to the construction of enlarged Gothic chapels at this point.

The *rinceau* sections between the piers are for the most part superbly executed, while the panels on the piers are, by comparison, inept and crude. There is a double explanation for this. In the first place, it is partly the distinction between ornamental and figural work, which has been noted elsewhere, and which is one of the characteristic features of this phase of Provençal development. However, there are instances where the dos-

---

[17] See above, p. 25, n. 23.

[18] There is no direct evidence for the aisles and wooden roof, but these features seem to me probable. The church has been the subject of only one, very brief, architectural study, by G. Barruol, *C.A.* (1963), pp. 328–36.

[19] All the nave panels are reproduced in H. Giraud and J. Igolen, *Pernes, ancienne capitale du Comtat Venaissin* (Paris, 1927).

serets bear a foliate design as well, and these seem to reflect a deterioration in quality from the longer sections of scroll on the lateral walls. The reason for this probably lies in the method of work. The sections of *rinceau* all occur on long monolithic blocks, which must have been extremely heavy to raise into place. The only reason for utilizing such blocks must have been that they were previously decorated in the workshop, and set in place in a finished condition. The figured panels on the pilasters were probably also done in the shop. On the other hand, the small connecting sections on the dosserets were not carved before, but were decorated in position. Working from the scaffolding, on a small and awkwardly projecting block, the results were rather less polished than those achieved on the ground. At any rate it is clear that the less-well-executed portions on the dosserets are of the same date and are by the same sculptors as the remainder, since they employ the same leaf types and arrangements, even though they are handled more clumsily.

As has been said, the form of the *rinceau* varies from bay to bay. One of the most revealing sections occurs in the fourth bay from the west on the north side, and consists of an inhabited semi-leaf scroll. The form of this is identical with the scroll fragment seen at S. Restitut, and the two are certainly the work of the same man (Pls. 87, 98). If the order of work proposed here is correct, then we can see how this sculptor, after a brief experiment at S. Restitut, brought his ideas to Pernes, but simplified his task by carving his frieze in the workshop instead of in position. He also improved upon the working methods employed at Cavaillon, by using long monolithic blocks instead of a number of short ones. In this way he avoided the difficulty of running the scroll smoothly over the joints, and averted the possibility of setting the blocks in the wrong order.

Other sections of the *rinceau* include a scroll formed from a leaf of palmette type, and a second semi-leaf scroll, which is given greater depth and an increased plasticity; the leaves, instead of being totally flat, become slightly convex, curling inwards at the edges. In this *rinceau* we can trace the beginning of the development which was to culminate in what may be termed the 'stylized naturalism' of the superb *rinceau* at S. Gilles or the acanthus capitals in the Arles cloister. The same movement away from a strictly linear, pattern-like approach can be observed on some of the figured panels. Stylistically as well as formally they remain close to the panels of the northern nave frieze at Cavaillon, as may be seen if we compare the Adam and Eve at Pernes with the Temptation of Eve from Cavaillon; at the same time there is a greater plasticity at Pernes. It is, as yet, only a very slight development, and the figural representations still appear to be far less competently handled than the purely decorative motifs. Undoubtedly the best figural work occurs within the ornamental framework, in the inhabited scrolls, which were still closely based upon Roman prototypes.[20] They witness once again that these sculptors were perfectly capable of producing acceptable and even expert human and animal representations; the pilaster panels at Pernes and the north

[20] There are any number of Roman examples of inhabited scrolls, although not a great many have been preserved in Provence itself. The Cavaillon scroll is inhabited by birds, while fragments of other inhabited scrolls are preserved in the museums of Arles and Avignon.

frieze at Cavaillon demonstrate not so much a lack of sculptural techniques, but rather the adoption of a conscious archaism.

Pernes must in fact be seen as a highly significant building, which stands at something of a turning-point in the development of Provençal decoration. The decision to abandon the nave capital system was to be accepted, with few exceptions, throughout the region. The slight move away from the adherence to linear and two-dimensional forms was part of a general evolution which was to bring spectacular results in later years. On the other hand, the interior frieze did not prove a great success, and the only major buildings to take up the idea were the cathedrals of Carpentras and S. Paul-Trois-Châteaux. Instead there was a reversion to the external frieze system of Cavaillon—a development which was, as we shall see, part of a more general concern with external decoration.

The date of the Pernes nave is again fairly easy to establish on a relative basis. The links with S. Restitut and Cavaillon are close, and, for the reasons set out above, I would place Pernes after both of these, and this gives a date of *c.* 1135–1140. An exception must be made for the south porch, which is rather later. A comparison of the nave and porch cornices reveals an immediate difference, which is confirmed by the capitals and the gable. The porch is in fact related to the nave at S. Paul-Trois-Châteaux, and it will be mentioned later in that connection.

7 Carpentras, Rosans, and the Vaison Atelier

No other major works survive of the Cavaillon–Pernes *atelier*, discussed in the previous chapter. Stylistically, the next clearly definable group of works are directly dependant upon the Cavaillon tradition, although there does not appear to be any continuance in personnel. The key monument in this next group, the major work of the *atelier*, is the nave of Vaison Cathedral, but before discussing this and the related buildings, we may turn to the two final examples of the nave capital system, as it occurs in S. Siffrein at Carpentras and S. André-de-Rosans.

These two buildings clearly descend from the nave capital tradition of church design, even though stylistically they are largely unconnected with the work previously considered. Both appear to be uncharacteristic survivors into an age when the norms of Provençal architecture and decoration had largely changed. The nature of these changes is first revealed in the cathedrals of Vaison and S. Paul-Trois-Châteaux, and so, logically, Carpentras and Rosans should be discussed later. However, it seemed best to consider all the nave capital churches as a group.

Both Carpentras and Rosans are unfortunately difficult to discuss in any very detailed fashion since both are in ruins, preserving only fragments of their decoration. In addition, they are hard to classify stylistically, and Carpentras in particular is the work of a distinctive but otherwise unknown *atelier*. Both employ the nave capital system, but both in a sense misunderstand it, and for this reason alone they appear somewhat outside the mainstream of Provençal developments.

The cathedral of S. Siffrein at Carpentras was rebuilt on a large scale in the fifteenth and sixteenth centuries.[1] The new building was slightly to the south of the Romanesque church, and sections of the north wall of this were left standing. Today these fragments consist of a cupola bay and the nave wall to the west of it; this wall is preserved to its full height only in the bay adjoining the cupola (Pl. 100). Originally the building comprised a five-bay nave, with chapels set between the buttresses. The single-storey

---

[1] The new cathedral was begun in 1405, but it was not consecrated until 1519, and even then the west front was unfinished. The main source for both the Romanesque and Gothic buildings is E. Andréoli and B. Lambert, *Monographie de l'église cathédrale de Carpentras* (Paris-Marseille, 1862); see also Labande, *C.A.* (1909), pp. 194–203, and J. Thirion, *C.A.* (1963), pp. 283–306.

elevation was covered by a broken barrel vault, supported by transverse arches. The nave was succeeded by the cupola bay, which in turn gave directly on to the apse. At the west end there was an additional narrow bay, forming a sort of narthex. Apart from this, the building was therefore similar to Cavaillon—that is, to the restored Cavaillon, after the reconstruction of the original east end. But undoubtedly the most striking feature of the church was the incorporation of the great Roman triumphal arch, to form a sort of north porch.

The decoration of the building included a series of nave capitals, only one of which now survives, and an elaborate connecting frieze in at least the easternmost bay,[2] a cornice of vine scroll, and finally the symbols of the Evangelists in the squinches of the cupola.

The surviving nave capital, at the east end of the nave, is historiated and it abandons the traditional bipartite form (Pl. 101). The subject represented is uncertain; it involves at least four persons, and it has been suggested that it shows two slaves beaten by their captors, but this seems most improbable.[3] The figures are stocky, with large heads and hands, and the drapery is indicated by broad, schematic folds. The connecting frieze consists of garlands of flowers supported by *putti*, treated in high relief (Pl. 102). The motif is undoubtedly of classical origin, and fragments of an almost identical Roman frieze can be found in the Musée de l'Art Païen at Arles, as well as on the mausoleum at S. Rémy-de-Provence. The Carpentras frieze is surmounted by a cornice consisting of an elaborate but untidy vine scroll (Pl. 102). The Gospel symbols in the squinches of the cupola are in the same high relief, and are treated in a somewhat grotesque fashion. The Lion and the Bull are shown as complete figures, viewed from the side, but strangely contorted to fit into the triangular space (Pl. 103). The majority of the Gospel symbols in the earlier buildings are shown as frontal half-figures, and although there are also a good number of full figures, viewed laterally, none seem to belong to the early period.[4]

Although there are no direct parallels for the Carpentras style elsewhere, the arrangement of the decoration, with the classicizing frieze, may be compared with the nave of S. Paul-Trois-Châteaux,[5] while the solid, large-headed figures suggest a connection with the cloister and façade of S. Trophime at Arles. The employment of a historiated nave capital also reveals a fundamental alteration in the concept of nave decoration, and the three-dimensional qualities of all the work are far removed from the linear forms with which we have so far been concerned. It is only necessary to compare the Carpentras work with the Cavaillon friezes, or with the figured panels at Pernes, to see that a fundamental change has taken place.

[2] Since the nave wall only survives to a sufficient height in the easternmost bay, it is impossible to tell if the frieze was continuous. Following the example of Pernes, and the intention of S. Paul-Trois-Châteaux, we may probably assume that it was.

[3] Andréoli and Lambert, op. cit. I would suggest that a more likely possibility is that the capital represents the offerings of Cain and Abel.

[4] The following churches including squinch figures portrayed laterally may be cited: S. Marcel-les-Sauzet; Notre-Dame-du-Groseau; La Major, Marseille; the parish church of Venasque, etc.   [5] See below, Ch. 8.

The precise date of Carpentras is difficult to establish, because of the lack of comparative evidence. On the basis of the decoration alone, it must be seen as a late revival of an earlier mode, treated in an uncharacteristic manner. In short, the building is an example of the traditionalism which is clearly a major factor in Provence. It has been argued that it may be dated on the basis of the epitaph of Bishop Geoffrey de Garosse, who died in 1211, which states that finding the church reduced to nothing he restored and expanded it.[6] This seems to give a somewhat too late date for the church, and Labande was probably right in suggesting that the epitaph refers to a spiritual rather than an actual edifice. The stylistic evidence, uncertain as it is, would suggest a date in the 1180s, and therefore Labande's proposed dating of *c.* 1175–80 appears reasonable.[7]

S. André-de-Rosans is situated in the Hautes-Alpes, and geographically is one of the most distant products of the central Provençal school. The building, to which Jean Vallery-Radot first drew attention,[8] is in ruins, and the apse and façade are destroyed. The lateral walls survive for a length of four bays (Pl. 104). It was covered by a broken barrel vault, with transverse arches, of which only the springing remains. The main arcade is supported by simple compound piers, and the lateral walls of the nave are set back behind the buttresses to produce a series of shallow chapels. The nave opened directly on to the apse, the outline of which is still visible, although no masonry survives above ground.

The decoration of the building consists of a series of nave capitals, originally in each bay but of which only four survive (Pls. 108–11).[9] The capitals are surmounted by a cornice, which runs the length of the nave, and consists of an egg-and-dart moulding. Immediately above the points at which the dosserets of the piers project from the wall the cornice is surmounted by an additional row of tall acanthus leaves (Pl. 109). The effect of this is to produce a sort of parody of the bipartite capitals of the Avignon type, with the two halves of the capital separated by the cornice proper. Three of the surviving capitals are more or less orthodox Corinthian in form, with a lower ring of acanthus, surmounted by pairs of semi-leaves the terminals of which form scroll volutes. The fourth capital, supported by a square rather than a round colonnette, is block-shaped and bears four large acanthus leaves, whose spines run along the edges of the block (Pl. 111). The leaves themselves are multi-lobed and rather spiky, and the serrated edge of the lobe is pressed up against the smooth edge of the adjoining lobe to produce triangles of shadow. The sections of acanthus above the cornice have leaves of similar formation.

The building also includes a series of decorated imposts, on the flanks of the main piers (Pls. 105–7). Those which survive include a variety of forms, notably animal masks

---

[6] 'Ecclesiam nimis iste suam nichil usque reductam
  Extulit et crevit, fecit et esse quod est.'
  The date of Bishop Geoffrey's election to the see is uncertain, but it appears to have been *c.* 1200.

[7] Labande, *C.A.* (1909), p. 197. Thirion, *C.A.* (1963), suggests that the building was restored by bishop Geoffrey, and that the decoration dates from his episcopate.

[8] 'Le Domaine de l'école romane de Provence', *B.M.* (1945), pp. 5–63.

[9] These are at the west end, including the first three on the north side and the second on the south side.

with pairs of leaves sprouting from their mouths, or a row of single leaves alone. Several of these leaves are treated in a near-naturalistic fashion, and this in itself suggests a fairly advanced date for the building.

Since documentary evidence is lacking, S. André can only be dated by reference to other works. The true bipartite form of the nave capitals has been abandoned in favour of a more orthodox treatment, and this suggests a connection with Carpentras, and perhaps ultimately with the nave of Arles. At the same time the extra acanthus above the capitals, but separated from them by the cornice, is a parody, conscious or unconscious, of the bipartite form, and therefore must be seen as a later development. Thus, while we cannot arrive at a firm dating on the basis of the internal evidence alone, the final third of the twelfth century seems certain. Rosans, like Carpentras, reveals a late revival of traditional forms.

Some confirmation of this is provided by another work which seems to be by the same or by a closely related *atelier*. This is the elegant belltower of Notre-Dame-d'Aubune, a rural chapel near Beaumes-de-Venise, south of Vaison. The colonnettes and capitals of this tower are close to those in the nave at Rosans, and could be by the same sculptors (Pl. 112). The Aubune chapel itself dates from several periods, and varying reconstructions of its development have been proposed.[10] However, there is general agreement that the tower is the latest element, and it may perhaps be dated to the 1170s or 1180s.[11]

I attribute the group of buildings next discussed to the Vaison *atelier*, and it is possible but not certain that the nave of Vaison cathedral was their first achievement. The cathedral is a complex building, including work of several different periods, although its development was probably not as involved as Labande maintained.[12] The nave was remodelled in the twelfth century to form a three-bay, aisled structure (Fig. 7). The outer (aisle) walls were re-used from the preceding church, although they were slightly raised (Pl. 118). The remainder of the work was completely new. The eastern bay of the nave was covered by a cupola, while the single-storey elevation of the two remaining bays received a broken barrel vault, with half barrels over the aisles. As at S. Trophime at Arles, the dimensions of this nave were determined by the pre-existing structures, and it was these that dictated the preservation of aisles, and perhaps also, by laying down in advance the positions of the nave piers, resulted in the most unusual architectural feature—the employment of lightly pointed arches in the main arcade, rather than the normal round-headed form.[13]

---

[10] The main alternatives are J. Sautel, *Les Chapelles de campagne de l'archévêché d'Avignon et de ses anciens diocèses* (Avignon–Lyon, 1938), pp. 135–60, and H. Sigros, *C.A.* (1963), pp. 407–32. Sautel regards the three eastern apses as eleventh century, with aisles added in the twelfth. Sigros regards the original plan as having only a central apse, and dating from the second quarter of the twelfth century, with modifications taking place in the second half of the same century.

[11] The belltower at Aubune can probably also be seen as a revival of a traditional form, since it can be related to the western tower of Notre-Dame-des-Doms, Avignon, which was originally decorated with fluted pilasters and colonnettes.

[12] Labande, *Vaison*, pp. 253–321. Also see above, pp. 24–5, for the eleventh-century capitals in the apse.

[13] The use of pointed arches in the main arcade, though rare, does also occur in the Cistercian churches of Silvacane and Le Thoronet.

The internal decoration is comparatively simple. The squinches of the cupola contain the Gospel symbols, while in the nave proper there is an acanthus cornice, and, at the summit of the pilasters of the compound piers, there are panels containing pairs of confronted griffons and swans, flanking a chalice (Pls. 113, 114). At the west end, adjoining the façade, are a pair of nave capitals, supported by squared colonnettes (Pls. 116, 117). The southern colonnette has a male figure attached to it. The exterior decoration consists of a pair of friezes, at the summit of the aisle walls (Pls. 118, 119).

On the south side the frieze is formed of a *rinceau*, while on the north it is made up of alternating palmettes, surmounting the famous mystic inscription relating to the life in the cloister.[14] The upper walls of the nave are pierced by single windows (two on each side) and these are decorated with capitals and ornamented hoods. Finally, the gable of the façade is articulated by fluted pilasters and recessed panels.

Labande observed that not only are the lower parts of the aisle walls composed of early masonry, but also that in the first two bays of the nave there is a clear change in the colour of the masonry just above the aisle, in the main arcade. Here, visible only on the interior, the upper parts are somewhat lighter than the lower. This change occurs throughout, at the same level, producing a horizontal line the length of the nave. Above this line the occurrence of masons' marks is reduced, and, according to Labande, the upper part of the wall is set back slightly.[15] This last point is, I think, an optical illusion caused by the change in the colour of the stonework. Certainly at the point at which one can follow the plane of the wall upwards, namely at the junctions with the piers, there is no such set back, although there does *appear* to be one at the centre of the bay. The point could only be verified by the erection of a scaffolding.

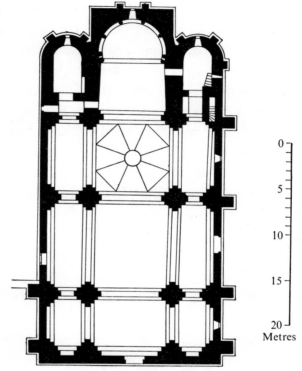

FIG. 7. Vaison cathedral. Plan

Having established this apparent break, Labande turned to the twelfth-century history of Vaison and discovered a convincing explanation for it. In 1142 Berengar de Mornas became bishop, and for almost twenty years he ruled over a peaceful and prosperous see. In 1152 he attended the solemn translation of the relics of St. Trophimus back into the

---

[14] The precise significance of this inscription remains obscure, despite many attempts to elucidate it. The most recent of such attempts are by M. Rambaud, 'Le Quatrain mystique de Vaison-la-Romaine', *B.M.* (1951), pp. 157–74, and W. Messerer, *Romanische Plastik in Frankreich* (Cologne, 1964), Ch. VIII, 'Ikonologischer Stil von Kreuzgängen'.

[15] Labande, *Vaison*, p. 273.

newly completed church at Arles, and this important event might well have inspired Berengar to inaugurate restoration work at Vaison. Unfortunately, however, the bishop shortly after fell foul of the powerful count Raymond V, Marquis of Provence. The exact cause of the trouble is unknown, but early in 1160 Raymond invaded the town, and, after being stubbornly resisted at the walls of the episcopal palace, he took over the city completely.[16] He refused to leave as long as Berengar was alive, and the luckless bishop remained for eighteen years in exile, dying at what must have been a great age in 1178. His successor, Bertrand de Lambesc, took up his cause, and re-took the city by force of arms in 1180. Raymond V was temporarily taken up with other affairs, but the quarrel was revived in 1185, and for a second time the bishop and his clergy were driven out. Bertrand too died in exile in 1190, but his successor, Guillaume de Laudun, came from a family which was on good terms with the Marquis, and with some difficulty a settlement was reached. Guillaume regained the city, but on his death some two years later it was again occupied by Raymond's forces. Indeed, it is said that the bishop's funeral service was interrupted by the returning troops. It was only after the new count, Raymond VI, had built himself a formidable fortress, which still dominates the rock of old Vaison, that a final truce was arranged, and the new bishop, Rambaud de Flotte, was permitted to establish himself in the city. Belated justice was done at the council of S. Gilles in 1209, when Raymond was publicly humiliated and made to confess his crimes, among which was the imprisonment of the bishop and clergy of Vaison, and the destruction of the episcopal palace and the canonical dwellings.[17]

This disastrous history (at least from the episcopal point of view) led Labande to conclude that building activity must have been impossible between the years 1160–96, and few would dispute this. Here, however, is the perfect explanation for the two nave campaigns; begun *c.* 1150, the restoration had reached a point just above the main arcade when the town fell into the hands of Count Raymond in 1160. Everyone then fled, and the work on the cathedral was only taken up again after 1196. It is from this period that the upper parts of the nave, including all the decoration, must be dated.

This is a splendid theory, apparently fitting all the evidence neatly, and it is with some regret that I find it unacceptable. The case for rejecting it is, however, equally strong.

The intrados of the arches of the main arcade, that is well below the apparent break in construction, consists of a plain, unmoulded element. The only embellishment occurs a few feet above the pier imposts, where we find a pair of small corbel-like projections, flanking the central element of the intrados (Pl. 115). This highly idiosyncratic detail also occurs in the apse of the nearby chapel of S. Quenin, which was undoubtedly built by the cathedral nave *atelier*. It is unthinkable that the builders of S. Quenin should, some thirty-five years later, have picked up this trick from the unfinished cathedral, yet the remainder of the decoration clearly goes with the upper parts of the cathedral nave. There is absolutely no suggestion that S. Quenin was built in two stages,

---

[16] The exact site of the episcopal palace is not known, but we may guess that it was in the vicinity of the cathedral.
[17] On the council of S. Gilles see A. Fliche, *Aigues-Mortes et S. Gilles* (Paris, 1961), pp. 31–2.

and it is obvious that these curious corbels were a stock-in-trade of this one *atelier*, especially as this detail hardly ever occurs elsewhere.[18] This in itself makes Labande's two-campaign theory unlikely, and in addition the pier imposts in the cathedral nave (again well below the presumed break) clearly go with the remainder of the decoration. It might be argued that these, together with the corbel projections, were added during the second campaign, but there is no sign of this, and a moment's reflection reveals the absurdity of the idea that a group of masons went round solemnly inserting pairs of semi-visible corbels, which do not alter the overall decorative effect in any way.[19]

We are of course still faced with the apparent break. It will be recalled that this consists of a change in colour of the stone, a reduction in the number of masons' marks, and an apparent set back of the upper nave walls. The reason for this change can only be guessed; it might represent a *short* break in construction, of months rather than years, or it might perhaps merely indicate that a new supply of stone was acquired, from a different quarry. The upper sections of the wall are built in the same fashion as the lower, employing the same size blocks set in the same manner. Whatever the reason for the break, Labande's thirty-six-year halt in construction is not compatible with the evidence.

Nevertheless, the first part of the historical argument still stands, and building operations cannot have been possible between the years 1160–96. Therefore the nave must date either before or after this, and here the decision must be based upon the stylistic evidence. We must also realize the implications of dating the nave and its decoration after 1196, since in this case all the related buildings must be of the same period. Other buildings which are stylistically advanced on Vaison, notably the nave of S. Paul-Trois-Châteaux, would then go well into the thirteenth century, and, since the decoration of S. Paul is dependent upon the cloister and façade of Arles,[20] that work too would have to date from this period. The objections to this view are too numerous to be listed here, and as far as Arles is concerned they have been sufficiently expressed by de Lasteyrie, in his rebuttal of Marignan's thirteenth-century dating of the work there.[21] We must therefore accept the alternative solution, and assign the Vaison nave to the period before 1160.

The internal ornamentation of this nave is comparatively simple; the acanthus cornice is similar to those at Pernes and S. Restitut, while the placing of panels on the pilasters of the piers can be seen as a simplification of the Pernes frieze system. The panels

[18] The only comparable treatment known to me occurs in the transepts of Montmajour, where the inserted corbels are larger and of somewhat different shape. The purpose of these corbels was almost certainly to support the wooden centring used in the erection of the arch.

[19] Another difficulty in Labande's theory is that the raising of the aisle walls belongs to the proposed first campaign, but he argues that the frieze decorating these walls was added during the second campaign. However, the frieze is set on long monolithic blocks, and I have previously argued that the usage of such blocks indicates that the work was done in the shop, and that the decoration was complete before they were raised into position.

[20] See below, Ch. 8.

[21] Lasteyrie, *Études*. This work was designed to refute both the very early datings proposed by Vöge and the late datings of Marignan.

themselves are in very low relief and are composed symmetrically, preserving the linear quality of the Aix–Cavaillon tradition. The most unexpected element in this scheme of internal decoration is the inclusion of the two nave capitals at the western end. The colonnettes are squared, and surmounted by single-storey capitals (Pls. 116, 117). These have four main acanthus leaves, rising to the full height and surmounted by rose and volutes. The southern colonnette has a male figure, one hand raised, attached to it; this is awkwardly executed, but it is certainly intended to achieve a three-dimensional effect. It belongs to the same world as the figure sculpture at Carpentras, breaking with the two-dimensional tradition, but exhibiting uncertainty and lack of expertise which suggest that the development was not as yet fully under control. But why is the figure included here, high up and almost out of sight, and why has provision been made for only two nave capitals? Nave capitals as such were clearly a throw-back to an older decorative scheme, and we may surmise that the builders of Vaison, having rejected the Pernes solution of an elaborate internal frieze, found that the cornice and linear panels alone gave too sober an effect. The nave capitals, used in this restricted way, give an extra touch of richness to the decorative scheme. A similar idea was adopted in the chapel of S. André-du-Gard, near Connaux. This does not explain the column figure, and there are no other instances of such an architectural usage in Provence. The explanation may well lie in the Vaison cloister, which was the work of the same *atelier*. Column figures are known from various Provençal cloisters, notably Avignon, Aix, and Ganagobie, and this raises the possibility that the nave capital shaft was originally designed for the Vaison cloister.

In terms of development, the exterior of Vaison is more interesting than the interior. We find a return to the Cavaillon system of external friezes, and this is only part of a greatly increased emphasis on the decoration and articulation of the exterior. This takes the form of a more elaborate treatment of the window openings, and an articulation of the upper façade wall with fluted pilasters and recessed panels. The frieze, which is at the summit of the aisle walls, consists on the south side of a semi-leaf *rinceau*, with a flower or human mask at the centre of each turn. As at Pernes, long blocks are used for this frieze, and the execution of the *rinceau* retains something of the flatness of the best work there. However, the relief is rather higher, and, though the quality is good, it does not have the elegance of the inhabited friezes of Pernes and S. Restitut, let alone the southern frieze at Cavaillon. The northern frieze consists of alternating palmettes, while on the buttresses there are recessed panels bearing human masks, clumsily executed. The whole aspect of this northern frieze is less accomplished than the *rinceau* on the south, but there is no doubt that it is of the same date, for the splayed terminals of both the palmette and *rinceau* friezes are treated in the same manner, and the surmounting corbels are identical on both sides. The variations in quality point to a number of hands within the *atelier*, and this is only to be expected.

The window openings receive a variety of decoration, and those on the south side are more elaborately treated. The arch is supported by capitals, which clearly go with the two nave capitals, and the hood bears a simple spoon-leaf ornament, with egg-and-dart and enlarged studs on the intrados.

In all, the decoration of Vaison takes an interesting step away from earlier conceptions. It is now the exterior rather than the interior which holds our attention, and although the style is still close to the Pernes mode, it is clumsier and somewhat uncertain. The sculptors were still obviously held by the linear tradition, but they felt pulled towards new experiments in three dimensions. The greater emphasis on the exterior reflects a growing realization that sculptural effects are enhanced by the effects of light, and that consequently external sculpture presents a range of possibilities which are unthinkable in the perpetual gloom of Provençal interiors. The same reason lies behind the comparatively large number of windows in the Vaison nave; the interior, though still obscure, is lighter than its predecessors, with openings at the base of the main vault, as well as in the aisles. Yet with all this, the sculptors felt unable to break too dramatically with the past, and their work remained strictly ornamental. The articulation of the upper façade, with fluted pilasters and the elaboration of the window openings were sufficient innovations. There was no attempt to create elaborate figure sculpture, or to concentrate attention on the doors and porches of the building.

Some mention should also be made of the mystic inscription on the north side of the church. This is executed in excellent Roman capitals, and the type and quality of the epigraphy are virtually unparalleled in the region in the Romanesque period. The only other occurrence of a similar script is the well-known inscription in the north aisle of S. Trophime at Arles.[22] This too is a mystic verse (were perhaps Roman capitals used normally and exclusively for such inscriptions?) occurring in the part of the building which Labande dated to the early eleventh century. The Vaison script is, by comparison, far superior, and must be seen as reflecting the growth of a true 'Renaissance' attitude on the part of the masons involved. This attitude reveals itself in other ways in the work of the Vaison *atelier*, and that this was in itself only part of a widespread development in Provence in the middle years of the twelfth century.

With regard to the dating of the Vaison nave, it must be seen as later than Pernes, but still under the influence of the ornamentalist tradition, and consequently it may be placed *c.* 1150–60, that is immediately before the outbreak of the quarrels between the bishop and the Count of Toulouse. This dating was proposed by Labande for the lower parts of the nave.

Support for a dating in the 1150s is provided by the conclusions of von Stockhausen regarding the cloister.[23] This was disastrously restored in the nineteenth century, but enough original fragments remain to reveal that its decoration was very close to that of the nave, employing the same foliage types, and using on the piers the chevron pattern seen on the nave colonnette on the north side. Stockhausen dated this cloister *c.* 1150–60.

A few hundred metres to the north of the cathedral is the chapel of S. Quenin, already

---

[22] For this inscription see Labande, *Arles*, ii, 17.   [23] Stockhausen, *Die Kreuzgänge*, ii, 148–57.

outside the walls of the town and set amidst fields. It is a curious building, with a seven-teenth-century nave and a famous triangular east end dating from the twelfth century.[24] This east end is richly decorated, and the character of the work reveals that it was certainly built by the cathedral nave *atelier*. The plan, which is without parallel, is externally triangular and contains on the interior a central apse flanked by two small apsidal chapels, set at an angle of forty-five degrees. The advantage of this plan over the traditional forms is that it provides on the exterior a considerable surface of flat wall, which could be decorated in the new manner of the cathedral nave. The walls are articulated with pilaster strips, fluted half-columns are placed at the angles, and at the summit of the walls is a series of frieze panels (Pl. 120). Given the small size of the building, this results in a very rich decorative effect.

The capitals of the half-columns are Corinthian in form, with a lower ring of leaves surmounted by cauliculi, rose, and volutes. The execution is somewhat clumsy, but the capitals relate more directly to classical forms than those produced in the nave capital tradition. One capital, on the north side, includes three small kneeling figures holding knives (Pl. 120). The frieze panels include a variety of foliate motifs, treated in the linear and stylized manner of the earlier friezes. There is, however, no reason to believe that these panels are re-used,[25] and the apparent stylistic differences between them and the adjoining capitals reveals once more the continuous dichotomy in Provençal decoration.

On the interior, the central apse is decorated with a blind arcade, the capitals of which may be closely compared with several of the window capitals of the cathedral nave (Pl. 121). Further links are provided by the corbel projections on the triumphal arch, which have already been noted.

A third work by the same group of masons is the southern portion of the chapel of Notre-Dame-du-Groseau, near Malaucène, on the slopes of Mont Ventoux.[26] This chapel is, like Notre-Dame-d'Aubune, a complex structure, and neither of the proposed reconstructions of its development seems very satisfactory.[27] Sections of the building appear to be early, and may well date from the mid-eleventh century, when the site came into the possession of S. Victor, Marseille.[28] I shall not propose an alternative reconstruction here, but simply note that the decoration of the southern portion, the chapel of the Baptist, was the work of the Vaison *atelier*. It includes a small apse, with a blind arcade, and a pair of male figures attached to the main piers, just below the impost. A comparison of the capitals of the arcade with those from the interior of S. Quenin immediately reveals the close links between them (Pls. 121, 122), while the simple figures on the piers may be compared with the column figure in the nave of

24 On S. Quenin see Labande, *C.A.* (1909), pp. 95–7; Sautel, op. cit.; and J. Vallery-Radot, *C.A.* (1963), pp. 264–73.
25 Sautel claims that certain of the panels are re-used Carolingian work.
26 On Notre-Dame-du-Groseau see Sautel, op. cit., pp. 225–49, and J. Vallery-Radot, *C.A.* (1963), pp. 274–82.
27 The building consists of a square, box-like structure, with a smaller rectangular chapel to the south of it. Sautel regards this smaller chapel as the original nucleus, but Vallery-Radot regards it as a later addition. In my view, the walls of this smaller chapel do contain early masonry, but the decoration is not contemporary with this.
28 The site was given to S. Victor by the Bishop of Vaison in 1059 or 1060, and this gift was confirmed by Pope Gregory VII in 1079, as 'monasterium Ste Marie de Grausello apud Malaucenam'.

Vaison cathedral. The decoration of the adjoining northern chapel, Notre-Dame, seems to be somewhat later, although there are fragments of a frieze at the summit of the walls on the exterior which again appear to be the work of the Vaison sculptors.

The Vaison *atelier* was active between *c.* 1150 and 1170. Its influence was considerable, for it led to new conceptions of decorative enrichment, particularly a growing tendency to elaborate external ornamentation, and an increasing usage of directly classicizing elements, such as Corinthian capitals and fluted pilasters. In this sense, the belltower at Notre-Dame-d'Aubune, already mentioned, was a product of the Vaison developments, for it is elaborately treated with pilaster strips, as well as colonnettes and capitals. In addition the individual capitals at Aubune appear to be later derivatives of the Vaison style. Similarly the small chapel in the Val des Nymphes, near La Garde Adhémar, reflects this influence, and we find the upper part of the façade treated with pilaster strips and recessed panels, very much in the Vaison manner. More generally, the tendency towards decorative enrichment recurs in other buildings which may be regarded as of the same period, such as S. Ruf at Avignon, where, although the work of a separate *atelier*, we find elaborate window openings, and an overall decorative conception which recalls the Vaison forms.[29]

There is also one specific decorative device which seems to originate with the Vaison *atelier*, and which may legitimately be considered as a legacy from the nave capital scheme. The first example occurs in the apse of the chapel of S. Quenin. Here the standard blind arcade is formed of colonnettes and capitals, but above the capitals and resting on them is a series of short pilasters which connect with the pilaster-ribs of the semi-dome proper. Visually therefore these pilasters play exactly the same sort of role as the nave capitals, acting as ostensible supports for vaulting ribs (Pl. 121), and there is a strong possibility that the one derived from the other. In addition to S. Quenin, the system occurs (employing either pilasters or half-columns) in the southern apse at Notre-Dame-du-Groseau, at Simiane-la-Rotonde, and at Bonlieu. A version of the scheme, where pilasters or colonnettes are placed only at the opening of the apse, occurs at Donzère, in the chapel of S. Martin near S. Victor-la-Coste,[30] and in the chapel of the Val des Nymphes, while a final variation is found at La Baume-de-Transit, where it occurs in the crossing.

---

[29] S. Ruf at Avignon is one of the most unusual and elaborate buildings in Provence, and it is puzzling in many ways. The cursory references to it here are really only intended to remind the reader of its existence, and of the fact that it holds an outstanding place among the many buildings in the region which deserve detailed study.

[30] Labande, *Études*, p. 202, dates this chapel to the first half of the eleventh century and regards the capitals it contains as important examples of early Romanesque sculpture. This appears to be one of Labande's very few total aberrations; the chapel and its sculpture are certainly of the second half of the twelfth century.

8 *S. Paul-Trois-Châteaux and Related* Ateliers

THE cathedral of S. Paul-Trois-Châteaux is perhaps the most handsome of all the major Provençal churches. Built of a warm, golden stone, and miraculously little damaged by the extensive restorations of the seventeenth century and the further alterations in the nineteenth, it is a beautiful and sadly little-known monument (Pls. 123, 128).[1] The church consists of an aisled nave of three bays of unequal length, covered by a barrel vault (with half-barrels over the aisles) (Fig. 8). The nave gives on to a projecting transept, with single absidioles in each arm, and a cupola over the crossing.[2] To the east of the crossing is the main apse, externally polygonal but internally semicircular. The elevation of the nave breaks with Provençal tradition by inserting a blind triforium, although this is combined with the clerestory to preserve the two-storey elevation (Pl. 128). The employment of a blind triforium suggests some sort of connection with Burgundian monuments in which similar forms occur.[3] On the other hand, it will be recalled that a form of blind triforium occurs in the early transepts of S. Trophime at Arles, and, since S. Paul follows the Arles plan, this may be the immediate source.

The interior decoration consists of a blind arcade around the apse, and capitals flanking the single windows in the transept chapels.[4] The nave is much more lavishly decorated. The central pilaster of the compound pier is cut, at half its height, and a column and

---

[1] There is a brief notice of the cathedral by Labande, *C.A.* (1909), pp. 112–21. The most extensive study is a small volume by Canon F. Vernet, *La Cathédrale de St. Paul-Trois-Châteaux* (*La Drôme monumentale et archéologique*, Romans, 1930). This is regrettably hard to obtain; however, it does not deal in any detail with the architectural history of the building. The available guidebook, L. Béchet, *Notice de la cathédrale de S. Paul-Trois-Châteaux* (Vaison, 1966), is little more than a résumé of Vernet's book. The most intelligent remarks about the architecture occur in a footnote (!) to Vallery-Radot's article on Mornas, in *C.A.* (1963), p. 263, n. 1.

[2] The present cupola is a restoration, constructed in 1841, which replaced the elegant lantern that was constructed in the time of Bishop Adhémar de Monteil (1630–45). This lantern, which itself replaced the original cupola, can be seen in a series of drawings made in 1841 for the proposed restorations, and now in the possession of the Monuments Historiques.

[3] The type of building which comes to mind is the cathedral of Langres, which employs a similar blind triforium (but not combined with the clerestory). In addition, Langres has other links with Provence in general and with S. Paul in particular; it employs an interior *rinceau* frieze in the choir, and the foliage capitals of the apse may be compared quite closely with some of those in the S. Paul nave. See *C.A.* (1928), pp. 483–510, for Langres. The cathedral was built between *c.* 1150 and 1220.

[4] There are capitals flanking the window in the south transept chapel only; it is not clear whether they were originally present in the north transept chapel.

capital inserted. Both visually and functionally (i.e. as a supporter of the transverse rib of the vault) it is clear that this form is related to the nave capital system. Directly above the main arcade, but below the triforium/clerestory, is a frieze, consisting of a draped curtain supported at either end of each bay by small human figures who pull on the curtain ropes (Pls. 133–6). This frieze occurs in the eastern bay on both sides of the nave, but it does not continue on the south, and is broken off in the middle of the adjoining bay on the north. At the eastern end of this frieze, on either side, are corbels bearing

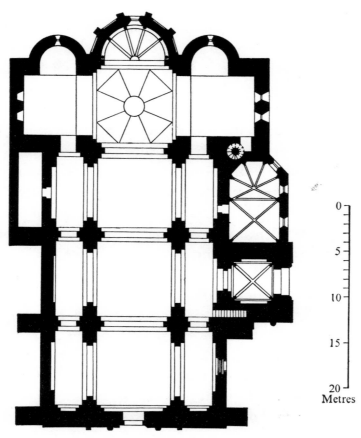

FIG. 8. S. Paul-Trois-Châteaux. Plan

the symbols of the Evangelists Mark (Pl. 132) and John, and these are balanced by the capitals of the columns adjoining the façade, which have the symbols of Matthew and Luke.[5] In the two western bays the blind triforium is made up of three simple rectangular panels per bay, formed by pilasters, with a single clerestory window pierced through the central panel (on the south side only). In the eastern bay the treatment is more elaborate, with arched recesses occupying each of the panels. These recesses are

---

[5] The symbol of St. Mark, at the south-east corner of the nave, is an extraordinary piece; below a well-executed head is an impossibly contorted body. It seems that the sculptor was under the impression that only a head-mask was necessary, and when requested to add a body as well he complied as best he could, given the limitations of a small single block. At the same time the distortion of the symbol may be compared with that which occurs at Carpentras, discussed in the previous chapter. The symbols of Matthew and Luke at the west end of the nave are crudely executed in an unrelated style, and appear to be restorations (? of the seventeenth century).

flanked by colonnettes and capitals; again the central recess on the south side is pierced to form a window. The nave is also highly decorated on the exterior; the voussoirs and hood of the west door are elaborately treated, and the door itself is flanked by pairs of half-columns and pilasters (one pair of each), which are curiously left without capitals or superstructure (Pl. 123). On the south side, giving on to the second bay of the nave, is a large porch, also elaborately decorated, and the south door itself originally possessed a sculpted tympanum.[6] In addition, on the south side only, the exteriors of the windows are embellished, and on the aisle and transept walls pilasters are used to increase the decorative effect.[7] Finally the nave walls on the south side are crowned by an elaborate cornice (Pl. 126). By contrast the north side of the nave is left entirely plain. The upper parts of the north transept include a blind arcading, resembling Lombard bands (Pl. 124). The three apses are externally fairly plain, although the central one is decorated with pilasters, and the central window is surrounded by a band of geometric ornament.

It is immediately clear, both on the basis of architectural and decorative features, that the building was constructed over a period of time in several distinct campaigns. It is less easy to define the precise limits of each campaign. The masonry is more or less uniform throughout, and there are few clear breaks. None the less, there are a large number of puzzling features which appear to indicate changes in plan. An analysis of the various campaigns leaves many points unanswered, but the general sequence of events is, I think, fairly clear. The church was begun at the east end, and the earliest extant sections are the apses and the north transept. The north wall of the north transept contains a pair of blocked windows, visible only on the interior, which suggests that even the initial plan underwent alteration in the course of construction. On the exterior of this transept, at a point just above two-thirds of its height, there is the decoration of paired blind arcading, resembling Lombard bands. On the west wall there is a buttress, which rises only to the height of this arcading—that is, still some way below the summit of the wall (Pl. 124). Closer inspection reveals that the masonry above the arcading is of rougher quality than the rest of the wall, and this strongly suggests that the whole transept has been raised. Support for this view is provided by an examination of the south transept. This is the same height as the north, but it is treated quite differently, decorated with pilaster strips resembling those which occur elsewhere on the south side of the nave. However, just above the aisle roof is a fragment of masonry which, from its shape and position, can be identified as the remains of a buttress, corresponding to that which survives on the west wall of the north transept (Pl. 127). Consequently, one may deduce that the upper parts of the south transept have been largely rebuilt, to conform with the more elaborate decoration of the south side of the building; it was not necessary to rebuild the north transept, since this side of the building is almost

---

[6] This apparently showed the Adoration of the Magi—a subject also found on tympana at S. Gilles and Beaucaire. It was in white marble, and was destroyed by the Protestants in 1561, appropriately enough on Christmas Eve. See Béchet, op. cit., p. 9.

[7] The façade and transept gables and the oculi of the façade are restorations, dating from the campaigns of 1850 and 1889.

entirely plain, so it was simply raised to conform with the new height of the south transept (a height which was itself dictated by the final scheme for the nave).[8]

The nave, like the transepts, appears to have been originally planned slightly lower than its present height. Two curious factors suggest this. The easternmost bay on the south side bears, on the exterior, a triple arcade. However, this arcade is not aligned with the triple arcade of the triforium/clerestory on the interior, the latter being placed somewhat lower. Consequently the single window in this bay breaks through the external arcade in an odd fashion (Pl. 125). In addition, the external arcade is surmounted by fragments of a cornice, which in fact runs the whole length of the nave on the south side. These fragments are distinct from, and much simpler than, the elaborate main cornice, which is separated from it by one clear course of masonry (Pl. 126). This again suggests that the nave was originally somewhat lower than it is now.

Between the south transept and the nave there does appear to be a masonry break; also the form of arcading on the eastern nave bay is somewhat different from that which survives on the north transept. Therefore it would seem that there were at least three campaigns of building:

(a) East end and transepts, lower than their present form.
(b) Nave walls, also lower.
(c) Heightening of nave and transepts, and vaulting of the whole.

In architectural terms, the most interesting problem here is whether or not stages (a) and (b) were, or were intended, to be vaulted. The occurrence of buttresses on the transept walls certainly would suggest an intention to vault, and equally the high blind arcading on the eastern nave bay suggests that originally no direct lighting was envisaged; this suggests that not only was vaulting intended for the nave also, but that this phase of the building belonged to the period when Provençal architects were not prepared to pierce any wall which carried a barrel vault (cf. Avignon and Cavaillon). In my view, although vaults were certainly intended from the beginning, they were probably never erected; consequently campaign (c) was primarily concerned with adding vaults to a pre-existing structure, and providing direct lighting on the south side of the nave. The slight all-round increase in the height of the building was no doubt occasioned by the introduction of the nave windows, since, in structural terms, the extra masonry does not raise the level of the springing of the vaults, but only increases the solidity of, and buttresses, the haunches of the vaults.

The third campaign did not end the long building history of the church, for this too appears to have been interrupted. The break in the nave decoration, together with the abandonment of the curtain frieze in the middle of the second bay, suggests this, as does the fact that the upper parts of the nave in the two western bays are much plainer than the easternmost bay. Finally, the two columns adjoining the façade in the western

---

[8] The belltower on the south transept was almost entirely rebuilt in the nineteenth century, but it does seem to have been an original feature of the cathedral; thus it may be associated with Vaison cathedral, which has a tower on the north transept, and also (if my reconstruction of it is correct) with Aix.

bay appear to be post-medieval (? seventeenth century); these are doubtless restorations, and it seems unlikely that the church remained unfinished during the medieval period. However, it does seem that the third major campaign was succeeded by a fourth, which completed the upper parts of the nave at the west end.

The main decoration of the nave may be attributed to the third campaign, since it relates directly to the positioning of the nave windows. Rather more of a problem is presented by the decoration of the west and south doors, since this is, as we shall see, by a hand that is distinct from, but related to, that found in the nave. The differences in these hands do not in this instance indicate that they are widely separated in time (see below).

The earliest decoration of the building, belonging to the first campaign, occurs in the east end and consists of the arcade around the interior of the main apse, together with the capitals flanking the window of the northern transept chapel. All these capitals are Corinthian in form, with one or two rows of leaves, surmounted by cauliculi, rose, and volutes. The leaves are small and somewhat untidily executed, with the lobe divisions drilled out in an apparently arbitrary fashion (Pls. 129, 130). They retain a chunky, inorganic feeling, which contrasts with the fairly accurate retention of an overall Corinthian form. These features seem to derive in part from the eleventh-century tradition of capital sculpture, as represented by both S. Victor at Marseille and the apse capitals of Vaison cathedral, but the S. Paul capitals remain largely unlike any other surviving work. The style of the external decoration of the east end is equally puzzling. This includes a continuous ornamental band which runs around the central apse window, and which contains a series of rosettes, a section of ribbon interlace, and a flat interlacing *rinceau* scroll—all of which looks back to the eleventh century and before.

The only Provençal work at all comparable with the apse capitals are those of the Avignon cupola and of the nave of S. Trophime at Arles. However, even this is a generalized comparison—all these capitals are treated in a similar manner and with the same sort of feeling, but in terms of precise manufacture the S. Paul works cannot be placed directly alongside those of Avignon or Arles. Nevertheless, since documentary and historical evidence is lacking, we have to rely upon what stylistic evidence there is. In addition to the capitals themselves, the only indications are the comparatively simple architectural forms, the lack of any elaborate external decoration, and the usage of the blind arcading on the north transept. This last point is not particularly helpful, since such arcading is found in the region throughout the twelfth century (e.g. Le Thor); however, taken together, all the evidence suggests that the east end of the church dates from the first half of the twelfth century, and it is probably somewhat earlier than the *c.* 1140 which Labande proposed as a starting date for construction.[9] The precise date of the capitals must remain uncertain, but, on the basis of the links with the Avignon and Arles works, *c.* 1120 seems very possible.

Despite the numerous signs of alteration and hesitation in the architecture, the main

[9] Labande, *C.A.* (1909), p. 120.

body of the nave decoration is stylistically coherent, suggesting that it is of uniform or near-uniform date; it has been suggested above that this decoration dates from the third major campaign on the church, although two hands are clearly involved.

The overall aspect of the nave decoration is itself revealing. On the interior, the employment of sizeable columns inserted into the piers can legitimately be seen as a reworking of the nave capital scheme, and in this sense a return to traditional concepts.[10] Similarly, the employment of an internal frieze looks back to Pernes, although the actual form and execution is totally different, and closer to the type found at Carpentras. The introduction of the false triforium provides an additional field for internal embellishment, but this is only fully exploited in the eastern bay, where the triple arcades on either side are richly decorated. In the two remaining bays the triforium is simply formed by the pilaster strips which divide the wall surface into panels (Pl. 128). Whether this was the original intention, or whether it represents a solution dictated by the necessity of completing the building rapidly, is uncertain.

On the exterior we find that the windows, occurring only on the south side, are lavishly decorated in the Vaison cathedral manner, with the added enrichment of flanking pilasters. The frieze as such is not employed, although the cornice at the summit of the nave walls is here greatly expanded, and assumes frieze-like proportions. The upper parts of the south transept and the façade have richly ornamented gables, and the latter also possesses decorated oculi (Pl. 123). However, the most important new element is that attention is concentrated on the two entrances into the building; the west door, flanked by half-columns and pilasters, has elaborate voussoirs and hood, the most striking feature of which is the usage of human masks set into the recess of the moulding (Pls. 151, 155), recalling some earlier Romanesque doorways, such as those of Monopoli and Acerenza in Apulia.[11] On the south side the entrance is set within the imposing porch. The door itself is treated in a similar fashion to that at the west, with the addition of a tympanum (now completely effaced). Thus the external decoration follows, in form at least, the pattern set by the Vaison *atelier*, and takes the logical additional step of enriching the entrances (although, as we shall see, the S. Paul *atelier* borrowed rather than invented this idea).

The style of all this work differs more markedly from previously established forms. The capitals in the nave are of superb quality (Pl. 131); orthodox Corinthian in form, they employ carefully executed acanthus leaves, undercut and with individual lobes clearly delineated. These leaves, together with those of the cornice and the window arches, have a depth and presence which distinguishes them from all the foliage decoration previously discussed; it is a quality which is perhaps best described as 'stylized naturalism'—they manage to convey that they are organic growths in stone.

A second though related hand was responsible for the two doors, the aisle windows,

[10] This scheme can of course be related to that found on the alternating piers at Conques, and to the rather more complex system in the nave of Cluny III.
[11] See A. K. Porter, *Romanesque Sculpture of the Pilgrimage Roads* (Boston, Mass., 1924), pp. 59 ff., and Pls. 158–62.

and perhaps also the exterior nave cornice (the latter is too worn to allow certainty). The distinction between these two hands is quite clear; the second hand employs a slightly flatter leaf, and uses drill holes in a distinctive way to emphasize the lobe divisions (Pl. 151). However, this second leaf type also achieves the 'stylized naturalism' of the first, and in addition the occurrence of the two types is not rigidly separated. Some imposts of the capitals in the nave are by the second hand, while much of the decoration of the south porch is in the style of the first artist. The distinction between the two is therefore most easily explained as individual hands within the same or succeeding *ateliers*, rather than as evidence of any significant chronological distinction. The fact that the first hand is more or less coincident with the eastern parts of the nave, and that the curtain frieze is broken off, while the second hand predominates in the western parts of the building, might suggest that one sculptor was replaced by another. But both worked within the same stylistic framework, and it is difficult to regard their work as of significantly different date. This conclusion is strengthened by the fact that both sculptors worked subsequently at S. Restitut (see below).

What is most significant is that, taken as a whole, the nave decoration is clearly distinct in style from all the major work so far discussed. The foliage sculpture reveals that the linear, pattern-making forms of the Aix–Cavaillon tradition had been completely abandoned. The same break with tradition can be found in the figure sculpture. The curtain frieze is treated as an illusionistic motif, including small figures tugging at realistic ropes. The use of the frieze itself is a traditional element, looking back to Pernes, where the precise motif of the curtain also occurs. However, the treatment of figural representations differs completely from Pernes; the small figures are distinguished by their comparatively high relief, their large round heads, and their bent-knee posture (Pls. 133–6).

Once again there is a distinction between the figure styles of the two main sculptors. The second hand is represented by the series of human masks set into the west and south doors, and these immediately reveal him as a sculptor of outstanding ability (Pls. 151, 155). The heads are in high relief, treated very expressively, lips slightly parted, eyes and nostrils drilled.

Thus, to recapitulate, the architectural evidence suggests that the church was built in four main campaigns; the decoration of the nave belongs to the third of these campaigns, but it comprises the work of at least two sculptors. The style of these two is related, although the second is perhaps the more competent artist, and handles the human form with increased ease. It is also perhaps significant that it is the second sculptor who formally breaks new ground and concentrates decorative attention on the doorways, while the first sculptor, with his internal frieze and his version of the nave capital scheme, is in formal terms still related to the traditional types of Provençal decoration. However, both sculptors clearly were highly accomplished and professional, and it is not surprising that we can find several other examples of their work elsewhere in Provence. Equally, it is no surprise to discover that here, for the first time, we have architectural sculpture which can be related stylistically to the major sculptural productions of the region, notably the cloister and façade of S. Trophime at Arles. But, before following up these links, we may turn to the internal evidence for dating the nave of S. Paul.

For Labande, the chevet dated from *c.* 1140–60, while the nave followed in the second half of the century, and was completed in the early thirteenth century. He associated the early work with a diploma of Frederick Barbarossa, dated 1154, which confirmed the Bishop of S. Paul in all his possessions and privileges, and also granted to him the quarry named Tudela.[12] This document is of doubtful authenticity,[13] but even if it is accepted there is no reason why it should mark the start of work on the church. On stylistic grounds I have argued that the eastern part of the building may be dated *c.* 1120.

The analysis of the nave decoration has shown that it is of uniform or near uniform date. However, it is extremely difficult to establish what this date is on the basis of internal evidence. There are no clear references to the church before April 1219, when a charter was witnessed before its door.[14] In September 1222, we hear of large numbers of people present in the church itself.[15] Furthermore, the establishment of an annual benefaction to the canons on the anniversary of the dedication of the church, which occurs in the will of Bishop Geoffrey de Voigne (1211–33) suggests, as Font-Reaulx has pointed out, that this prelate was directly connected with the event so commemorated.

All this is of little use for dating the nave decoration, since it presumably relates to the fourth campaign and the completion of the building. In addition it provides only a *terminus ante quem* of *c.* 1220, and the dedication of the church does not necessarily relate to its immediate completion. According to *Gallia christiana*, the town was besieged and partly burnt in the course of a feud between the bishop and Raymond VI, Count of Toulouse, in 1202, and this would provide a plausible explanation for the break between the third and fourth campaigns. Unfortunately, however, the authenticity of this story is doubtful.[16] Thus virtually all one can say about the nave decoration is that it dates from before *c.* 1220; in order to date it more closely we must turn to comparison with other works.

The first of the S. Paul nave sculptors (the curtain frieze hand) may be associated with, and almost certainly identified as, one of the *atelier* which worked on the cathedral of Nîmes. This building is extremely difficult to study; it has been largely rebuilt and drastically altered, and only the façade retains extensive traces of twelfth-century construction.[17] The major surviving decorative element is the external frieze at the summit

---

[12] *Gallia christiana*, i, Instrumenta, pp. 120–1.

[13] J. Font-Reaulx (ed.), *Cartulaire de l'évêché de S. Paul-Trois-Châteaux* (Valence, 1946), p. 11, no. 6.

[14] Font-Reaulx, op. cit., no. 17.   [15] Font-Reaulx, op. cit., no. 67.

[16] *Gallia christiana*, i, col. 714, and Instrumenta, p. 121. See criticism of C. L. Devic and J. Vaissete, *Histoire générale de Languedoc* (Toulouse, 1874–92), vol. vi, p. 199.

[17] See M. Louis, 'La façade de la cathédrale de Nîmes', *Mém. de l'Institut Historique de Provence*, xi (1934), 81–3; M. Gouron, *La Cathédrale romane de Nîmes* (extrait du *Bulletin Archéologique*, 1936–7); P. Pradel, 'Vestiges d'un zodiaque-calendrier Nîmois du XIIIe siècle', *Mon. Piot*, lv (1967), 105–13. These authors assume, for no apparent reason, that the frieze is earlier work which was re-set in its present position.

of this façade, but even this, and the elaborate gable above it, was largely renewed in the seventeenth century. A few Romanesque sections have survived, but these too have probably been somewhat recut (Pl. 137). The only other extant sculptures are some damaged panels on the lower portion of the façade,[18] and a few fragments now in the municipal museum.[19]

Even on the basis of this fragmentary evidence, the relationship between Nîmes and S. Paul is clear. In a general way, both employ friezes, although they are differently situated. More specifically, the figure style within these friezes is similar, employing small but heavily built figures, with over-large heads and hands. The figures are all in a semi-crouching position, with knees bent, as though confined by the narrow limits of the frieze (Pls. 133, 137). The precise treatment of the drapery and of the facial types also reveals connections, as for example in the thick swathe of material around the waist, treated as a series of horizontal folds, and common to both groups. However, the value of these detailed connections does rely largely upon the authenticity of the Nîmes figures, and the comparison is probably best restricted to one of general aspect. In addition, the closest connection in detail with the S. Paul sculpture is made by a capital fragment preserved in the Nîmes museum (Pl. 138). In this fragment, which clearly comes from a Sacrifice of Isaac, we find again the general connections of body type already noted. But the links become much more precise if we compare the head of Isaac at Nîmes with that of one of the rope-pullers from S. Paul (Pls. 133, 138)— here the work of the same sculptor seems a strong possibility. A further detail reinforces this link. The Nîmes fragment includes a section of the sleeve of the angel, which terminates in a crescent-shaped hem that is decorated with a row of rectangular punch-holes. This again recurs on the sleeve of one of the S. Paul curtain-pullers (Pl. 134).

In a study of the capital fragment from Nîmes, Lassalle pointed out that it is linked, both iconographically and stylistically, with the capitals of the apse arcade at Les-Saintes-Maries-de-la-Mer. There is no need to re-state those links here (cf. Pls. 138, 139); their reality is further demonstrated by the fact that they can be extended to S. Paul as well, and a comparison of this work with the capitals of Les-Saintes-Maries at once reveals a close affinity (Pls. 133–40). Again the same figure types appear, stocky and large-headed, with the familiar bent-knee stance. The facial types are similar, occasionally markedly so, and there are close parallels in the drapery treatment (the row of punch-holes on a crescent-shaped hem also occurs at Les-Saintes-Maries). Another factor linking the decoration of all three buildings is the foliage sculpture, and again the connections are both general and specific. All employ excellent stylized acanthus leaves, formed in a similar manner, crisply executed with considerable expertise. Individual lobes are undercut and drilled. More specifically one of the capitals at Les-Saintes-Maries has a central rose consisting of a five-petalled flower the centre of which is made

---

[18] These represented the Ascension of Alexander, Gouron, op. cit.

[19] V. Lassalle, 'Fragment roman d'un Sacrifice d'Abraham au Musée archéologique de Nîmes', *Revue du Louvre* (1965), pp. 165–70.

up of a protruding convolute tendril. This highly unusual form turns up again in the nave cornice at S. Paul. It is probably unwise to allow very great significance to such a small detail, but it occurs only exceptionally at S. Gilles, on two of the capitals in the nave,[20] while it can be found several times in the foliage sculpture of the north gallery of the cloister at Arles.

It is in fact clear that the sculptor of the capitals at Les-Saintes-Maries was a member of the *atelier* responsible for the sculpture of the north gallery of the cloister of S. Trophime. The connections with the Arles work are very numerous (Pls. 141–8); at both we find corner capitals decorated with (almost identical) devilish masks with tendrils emerging from their mouths;[21] both employ capitals on which busts or heads replace the volutes or the rose, and in several instances the treatment of the heads is very similar. The foliage sculpture is still closer, and the leaf-forms and arrangements found at Les-Saintes-Maries can be matched exactly in the Arles work.

There is one apparent objection to the close connection between Arles and Les-Saintes-Maries; both series include capitals showing the Sacrifice of Isaac, which are clearly by different hands, and which follow different iconographic modes (Pls. 149, 150). In comparison with Arles, the figures in the Saintes-Maries version are more contorted and more mannered, sharing something of the movemented style of the marble capitals from Avignon.[22] The explanation for this lies, I believe, in an analysis of the work of the Arles north gallery *atelier*; I do not propose to undertake such an analysis here in detail, but it can be shown that at least two men were involved, together with a number of assistants. The capitals of Les-Saintes-Maries are not the work of the Arles north master-sculptor, but of his assistant. Whether or not this is correct, there can be no doubt that a close link exists between the Saintes-Maries capitals and the Arles north style, and that this link stands despite the differences in the two versions of the Sacrifice. Consequently there is also a link between Arles north and the nave of S. Paul-Trois-Châteaux. The nature of this link is immediately clear if we compare the frieze and cornice at S. Paul with the capitals and abaci in the Arles north gallery; in terms of formal conception, of the handling of the human figure, and particularly in the nature of foliage carving, the two are directly comparable. It is not in this case a question of whether or not the same artists are involved; it is simply that both sets of decoration share the same stylistic and technical base.

The first S. Paul sculptor can be considered as an artist descended from the Arles north gallery tradition; one line of this tradition is represented by the filiation Arles:

[20] Hamann, *S. Gilles*, iii, Pl. 165c, d.

[21] This type is found in the arcade of the north wall of the cloister at Arles, where almost all of the capitals are restorations. However, there is no reason to think that they do not follow, at least in general terms, the form of the original work. In July 1844, Merimée wrote 'on me dit que les chapiteaux nouveaux du cloître de S. Trophime ne sont pas très bons . . .', but the following year, when he had actually seen the work, he wrote 'Je suis très content de la restauration du cloître de S. Trophime, sauf quelques détails d'ornementation, comme à S. Gilles.' See P. Merimée, *Correspondance générale* (Paris, 1941–64) (2 series, 17 vols.), vol. iv, p. 121 (to Requien) and p. 356 (to Vitet).

[22] For the Avignon capitals see primarily Stockhausen, *Die Kreuzgänge*, ii, 124–34. The Saintes-Maries capitals are of course also in marble, but the stylistic connections with the Avignon work are not, in my opinion, very close.

Saintes-Maries: Nîmes: S. Paul. The underlying relationship between S. Paul and Arles is further stressed by the fact that the former adopted the plan of S. Trophime, and introduces a blind triforium, related to the earlier form found in the Arles transepts. At the same time, S. Paul seems to be slightly later than Nîmes, since the connections with Les-Saintes-Maries are not quite so close.[23]

The second hand at S. Paul, the portal sculptor, can also be shown to be directly related to the Arles *ateliers*. In this instance we can again work back from S. Paul to Arles by way of at least one intermediate stage. This is the small chapel of S. Gabriel near Tarascon,[24] where the work of the S. Paul sculptor occurs on the oculus of the façade. This façade consists of a central doorway, surmounted by a tympanum, and flanked by half-columns supporting a gable. The latter encloses a rectangular panel, showing the Annunciation and the Visitation.[25] At the apex of the gable is an Agnus Dei. The whole doorway is set back deeply into the façade, and enclosed in a large single arch (Pl. 157). Above this there is the elaborately decorated oculus, flanked by the four Gospel symbols, which provides the only direct lighting for the simple interior. The remainder of the building is completely plain.

For such a small building this lavish treatment of the façade is exceptional. Moreover the decoration is not of uniform style or quality. The tympanum includes two clumsily executed subjects: Adam and Eve, and Daniel in the Lions' Den, with the angel bearing Habakkuk to him by the hair (Pl. 158). This, and the rectangular panel above, are carved in shallow relief, in a manner that looks back to the northern frieze at Cavaillon, and ultimately to the panels of the tower at S. Restitut. However, as noted in a previous chapter, there is a significant difference. The true linear style of the eleventh-century tradition was uncompromising in its acceptance of two-dimensional form; the S. Gabriel work is ambiguous in its linear style, and by the use of certain devices, notably increasing the relief of the heads, has attempted to convey a feeling for the third dimension. Other works which we have come across in this linear style have exhibited a similar tendency towards more plastic, less rigid forms within an essentially planar tradition—notably the nave panels at Pernes, with which the S. Gabriel tympanum is closely comparable. This would suggest a date in the second quarter of the twelfth century for the tympanum.[26] However, it is clear that this tympanum was not designed for the doorway in which it is now located. The door is flanked by columns, with capitals

---

[23] There are other factors linking Arles, Nîmes, and S. Paul. Nîmes too was an aisled building, terminating in three apses (but apparently without transepts). Gouron, op. cit., states that the floor was covered with a magnificent mosaic. The remains of what must have been a splendid mosaic decoration still exist on the floor of the choir at S. Paul, and the lower of the two floor levels discovered by Revoil in S. Trophime in 1870 revealed traces of what seems to have been extensive mosaic decoration.

[24] See Labande, *C.A.* (1909), pp. 259–62.

[25] This is surmounted by an inscription, apparently done after the panel was placed in its present position, which reads:

AVE MARIA GRĀ PLENA DŇ TECV̄   (Luke 1:28)

Below this the figures are identified as:

ANGELVS GABRIHEL : S MARIA MATER DŇĪ : ELIZABETH.

[26] See above, pp. 80–2.

and abaci, and the tympanum should rest directly on these. Instead two extra courses of masonry are inserted, followed by a second pair of abaci, and it is on these that the tympanum rests (Pl. 158). This is a curious arrangement, and suggests that the tympanum was not designed for the present scheme, in which the height of the doorway is determined by its location in the gabled portico. It is possible that the tympanum was intended to have a lintel, fitting into the space between the two sets of abaci, and in this case the obvious candidate would be the panel now inserted into the gable. However, this block is too short for the space presently available, and it shows no sign of being cut. It is also too broad, and so it cannot be seen as part of a lintel for the present scheme, although it remains possible that it comprised a lintel in the previous arrangement.

These facts, together with the clear stylistic differences in the decoration, make it certain that the tympanum and gable panel above were re-used. The masonry of the chapel is fairly uniform, and it is not clear whether the present structure and decoration represent a reworking of a pre-existing chapel on the site, or a new building employing decorative elements from elsewhere.

The reason for re-using these elements, which to modern eyes are markedly inferior to the excellent decoration of the oculus, probably lies in the very fact of their traditional and *retardataire* nature. The figures on the tympanum are placed between two horizontal lines (with the exception of the angel); the figures on the panel are placed under an arcade. Both immediately suggest—and are no doubt intended to suggest—sarcophagi. The iconography of the tympanum reinforces this impression,[27] and it is possible that the pieces were re-used because they were taken for Antique work.

The different style revealed on the oculus at the summit of the façade is undoubtedly the work of the portal sculptor at S. Paul-Trois-Châteaux (Pls. 155, 156). The frame of the window consists of two rows of foliage, separated by a row of alternating rosettes and masks, which are set into the moulding. This is of course the form employed on both doors at S. Paul. Moreover the style is identical; characteristic broad acanthus leaves, with drill-holes scattered at the lobe ends, and distinctive facial types, high-cheeked and wide-eyed, but tensely controlled. A comparison of the two leaves no doubt that they are the work of the same sculptor. The same hand can be recognized elsewhere on the S. Gabriel façade—in the four Gospel symbols, and in the Agnus Dei.

The chapel of S. Gabriel includes decoration of two distinct types and dates, and the S. Paul sculptor planned a façade which re-used older material. It is significant that we also find re-used panels at S. Paul, on the south transept, which was rebuilt by the nave *atelier*.[28] In both cases this re-use can be connected with the growing 'Renaissance' attitude, first noticed in the work of the Vaison *atelier*.[29]

As has already been mentioned, the S. Paul artist can be traced back a step further, to the north gallery of the cloister at Arles. The fact that he worked at S. Gabriel, a

---

[27] The two subjects frequently occur on early Christian sarcophagi, and are sometimes placed alongside each other. See J. Wilpert, *I Sarcofagi cristiani antichi* (Rome, 1929–36).

[28] See above, pp. 28–9.

[29] See above, pp. 86 ff.

comparatively obscure rural chapel, probably derives from its location on the old Roman road from Arles to Avignon.[30] We can imagine a sculptor leaving Arles, perhaps with the offer of a job on the major new project at S. Paul, but stopping off on the way to work at S. Gabriel. Implicit in this theory is the close connection between the S. Paul portal sculptor and the *ateliers* of S. Trophime. One of the most distinctive features of the S. Paul artist is his treatment of foliage—broad leaves with drill-holes scattered at the lobe ends. This leaf turns up several times in the north gallery of the cloister at Arles, especially on abaci. Moreover, the tense, staring faces done by the S. Paul sculptor, with their drooping, slightly open mouths, can be closely related to the head style of the great artist who made the figure of S. Peter for the Arles cloister. Similar connections can be found in heads on capitals in the same north gallery of the cloister (Pls. 151–4).

Here again we are faced with the problem of the precise stylistic analysis of the sculpture at Arles (a task which has yet to be seriously tackled in print).[31] In order to clarify the position with regard to S. Paul, I shall briefly summarize my own conclusions about Arles, but without giving the evidence on which they are based in detail.

The earliest sculpture at Arles (apart from the nave capitals) is in the north gallery of the cloister.[32] This was built from west to east,[33] and involved the work of a small and closely knit *atelier*, perhaps of two main sculptors, each with an assistant or pupil. This *atelier* broke up before the north gallery was finally completed, since the north-east pier includes unfinished work, and one large figure in a totally new style. The next work was on the façade of the church.[34] At least one of the assistants (perhaps the S. Paul portal sculptor) continued to work in Arles, but the other members of the *atelier* left—one for Les-Saintes-Maries, another for Montmajour.[35]

The façade of S. Trophime includes a variety of sculpture, all of which is technically well produced. However, much of it (with the notable exception of the upper frieze) is dull and repetitive—qualities which have led some to regard it as considerably later

[30] For the Roman roads to Arles see L. A. Constans, *Arles antique* (Bibl. des Écoles françaises d'Athènes et de Rome, vol. cxix, 1921).

[31] Professor W. S. Stoddard will shortly publish a major study of the sculptures of S. Gilles and Arles, which will include a lengthy stylistic analysis. Although I have had many fruitful discussions with Professor Stoddard, I am unable to accept all of his conclusions.

[32] This view has been accepted by all those who have studied the cloister.

[33] The suggestion that the north gallery was built from west to east is based upon the stylistic analysis of the sculpture, and also upon the fact that the north-west pier is unified and clearly erected at one time, whereas the north-east pier contains unfinished work (notably the relief of the Stoning of Stephen). The apostle figure which adjoins the Stephen relief is executed in a style unlike that of the remainder of the north gallery.

[34] The connections between the sculpture of the north gallery and that on the façade are most apparent if one compares the relief panels in the former with the upper frieze of the latter. At the same time a great deal of the façade sculpture, notably the large apostle figures, is by artists who are not directly connected with the north gallery *atelier*. One of these new artists produced the Stoning of Stephen panel for the façade, in which he borrowed from and combined the iconographic and compositional schemes of two of the cloister panels. The façade Stoning takes the upper half of the cloister Ascension panel (on the north face of the north-east pier) and combines it with the lower half of the (unfinished) Stoning of Stephen panel (on the east face of the same pier).

[35] For the connections between the cloisters of Arles, Montmajour, S. Paul-de-Mausole, and Aix-en-Provence, see Stockhausen, *Die Kreuzgänge*, vol. ii, and also my M.A. thesis (London University, 1967), 'The Cloister of the Cathedral of St. Sauveur, Aix-en-Provence'.

than the more expressive and individualized work in the north gallery of the cloister. The distinctive and, it must be admitted, somewhat unattractive appearance of the portal probably arises from the fact that it is a rushed work. The monotony of much of the sculpture suggests rapid execution and a form of mass production.

By the time the façade was completed, and probably before, all the members of the cloister north gallery *atelier* had left. Subsequently work was resumed on the east gallery of the cloister, by an *atelier* which included some of those who had worked on parts of the façade. Thus the major sculpture at Arles represents in some sense a continuing programme, and the links between the various parts of the work are close and sometimes confusing. The dating of the work on internal evidence is, to my mind, fairly clear, but it cannot be accepted unequivocally since it has been rejected by several scholars.[36] None the less, the arguments of R. de Lasteyrie, based upon the inscriptions in the cloister walls, are very strong, and they have yet to be disproved (rather than simply rejected).[37] The inscriptions suggest that the north walk was not built before the 1160s. My analysis of the sculpture suggests that it is all stylistically related, and represents a continuing programme. It is not possible to separate the sculpture of the two Romanesque cloister walks by more than a few years (and certainly not by the half-century proposed by von Stockhausen).[38] In addition, the excavations of Revoil and Véran prove, as Labande pointed out,[39] that the portal dates from after—presumably some time after—the translation of St. Trophimus in 1152; this means that, if my analysis is right, the north gallery of the cloister also dates after this time. The previous study of the nave capitals of S. Trophime[40] has shown that they are totally different from the work in the cloister and on the façade. These capitals can be dated to *c.* 1120, and it would seem certain that the cloister capitals are of markedly different date.

The work on the north gallery of the cloister was somewhat abruptly halted, and work was then taken up on the façade. The latter, with its repetitive forms, looks like rapidly executed work. It is by no means impossible that it was completed quickly so as to be ready for the most important and spectacular event in the twelfth-century history of Arles, the coronation of Frederick Barbarossa in S. Trophime in 1178.[41]

[36] The internal evidence for dating Arles was notably disregarded by Porter, *Pilgrimage Roads*, by Hamann, *S. Gilles*, and by G. de Francovich, *Benedetto Antelami, architetto e scultore e l'arte del suo tempo* (Milan–Florence, 1952), pp. 45 ff.

[37] R. de Lasteyrie, 'Études sur la sculpture française au moyen âge', *Mon. Piot* (1902), viii, 1. Stoddard believes that Lasteyrie misread the inscription of Pons de Bascle. He claims that the name is Poncius de Barcia and the date is 1201 rather than 1165. I do not find Stoddard's argument convincing, but if it is correct it would make the earliest inscription in the north gallery that of 1183. Nevertheless Lasteyrie's main argument still holds good; in addition, it is difficult to see why, if the cloister had been standing for years already, people should suddenly start being buried in it. Presumably some canons died before the latter part of the century, and presumably also if the cloister had existed they would have been buried in it.

[38] He dates the north gallery to *c.* 1120–40, and regards the east gallery as started in the third quarter of the century and finished by the beginning of the thirteenth. Stockhausen, *Die Kreuzgänge*, ii, 168.

[39] Labande, *Arles*, pp. 30–1. The evidence is provided by the two floor levels in the church, the first of which corresponds to the 1152 crypt, the second to the portal.

[40] See above, pp. 63 ff.

[41] According to Fournier (*Royaume d'Arles et de Vienne*, p. 37, n. 2) the idea of the coronation may have been mooted as early as 1162. However, it seems that the actual decision cannot have been taken until after the Peace of Venice in

This would certainly conform with the dating and development of the Arles *ateliers* suggested here.

The internal evidence for the dating of the Arles work may be compared with that available for the related works—Les-Saintes-Maries, Nîmes, S. Gabriel, and S. Paul. Unfortunately none of these are in any way certainly dated, and there appears to be no evidence of any sort for dating S. Gabriel. For Les-Saintes-Maries there are two references in wills, of 1172 and 1175, to donations 'ad opus', but this need not refer to a building operation.[42] There is more evidence for the cathedral at Nîmes, but it is no more helpful.[43] There was a consecration by Urban II in 1096, and bishops were buried in the church in 1112 and 1141. However, it is known that a Petrus Brunus was working as a sculptor in the city in 1186, and this would provide a convenient date for the frieze and the capital fragment.[44] Finally, the S. Paul nave was decorated before *c.* 1220, but after (and by implication some time after) *c.* 1120. Therefore a date in the 1180s would be quite possible.

It would probably be a mistake to think that a series of individually uncertain dates become any stronger because collectively they make chronological sense; equally it is dangerous to ignore such evidence completely. Ultimately the strongest argument is that the S. Paul nave is clearly post-Vaison, and therefore it *must* date from the second half of the century. However, these considerations may be reserved for our final conclusions. To recapitulate, the two nave sculptors at S. Paul may both be traced back to Arles, via different routes. The curtain frieze sculptor was probably not an actual member of the Arles *ateliers*, but was perhaps trained at Nîmes. The portal sculptor may well have been trained at Arles, and certainly worked at S. Gabriel on his way north. In addition to the stylistic links, there are also formal elements derived from Arles, notably the fashion for decorated portals and tympana. Les-Saintes-Maries originally had two doors, one on each side of the nave.[45] That on the south side can be seen to have included socles in the form of lions. At Nîmes there was a tympanum, showing the Virgin and Child with angels, which was destroyed in 1610.[46] Both doors at S. Paul are decorated, and that to the south had a tympanum with the Adoration of the Magi.[47] By contrast, it has already been observed that Provençal buildings of the first half of the twelfth century have simple entrances, and do not normally employ tympana.

The two sculptors who worked in the S. Paul nave also worked in the nearby chapel

August, 1177. Frederick then remained in Italy for the winter, and we can trace his progress from 15 June 1178, when he was at Turin, to Embrun on 14 July, to Gap on 18 July, and finally to Arles on 28 July, where the coronation took place two days later. It is by no means impossible that a team of sculptors (perhaps five or six men) could have produced the sculpture for the façade in the time available; the actual carving could have been done indoors during the winter months, and the façade erected and finished in the spring of 1178.

42 F. Benoit, 'Église des Saintes-Maries-de-la-Mer', *B.M.* (1936), pp. 145–80.

43 Gouron, op. cit., pp. 6–7.

44 Brunus signed himself 'artifex in opere ligneo et lapideo', Gouron, op. cit., p. 17.

45 Benoit, op. cit., pp. 154–6. This information is given in the report of the excavations carried out in 1448 to search for the relics of the saints. The door referred to on the north side was doubtless that which still exists in the choir.

46 Gouron, op. cit.   47 See above, n. 6.

of S. Restitut. I have argued that the final transformation of the church at S. Restitut consisted of the addition of a new eastern apse and a new south porch. These two sections are clearly stylistically unified, and are equally clearly decorated by the S. Paul sculptors. The same workshop also created the south porch of Notre-Dame-de-Nazareth at Pernes,[48] which has a similar architectural form to that at S. Restitut, and which includes the now familiar decorative elements.

The porch at Pernes appears to be the last preserved work of this *atelier*. Even so, together with the Vaison *atelier*, it represents the most widespread Romanesque group traceable in Provence. The indirect influence of the S. Paul style is equally marked. It can now be more clearly appreciated that buildings such as Carpentras and Rosans, discussed in the previous chapter, are heavily indebted to the new modes of decoration introduced at S. Paul, and in the case of Carpentras it appears that the style of the S. Paul nave was directly influential (Pls. 101, 135). Ultimately the decorative forms at both Rosans and Carpentras, despite their allegiance to traditional concepts, are the result of the major developments at Arles, but the Arles influence appears indirect, and S. Paul-Trois-Châteaux played a major role in its transmission.

[48] This connection was observed by G. Barruol, *C.A.* (1963), p. 329.

9 *The Architectural Origins of the Nave Capital Churches*

WE have now considered all the churches in Provence employing what I have termed the nave capital system. On the basis of the chronology and the development proposed, we now turn to some of the more general questions posed by this series of buildings. The first of them, Avignon, emerges in the second half of the eleventh century, with a fully developed plan, elevation, and constructional system. There are apparently no forerunners or prototypes for this form in Provence itself (see below). The most direct successors to Avignon were S. Sauveur at Aix, and Notre-Dame at Cavaillon, which adopted precisely the same forms, with the modification at Cavaillon of setting chapels between the buttresses. The major decorative elements in these churches were the nave colonnettes and capitals, and these were taken up by the builders of S. Trophime at Arles, although the church here is otherwise unrelated to the Avignon type. As the twelfth century progressed, the Avignon/Cavaillon plan came to be commonly adopted, but the nave capital scheme was gradually abandoned, in favour of more elaborate decorative solutions. It reappears in some later monuments, notably Carpentras and Rosans, but in these it is misunderstood and appears anachronistic.

The date proposed for the cathedral of Avignon (second half of the eleventh century) puts it firmly into the period of great architectural experiments—a period which includes the gradual evolution of the pilgrimage churches,[1] the prodigious development of Norman architecture, the construction of massive semi-vaulted structures such as Speyer and Durham,[2] and the vaulting experiments of the Lombard masons.[3] In this sort of context Avignon is hardly out of place, nor is it particularly exceptional. It is a comparatively small building, and neither its elevation nor its vaulting can be

---

[1] The view that the pilgrimage type was a coherent and unified development is no longer seriously tenable. The most recent debate concerns Ste Foy at Conques; see the contributions of M. Deyres and F. Leseur in *B.M.* (1965, 1966, 1968, and 1969). Note also E. Delaruelle, 'A la recherche du S. Sernin gallo-romain', *Actes du Vᵉ. Congrès international d'archéologie chrétienne* (Paris–Vatican, 1957), pp. 265–78, and M. Chamoso Lamas, 'Excavaciones en la Catedral de Santiago de Compostela', *Archivo español de arte* (1954), pp. 183–6 (1958) pp. 39–47.

[2] The view that only the choir of Durham was initially intended to receive vaults is given by J. Bony, 'Le projet premier de Durham. Voûtement partiel ou voûtement total?', *Urbanisme et architecture; études écrites et publiées en l'honneur de Pierre Lavedan* (Paris, 1954), pp. 27–35.

[3] A. K. Porter, *Lombard Architecture* (New Haven, Conn., 1915–17), 4 vols. Many scholars now deny, to my mind wrongly, that there were any early ribbed vaults in Italy.

considered especially adventurous. At the same time, it would no doubt have been considered a very modern and very smart edifice, constructed with great expertise. Moreover, if Avignon is not out of place in a European context, it is much more unexpected in terms of what we know of eleventh-century Provençal architecture. It is true that this may be partially because our knowledge is deficient, but it does seem that during the tenth and eleventh centuries the normal type of building was a simple structure, largely or wholly devoid of decoration, vaulted only over very small areas, and constructed in a competent but by no means exceptional manner. The church of St. Peter and St. Paul at Sarrians (Vaucluse, near Orange), which is now disastrously restored, appears to be the building constructed between 1031 and 1048 and consecrated by Regimbald, Archbishop of Arles.[4] It is constructed of small roughly shaped stones, and it has a crude and rustic look about it, which no doubt derives as much from its isolated situation as from its early date.

A group of buildings, seemingly of eleventh-century date, have survived in Haute Provence, and these are for the most part equally simple and plain. The aisled church of S. Donat (diocese of Digne) has a main arcade supported by monolithic columns, and is covered, somewhat exceptionally for a church of this size, by a simple barrel vault.[5] More typical perhaps is the unvaulted chapel of S. Martin-de-Volonne (diocese of Gap) which adopts the same plan as S. Donat. Elsewhere in the region occasional buildings survive which witness a similar type of construction; one can cite Notre-Dame-de-Caseneuve at Goudargues, together with several other chapels mentioned in Chapter 2 in connection with the eleventh-century capitals.[6]

It would be a mistake to regard these occasional survivors, mostly small country chapels, as typical of Provençal eleventh-century building—especially as in most cases their twelfth-century equivalents preserve exactly the same constructional forms. It is probably fair enough to assume that the best and most up-to-date buildings were the major churches, and where sections of these survive, notably in the transepts of S. Trophime at Arles and in the narthex of S. Victor at Marseille,[7] we do find a superior type of construction. Yet even here there is nothing which does not fall into the framework of First Romanesque.[8] The most distinctive feature of the Provençal ecclesiastical landscape at this period was probably still the late Antique baptisteries, standing, like that at Aix,[9] isolated from the cathedral building. Several of these, such as that at

---

[4] Manteyer, *La Provence du premier au douzième siècle*, believed that this was the church which Count William of Provence (d. 993) gave to Cluny. Vallery-Radot has pointed out that it is more probably that constructed by the Cluniac monk Leodegar and consecrated by Regimbald. See *C.A.* (1963), pp. 21–2.

[5] For this and other early buildings in Haute Provence see *Sites et Monuments de Haute Provence; Inventaire* (*Les Alpes de Lumière*, no. 34, 1964); R. Collier and J. P. Ehrmann, 'L'art roman primitif en Haute Provence', *Provence Historique*, fasc. 59 (Jan.–Mar. 1965), pp. 3–24; R. Collier, *Monuments et art de Haute Provence* (Digne, 1966); J. Thirion, 'L'influence lombarde dans les Alpes françaises du Sud', *B.M.* (1970), pp. 7–40.

[6] See above, pp. 22 ff.

[7] See above, pp. 21–5, 61 ff.

[8] J. Puig y Cadafalch, *La Géographie et les origines du premier art roman* (Paris, 1935), pp. 20–2, 310–13.

[9] See above, p. 48, and P. A. Fevrier, 'Les baptistères de Provence pendant le moyen âge', *Actes du Vᵉ congrès d'archéologie chrétienne* (Paris–Vatican, 1957), pp. 423–32.

Venasque, appear to have been largely remodelled in the course of the eleventh century.[10]

In short, it seems unlikely that a church of the Avignon type could have arisen unheralded in Provence, and since there is no real evidence of 'experimental' work in the area, one must look for external stimuli. At the same time we must remember that the ever present examples of Roman architecture must have served as continual sources of inspiration and information. The temple of Diana at Nîmes is frequently cited as the ultimate ancestor of the southern Romanesque church, and it certainly provides a splendid lesson in the construction of a barrel vault. However, perhaps more influential were the great arenas, which habitually served as medieval fortresses,[11] and which include an amazing variety of constructional forms. From such sources Provençal masons could learn many basic techniques, as well as the value (both structural and aesthetic) of employing ashlar masonry.

In considering the antecedents of the Avignon/Cavaillon type we may concentrate on three specific and distinctive aspects; the plan, the nave capital system, and the bipartite form of the capitals. In considering the plan we are limited to the nave, since none of the extant examples preserve their original east ends. The reconstruction which Labande proposed for Avignon is very probably correct, but we cannot take it as evidence.[12] This is again a case where excavation would be valuable.

The simple unaisled nave had existed in Provence from an early date; the church of St. Peter excavated at S. Blaise, and datable to the fifth or sixth century, was of this type.[13] The original cathedral of Notre-Dame at Aix seems to have been a similar sort of building.[14] However, this was by no means the only type of plan in early medieval Provence; S. Trophime at Arles, Notre-Dame at Vaison, and the first cathedral of Nice, were all aisled basilicas, and occasionally also centralized plans were employed.[15]

The crucial differences in the Avignon/Cavaillon type are the use of compound piers, the placement of chapels between the buttresses, and the introduction of broken barrel vaulting. The adoption of the compound pier may be seen as a consequence of the widespread introduction of vaulting, and it is certainly in no way surprising in an eleventh-century context. We have already seen that a simpler cruciform pier was

---

[10] Fevrier, loc. cit.

[11] See R. Michel, 'Les chevaliers du château des arènes de Nîmes aux xiie et xiiie siècles', *Mélanges d'histoire et d'archéologie* (Paris, 1926), pp. 115–35; also G. Duby, 'Les villes du sud-est de la Gaule du viiie au xie siècle', *La Città nell'alto medioevo* (Centro Italiano di studi sull'alto medioevo, Spoleto, 1959), pp. 231–76. On Roman influence in Provence see the recent book by Lassalle, cited on p. 74, n. 9.

[12] The instructions for the rebuilding of 1671–2 do not specify the form of the original east end: 'lesdits entrepreneurs seront tenus de faire et dresser après la croisée qui porte le dôme de ladite église, un croisier fait en berceau, conformément au vieux de la nef, de la hauteur et longueur des autres, avec les mêmes ornements et moulures, impostes, colonnes, chapiteaux, soubassements, etc.', Archives de Vaucluse, G451, quoted in *C.A.* (1963), p. 45, n. 1.

[13] H. Rolland, *Fouilles de Saint-Blaise (Bouches-du-Rhône)*, Supplément à Gallia, iii (1951), and vii (1956), especially pp. 61–70 of the latter.   [14] See above, pp. 56–7.

[15] For the cathedral of Nice see J. Thirion, 'L'ancienne cathédrale de Nice et sa clôture de chœur du xie siècle, d'après des découvertes récentes', *Cahiers Archéologiques*, xvii (1967), pp. 121–60. The author regards the first church found (église A) as that consecrated in 1049, but, as he himself admits (pp. 150–1), a case can be made out for a much earlier dating. For buildings of centralized plan see again Thirion, 'Note sur trois chapelles polygonales de l'ancien diocèse de Grasse (Alpes-Maritimes)', *Actes du Ve congrès d'archéologie chrétienne* (Paris–Vatican, 1957), pp. 589–97.

employed at S. Trophime in the late tenth or early eleventh century.[16] It is more difficult to explain the chapels set between the buttresses, and while it is certainly possible
that this was a Provençal 'invention', the idea does in fact have a long history. It is of
course one way, and probably the simplest way, of increasing the width of a barrel-
vaulted building without increasing the width (and therefore also the weight) of the
barrel vault itself. Some of the earliest examples of this technique occur in the early
Christian churches of southern Syria, where they were classified as a specific type by
Butler.[17] Several other examples, dating from the seventh to the ninth century, may be
found in Mesopotamia. Ctesiphon, Kefr Zeh, and Arnās are the major examples, and
in his study of these churches Monneret de Villard related their plans back to the royal
halls of Sassanian and Umayyad palaces.[18]

Perhaps the most directly related of all the Mesopotamian churches is the Palatine
chapel at Ani.[19] It consists of a three-bay nave, giving on to a single apse. The nave is
covered by a barrel vault, with transverse ribs, supported on compound piers which
project from the lateral walls of the nave. In other words, it anticipates almost exactly
the Avignon/Cavaillon church type. Another related building is the church at Ptghavank
(Armenia), where recessed chapels and compound piers recur, although in this case the
central bay of the three bay nave appears to have carried a cupola.[20]

This, however, suggests a further consideration; the distinctive appearance of Provençal buildings such as Cavaillon results from the occurrence of recessed chapels in a
building covered by a broken barrel vault. The majority of early medieval barrel vaults
in the Near East appear to have been semi-ovoid, but not broken. The widespread
pre-Romanesque usage of broken barrel vaults was in Muslim architecture, and visually
one of the closest parallels for the Provençal church type is provided by the great hall
of the fortified palace of Ukhaidir, remotely situated in the desert, some 120 km. south-
west of Baghdad.[21] This hall, which has been dated by Creswell to the eighth century,
and which Monneret de Villard has related to the Mesopotamian churches mentioned
above, employs walls set back behind the buttresses to produce lateral 'chapels', and it
is covered by a broken barrel vault. The similarity to Provençal buildings is quite
striking, although Ukhaidir lacks compound piers and transverse ribs.

I would not of course suggest that Umayyad architecture (let alone Ukhaidir in
particular) provided the direct models for Provençal churches. At the same time, the

---

[16] See *Revoil*, ii, 33–47.

[17] H. C. Butler, *Early Churches in Syria* (Princeton Monographs in Art and Archaeology, Princeton, N.J., 1929),
pp. 20–1.

[18] U. Monneret de Villard, *Le Chiese della Mesopotamia* (*Orientalia Christiana Analecta*, no. 128, Rome, 1940), pp.
12–13, 48–51. The system of recessed chapels did not originate in places such as Firouzabad and Sarvistan, since they
are prefigured by some of the early Christian examples in Syria, such as Umm-idj-Djimāl. The two earliest examples
seem to be the small temple of Dāt Rās (cited by Monneret de Villard, op. cit., p. 49, Fig. 43, who dates it to the
second or third century A.D.) and the south līwān of the main palace at Hatra (cited by K. A. C. Creswell, *Early
Muslim Architecture* (Oxford, 1940), ii, 87, Fig. 73. It is here dated to the second century A.D.)

[19] Monneret de Villard, op. cit., p. 67, Fig. 66.

[20] R. Krautheimer, *Early Christian and Byzantine Architecture* (London, 1965), p. 230, Fig. 229B.

[21] Creswell, op. cit., ii, 50–100.

striking similarities which exist between several Mesopotamian buildings and the Avignon/Cavaillon type does imply that some sort of connection, direct or indirect, exists between them. The nature of this connection can only be guessed. Since Avignon can now be dated before 1101, the convenient explanation of the Crusades is not possible. However, trade rather than warfare probably always played the greatest role in the transmission of cultural and artistic ideas, and, given the cosmopolitan nature of Marseille and Arles, it is by no means impossible that a knowledge of eastern Mediterranean architectural forms could have reached Provence in the eleventh century. The lack of any indigenous architectural traditions to which Notre-Dame-des-Doms can convincingly be traced strengthens the supposition that external influences, however distant, were involved.

The second feature is the employment of colonnettes and capitals, set into compound piers, as supports for the transverse arches of the vault. Again the earliest and also some of the most direct parallels for this type of arrangement are found in the eastern Mediterranean, and particularly in Syria. Here a group of basilican churches supported the cross-beams of their wooden roofs on a series of colonnettes on corbels. The best-preserved example occurs at Qalb Louzeh, datable to c. 500.[22] A similar system was employed in the basilican church of St. Sergius at R'safah, and at Qalat-Siman. However, the specific connection of this system with Syria seems dubious, and derives mainly from the fact that a number of Syrian buildings have survived to their full height. That the system was not limited to this region is witnessed by the fifth- to sixth-century church of Alahan Manistiri (Khoja Kalessi), in Turkey.[23] In addition, the significance for present purposes of the occurrence of the system in Syria is lessened by the fact that it was not, to my knowledge, employed in any church which also had recessed lateral chapels.

Another objection to any suggestion of a direct link between Syrian and Provençal buildings is of course that by the eleventh century the whole of this area was in Muslim hands, and the buildings in question were already in ruins. Also the colonnettes involved are not inserted into piers, and they support wooden beams, not transverse arches of a vault. Nevertheless, in visual terms, the form found in these early Christian buildings does recall the subsequent Provençal development: in both cases we are dealing with a 'false' architectural member, which appears to play an active supporting role, but in fact is purely decorative.

The system was not taken over by Muslim architects, whose buildings were for the most part vaulted. Occasionally colonnettes were used to support arches, as for example below the ninth-century dome in the Great Mosque at Qairawan,[24] but these cannot be related either to the Syrian or to the Provençal forms.

The uncertain nature of these connections is the more apparent since it is also possible to discover western parallels for a system of colonnettes supporting brackets or arches.

---

[22] Cte. de Vogüé, *Syrie centrale, architecture civile et religieuse du Ier au VIIe siècle* (Paris, 1865–77), vol. ii, Pl. 126. I am grateful to Professor Krautheimer of New York University for confirming to me the accuracy of de Vogüé's drawing in this respect.

[23] Krautheimer, op. cit., pp. 177–9.   [24] Creswell, op. cit., ii, 315–16.

In the Carolingian church of Germigny-des-Prés pairs of colonnettes are inserted on either side of the triumphal arch, and single colonnettes are inserted into the aisle piers, just below the springing.[25] A very similar form occurs in the so-called crypt of S. Laurent at Grenoble.[26] In this case it may also be noted that the capitals are provided with large Ravenna-type impost blocks (see below). A still closer analogy, if only in terms of the size of the building, is provided by the nave of San Pere de Roda in Catalonia. The church here was consecrated in 1022, and the nave is normally assumed to be of around the same date.[27] The nave piers have pairs of short columns inserted into them, one above the other, and the upper one supports the transverse arch of the barrel vault. However, this connection raises rather more problems than it solves, for Roda is a largely exceptional Spanish church; it is an aisled building, with small transepts, and an eastern ambulatory without chapels, and all these features are unusual (and the ambulatory unparalleled) in eleventh-century Spanish building. Equally, there are no other Spanish churches which adopt this nave system. Earlier Visigothic churches sometimes supported transverse arches on columns which rose directly from the floor (e.g. San Pedro de la Nave),[28] but the conception of superimposed columns is really only paralleled in the Great Mosque of Cordova. In the latter the double tier of arches has itself been compared, not very convincingly, to Roman structures such as the aqueduct at Merida.[29]

One can find other examples which are more or less comparable to the system as it occurs in Provence—for example, the nave at Tournus employs half-columns atop the great cylindrical piers as supports for the diaphragm arches[30]—but nowhere does the exact system used in Provence appear.[31] It is perhaps equally revealing that certain areas which one might have expected to influence the development of Provençal architecture, notably northern Italy, do not seem to have used any comparable arrangement. The only remotely related form of pre-twelfth-century date would seem to be half-columns placed above the alternating piers in S. Ambrogio, Milan.[32] Here, however, all they 'support' is an arched corbel table at the level of the triforium. It is not until the twelfth century that a system closely comparable to that used in Provence is found elsewhere, in several churches of the Burgundian school. Perhaps the earliest directly comparable example is in the nave of the cathedral of Autun, dating from the second quarter of the

[25] J. Hubert, 'Germigny-des-Prés', C.A. (1930).

[26] J. Hubert, 'La "crypte" de Saint-Laurent de Grenoble et l'art du sud-est de la Gaule au début de l'époque carolingienne', *Arte del primo millennio* (*Atti del IIo convegno per lo studio dell'arte dell'alto medio evo, Pavia, 1950*, Turin, n.d.), pp. 327–34.

[27] See *Ars Hispaniae, Historia universal del arte Hispánico* (Madrid), v (1948), p. 17.

[28] *Ars Hispaniae*, ii (1947), pp. 289–99.

[29] Creswell, op. cit., ii, p. 157.

[30] The dating of the nave vaults at Tournus is by no means certain, but they are probably twelfth century. The most recent study of the building is J. Vallery-Radot, *S. Philibert de Tournus* (Paris, 1955).

[31] The half-columns which surmount the main arcade on the alternating piers in the nave at Conques might also be cited in this context. The system here is more closely comparable to that found at S. Paul-Trois-Châteaux—a connection that has already been made by Aubert (see his article on Conques, C.A., 1936).

[32] For S. Ambrogio see Porter, *Lombard Arch.*, ii, pp. 532–95. The clustered colonnettes on the alternate drum columns of S. Eustorgio date from the late-twelfth-century restoration of the church.

century.[33] In this building we find the use of pointed arches and of a broken barrel vault—features derived no doubt from the third church at Cluny.[34] It is of course possible to use the occurrence of such colonnettes in Burgundian churches of the twelfth century as evidence for adhering to a late dating of the Provençal buildings. However, the unreality of such a view is immediately apparent; the nave colonnettes are one of the least important features in buildings which employ a wide variety of decorative devices—fluted pilasters, blind triforia, historiated capitals in the main arcade, etc. It is hardly likely that Provençal builders would have taken over this one small feature from Burgundian churches, and have ignored all the others. Indeed, if one influenced the other it would seem much more probable that the direction in which this influence travelled was from Provence to Burgundy.[35]

In short, there do not seem to be any direct predecessors employing the nave capital system as it is found in Provence. If the idea goes back ultimately to fifth-century Syria, it does not seem to pass directly from there into Romanesque architecture. Perhaps the idea of using colonnettes as a support for an arch is in itself too common a feature to be considered significant at all; on the other hand, there persists the feeling that the particular Provençal usage is more than a regional idiosyncrasy.

It has been observed that the capitals which crown the colonnettes in the Provençal churches are of highly unusual form. The bipartite form, with the distinct and extensive upper section, would suggest a distant connection with early Byzantine capitals and imposts, of the type familiar to western artists from Ravenna. However, the Byzantines always retained the distinction between the two sections—that is, of a capital surmounted by an enlarged impost—although, when the upper part was decorated, the whole did take on something of the appearance of a bipartite capital. The two parts were never fused, and indeed the closest Byzantine parallels occur in the great cisterns of Constantinople, and consist of two independent capitals superimposed.[36] But this was almost certainly a practical solution to a particular problem (i.e., the column was not long enough).

The extended impost block, introduced to the west at San Vitale, does survive into the Middle Ages proper, but it tends to become less rather than more decorated. Capitals of this type occur in the crypt of S. Laurent at Grenoble. There are in fact two groups of capitals in this building; six marble ones, dated by Hubert to the early seventh century, and the remainder of stone, dating from the period when the chapel was

---

[33] See D. Grivot and G. Zarnecki, *Gislebertus, Sculptor of Autun* (London, 1960).

[34] The system at Cluny has been compared by Deyres to that at Conques (*B.M.* (1968), p. 50), although it combines colonnettes in the dosserets above the main arcade with half columns on the pilasters at the level of the triforium and clerestory. The date of Cluny is also open to question. For a recent contribution to the debate see F. Salet, 'Cluny III', *B.M.* (1968), pp. 235–92, which argues that little more than a plan and foundations date from the consecration of 1095.

[35] It also seems possible that the broken barrel vault entered Burgundian architecture from Provence. It is the one feature in buildings such as Cluny and Autun which cannot be derived from Roman monuments (no Roman examples of broken barrel vaults are known to me), and the Provençal examples provide the only obvious forerunners.

[36] R. Kautzch, *Kapitellstudien* (*Studien zur Spätantiken Kunstgeschichte*, no. 9, Berlin–Leipzig, 1936), Pl. 40, nos. 669*a* and *b*.

constructed.[37] The later capitals follow the form of the earlier ones, illustrating how firmly the Ravennate form was entrenched. It is therefore worth recalling the Byzantine rams' head capital found in Arles, and which suggests the possibility of a body of Ravennate work in Provence.[38]

Nevertheless, the connections between the Provençal nave capitals and those of the Ravenna tradition, with enlarged impost blocks, is at best a general one. No extant Ravenna tradition capitals really look much like those in the naves of Avignon or Aix, and this is especially true if we consider not only the form but also the content of the Provençal capitals—that is as asymmetrical and 'anti-classical' foliage capitals. The anti-classicism is markedly different from that which occurs in the Ravennate capitals; the latter reject the Corinthian form and arrangement, substituting for it a carefully structured and tightly controlled surface pattern. By comparison the Provençal capitals appear as intentional revisions, even distortions of Corinthian forms, and the origins of this tradition lie, I suspect, not in stone but in stucco.

It has long been apparent that stucco was a major medium for architectural decoration in the early medieval period, although the nature of the material has resulted in its almost complete destruction. Our knowledge is confined to a few fragments of once elaborate programmes, and to a few pieces of church furniture and smaller objects. The few more extensive survivals, most notably Cividale, have therefore acquired a reputation which almost certainly goes far beyond their true significance.[39]

The arbitrary pattern of survival makes it difficult to substantiate the suggestion that the origins of the Provençal nave capitals lie in stucco carving. None the less, the capitals themselves, their fantastic and virtuosic forms, their combination of plasticity and precision, and the manner in which they are cut, are readily translatable into and suggestive of stucco. It is therefore no surprise to discover that the two buildings in France which have been cited as anticipating the inserted colonnettes of Provence, S. Laurent at Grenoble and Germigny-des-Prés, both included extensive stucco decoration.[40] Indeed the western medieval usage of stucco goes back at least to Ravenna, where it occurs in both the orthodox baptistery and in San Vitale.[41] In Provence itself there is evidence of stucco decoration at an equally early date, in the oratory of Notre-Dame in the crypt of S. Victor at Marseille.[42] The most extensive traces of early medieval stucco decorations survive at Santa Maria in Valle, Cividale, at San Salvatore in Brescia, and at San Benedetto at Malles.[43] Further north, excepting the examples at Grenoble and Germigny mentioned above (which are fragmentary and restored), little survives before the

---

[37] Hubert, 'La "crypte" de Saint-Laurent de Grenoble', pp. 327–34.

[38] F. Benoit, 'Chapiteau byzantin à têtes de bélier du musée d'Arles', *B.M.* (1938), pp. 137–44.

[39] For stuccos in general see *Stucchi e mosaici alto medioevali (Atti dell'ottavo congresso di studi sull'arte dell'alto medioevo, Milan, 1962)*; hereafter cited as *Stucchi*.

[40] Hubert, 'La "crypte" de Saint-Laurent de Grenoble', and M. Vieillard-Troiekouroff, 'Tables de canons et stucs carolingiens', *Stucchi*, pp. 154–78.

[41] S. K. Kostof, *The Orthodox Baptistery of Ravenna* (New Haven, Conn., 1965).

[42] P. Deschamps, 'Quelques témoins de décors de stuc en France pendant le haut moyen âge et l'époque romane', *Stucchi*, pp. 179–85.

[43] N. Rasmo, 'Note preliminari su S. Benedetto di Malles', *Stucchi*, pp. 86–110.

extensive series of eleventh-century capitals in S. Remi at Reims.[44] There are in addition numerous even smaller and more fragmentary survivals, but the sum total remains extremely small, and it is impossible to build up any coherent picture of the nature of stucco developments. The programme at Cividale contains little that can be directly related to Provençal forms. On the other hand, the fragments of the stucco arcades which decorated the apse walls at Malles do include capitals which emerge from the decorated colonnette in a way that suggests a bipartite form.[45] The relationship is admittedly distant, and the Malles work relies largely on interlace patterns which are absent from Provence.[46] It would be unwise to press this particular comparison too far, and the dependence of the Provençal nave capital type on stuccos can probably never be more than a hypothesis. At the same time, it is a hypothesis which gains some strength from the fact that no convincing forerunners have been found in the field of stone sculpture. It may also be mentioned that the bipartite capitals of Provence resemble the 'fantasy' capitals which frequently occur in the canon tables of Carolingian and Ottonian manuscripts. It is difficult, if not impossible, to imagine a Romanesque sculptor borrowing the form of his capitals from a manuscript source; if it operated at all, the process must surely have been in reverse. Indeed it has been suggested that the elaborated forms found in canon tables themselves follow current tastes in plastic decoration, particularly stucco.[47]

The foregoing discussion has not lead to any very definite conclusions. There does not seem to be any complete prototype for Avignon, Aix, or Cavaillon, and clearly we must allow Provençal masons a measure of originality. At the same time, all the individual features considered can be derived from pre-existing forms, and it does seem that the recessed lateral chapels, the broken barrel vaults, and perhaps also the nave colonnettes, can most easily be explained in terms of a knowledge of eastern Mediterranean architecture. The precise way in which such knowledge may have been acquired is, as I have said, obscure, but it may probably be seen as a by-product of flourishing commercial activity. The existence of a small group of buildings in the Salon region which employ a characteristic Syrian roofing system suggests, as R. Doré pointed out,[48] that in some cases first-hand knowledge of non-European monuments was involved. It is not necessary to postulate such direct links for the Avignon/Cavaillon group, but their development indicates at least an awareness of a variety of architectural styles.

[44] L. Grodecki, 'Les chapiteaux en stuc de Saint-Remi de Reims', *Stucchi*, pp. 186–208.

[45] Rasmo, op. cit., Figs. 13, 14, 17.

[46] However, some support for this theory is provided by the transept capitals in the Cluniac abbey of Payerne in Switzerland. These can be stylistically related to the Malles stuccos. The south-east corner capital of the south transept (a capital which has enabled Professor Zarnecki to date the series to the second half of the eleventh century) has a greatly enlarged abacus or impost, and in general conception it may be directly compared with the Provençal form.

[47] Vieillard-Troiekouroff, op. cit.

[48] See Les Bouches du Rhône, *Encyclopédie Départementale*, vol. iv: 1, *Archéologie* (Paris–Marseille, 1932), with the section 'Moyen âge' by Robert Doré. The buildings concerned include the parish church of Marignane, the chapel of S. Jean de Bernasse, near Salon, and one room in the Château of Salon. All these are vaulted by a series of transverse arches placed very close together, on which the large roofing tiles are directly laid. This system (though applied to a flat rather than an arched roof) was relatively common in fifth- and sixth-century Syria; e.g. the case cited by Butler, op. cit., Fig. 11, the church of Iulanos at Umn-idj-Djimâl.

10 *The Nave Capitals and* L'Art roman de Provence

IN the preceding chapters I have presented a revised view of the development of Provençal Romanesque. It has been suggested that the documentary and stylistic evidence for dating buildings such as Avignon, Aix, or Cavaillon, is good, and that this cannot be set aside or ignored; however, if it is accepted it entails a revision of the whole picture. This interpretation conflicts with what might be termed the orthodox French opinion, based largely upon the studies of Labande, which regards the Provençal school as an exclusively late development. At the same time, an integral feature of my revised chronology is the view that both the style and the form of the decoration at S. Paul-Trois-Châteaux suggest a date in the last quarter of the twelfth century, and this means a 'late' date for the major sculpture at Arles as well. Consequently this interpretation also conflicts with that of the group of German and American scholars who accept an earlier twelfth-century dating for the façade of S. Gilles and for at least the north gallery of the cloister at Arles.

The arguments in favour of the late dating of the whole school arise partly from the fact that there are several monuments in the region which are certainly datable to the second half of the twelfth century. These include the three major Cistercian houses, and the churches of Tarascon and Le Thor. These are all well-dated monuments, and no amount of special pleading can possibly place them before *c.* 1150. At the same time none of them are in fact at all closely related to the Avignon/Cavaillon type of building. None the less, some consideration of them is essential, since they are frequently included in the argument.

It is clearly impossible to maintain that any of the Cistercian houses predate their foundations. These were *c.* 1144 for Silvacane, 1148 for Sénanque, and *c.* 1160 for Le Thoronet.[1] All three church buildings are related to each other, and all diverge from the Avignon/Cavaillon plan. They are aisled buildings, with projecting transepts and a pair of chapels in each arm. At Silvacane the chapels and the choir are rectangular, while at the other two they are apsidal. At Thoronet and Silvacane the nave is covered by a broken barrel vault, with transverse arches supported on half-columns. At Sénanque

---

[1] For Silvacane and Le Thoronet see the articles by M. Aubert, *C.A.* (1932), pp. 123–43 and 224–43. For Sénanque see the article by M. Thibout, *C.A.* (1963), pp. 365–76.

the vault is devoid of transverse ribs. The crossing at Silvacane has a ribbed vault, although this was not originally envisaged. All three are entirely plain, with no superficial decoration, in accordance with Cistercian custom. Thoronet and Sénanque appear to have been begun *c.* 1160, while Silvacane was probably started a little later.

There is no reason why these buildings should be contemporary with Avignon, Aix, or Cavaillon. They represent a largely unrelated type, following a plan and design which is otherwise unknown in the region. In a very general way both groups share similar features—e.g. the use of a single-storey elevation—but the details are handled quite differently. Thus the Cistercian buildings employ half-columns and roll mouldings, whereas only angular profiles occur in the nave capital group of churches. In short, the Cistercian buildings are only superficially related to the type of church which has been discussed here, and as such they can hardly be used as significant dated examples of 'Provençal' Romanesque. It is perhaps more significant to point out that, while one can find elements in all three Cistercian churches which might be derived from churches of the nave capital type, the Avignon/Cavaillon group show no evidence of knowledge of the Cistercian buildings.

An equally misleading instance is the church of Le Thor.[2] This can be regarded as a firmly dated building, on the basis of a reference to it as 'ecclesiam novam' in 1202; this evidence is supported by the stylistic analysis of the decoration of the building.[3] Le Thor is closer to the Avignon plan, having a single nave of three bays, succeeded by a cupola bay and an apse. However, the nave is covered by a ribbed vault, and the cupola and the semi-dome of the apse also employ ribs. The interior of the building is fairly plain, but for a blind arcade around the apse. On the exterior, the windows are flanked by colonnettes, the west and south doors are decorated, and the latter is enclosed in a rib-vaulted porch. The form and extent of this decoration imply that it is post-Vaison, and the overall effect suggests a date similar to or even later than that of the nave of S. Paul-Trois-Châteaux. The Le Thor *atelier* was also responsible for building the parish church at Venasque.[4]

In terms of the decoration alone, this *atelier* has no connection with the Avignon/Cavaillon school. The use of rib vaults and roll mouldings is again a distinguishing feature of Le Thor. The only things it shares with the Avignon group are the plan (shortened at Le Thor) and certain decorative devices—e.g. the placement of the symbols of the Evangelists in the squinches of the cupola. But to regard these very general connections as significant is clearly a mistake; the conservatism of the region is well known, and one can cite buildings which are more closely related to the plan and form of the cathedral at Avignon which were built considerably later. Such is the parish church at Malaucène, a near-perfect example of Provençal 'Romanesque' dating from the

---

[2] See E. Lefevre-Pontalis, *C.A.* (1909), ii, 275–98.

[3] In addition to the article by Lefevre-Pontalis cited above, see also my M.A. thesis, 'The Cloister of the Cathedral of St. Sauveur, Aix-en-Provence' (London University, 1967) (unpublished).

[4] The connection was noted by Labande, *C.A.* (1909), pp. 285–7, but he did not point out that they are undoubtedly the work of the same *atelier*.

fourteenth century.[5] The sixteenth-century rebuilding at Avignon reveals that this mode still survived, and indeed it can be argued that when men such as Revoil came to restore these buildings in the nineteenth century they were working within a tradition which had never really died out. This applies not only to general features such as the plan and elevation, but also to specific forms of embellishment; thus there are symbols of the Evangelists in the squinches in the Mas de la Brune at Eygalières, which was built in 1572.[6]

What this amounts to is that valid connections between Provençal monuments must depend upon something more than generalized features, and that on this basis it is clear that Le Thor is in no way directly related to the Avignon/Cavaillon group. At the same time, it would be unfair to the memory of such an excellent scholar as Labande to suggest that he ever used Le Thor as in any way direct evidence for dating the Avignon/Cavaillon group. Nevertheless, once these buildings had come to be accepted as later-twelfth-century monuments, it proved almost impossible not to find confirmation of this opinion in buildings such as Le Thor. This is perhaps why the Labande dating of Provençal monuments has stood for so long unchallenged; a series of generalized connections have come to be regarded as particular, and consequently no one has reconsidered the basis for dating Avignon and Aix to the mid-twelfth century.

There are other dated buildings to consider, such as the small chapel of S. Nicolas on the Pont-S.-Bénézet at Avignon.[7] This is not a particularly distinctive building, and it has been much rebuilt, but the lower apse appears to date from the period of the construction of the bridge, 1177–85. The large and rather clumsy apse capitals employ a leaf type clearly derived from the Arles cloister, and the work is close to that found in the west gallery of the cloister at Aix.

A rather more problematic building is the main church at Montmajour.[8] The crypt, with its rotunda-like ambulatory and radiating chapels, is unique in the region. The upper church ignores the crypt plan, and it is in fact difficult to believe that, as is normally stated, they are contemporary. The upper church has a polygonal apse, projecting transepts, and a nave, of which only two bays were constructed. The crossing is rib-vaulted, although the ribs were probably not originally envisaged. The adjoining cloister is very closely related to, but slightly later than the north gallery of the cloister at S. Trophime. The north wall of this cloister was also intended to form the south wall of the nave, and the compound piers for this unfinished nave remain on its north face. However, the cloister corbels on the south face of the same wall do not appear to be insertions, but are part of its original fabric, and consequently it would seem that the nave was under construction, or rather its construction was abandoned, when the cloister was being built. This was most probably in the late 1170s or 1180s, and so we may accept the traditional view that the building of the upper church began at the

---

[5] The parish church at Malaucène was begun in the time of Pope Clement V (1305–14), who frequently visited the town.

[6] See M. Pezet, *Les Alpilles; Eygalières et Mollèges des origines au XVIᵉ siècle* (Cavaillon, 1949), pp. 101–2.

[7] See *C.A.* (1909), pp. 48–52.

[8] For Montmajour see above, Ch. 2, n. 2.

east end after the middle of the century, perhaps *c.* 1160. The upper church also reflects the plan of S. Ruf, Avignon, with which it is, in my opinion, contemporary. At any rate, at the risk of labouring the point, Montmajour is clearly not directly related to buildings of the nave capital group.

Turning to another of the main 'dated' monuments, Ste Marthe at Tarascon, we find a somewhat different situation. Here the south porch, which is almost all that remains intact of the twelfth-century building, is firmly dated by two inscriptions to 1187–97.[9] This porch is richly decorated, and, despite the destruction of the tympanum, it is a key monument of Provençal sculpture. The form of the capitals is closely comparable to those of the Arles façade, and must be seen as confirming a later twelfth-century date for that. French scholars have always maintained that all the major sculpture at Arles is relatively close in date, and here I readily concur. The reasons for this, which are to some extent set out above,[10] are basically the stylistic analysis of the work itself, and the evidence of the nave capital churches (including of course S. Trophime). The latter suggests that neither the forms nor the style of the Arles cloister and façade were current in Provence in the first half of the twelfth century.

Up to this point I have studiously avoided any consideration of S. Gilles-du-Gard, on the technical grounds that it is in Languedoc rather than Provence. Nevertheless, it is only some 16 km. distant from Arles, and possesses by any standards the most spectacular façade in the region. There can be little doubt that it provided the direct inspiration for Arles. Since the interpretation of Provençal developments proposed here to some extent reflects upon and itself reflects the problems of S. Gilles, some consideration of those problems is essential.

I shall not go into the various complex questions in great detail here; the one thing that has emerged clearly from all the discussions is that the evidence is open to widely differing interpretation, and it would only complicate the issue to enter into specific problems now. I prefer rather to offer some general thoughts on the problems involved.

Gilles (Aegidius, Giles) was a popular and widely known saint.[11] In the eleventh and more particularly the twelfth century the pilgrimage to his tomb became increasingly popular. The most southerly of the French routes to Santiago became known as the Via Aegidiana, and the author of the pilgrim's guide devotes more time to the shrine of this saint than to any other except James himself. Aimery has, however, his priorities right on this occasion; he passes over the church with the briefest mention ('Quis Deum adorabit in ejus sacratissima basilica?') and devotes himself to the saint and his shrine.[12] It is worth remembering that the point of the pilgrimage was at all times the shrine, and it was this not the façade which really mattered. There can be no doubt that the first consideration of the Cluniac monks installed there was to provide a fitting surrounding for the tomb. In all probability the altar which Urban II consecrated in

---

[9] The texts of these inscriptions are given by Porter, *Romanesque Sculpture*, p. 299.
[10] See above, pp. 106–108.
[11] *Acta Sanctorum*, vol. xli, 1 September. See also above, Ch. 1, p. 15.
[12] J. Vielliard (ed.) *Le Guide du pèlerin de Saint-Jacques de Compostelle* (Mâcon, 1963), pp. 36–46.

1096 was in or near the *confessio* chapel which now forms the central bay of the crypt.[13] There seems little doubt that a major building campaign began in 1116, as the well-known inscription states.[14] The object of this must have been to surround and enclose the shrine in a fitting setting—that is, to build the crypt or lower church. The basic disagreement between what may be termed the French and the German views concerns the nature and intention of this campaign: was it intended to produce a crypt which would act as substructure for the main church, or was it intended as a real lower church, which was subsequently converted into a crypt? Yet this seems to me to miss the point, for (as Labande pointed out long ago)[15] all the physical evidence suggests that this lower section was built over a considerable period of time, with numerous interruptions. The evidence brought forward by Schapiro proves, I think, that the west wall of the crypt existed in 1129, and may also indicate that some form of upper façade was already envisaged.[16] It certainly does not prove that work was already started on that upper façade.[17] A second factor is that even if we allow that the western wall of the crypt was built by 1129 one can hardly envisage a building programme which erects a highly elaborate façade on this wall, with nothing at all behind it—i.e. we cannot divorce the façade from the rest of the upper church. It is worth remembering that all the dated and datable inscriptions on the building occur in the lower church. Furthermore, only the first western pier of the nave of the upper church rests directly on the crypt piers; the others are progressively off-centre, and this implies not only a west to east building, but also strongly suggests that the crypt was finished first.[18]

At this point I think one may legitimately question the basic assumption of almost all those who have written on the subject of S. Gilles—namely that the façade has been in some way reconstructed. The 'Proto-Renaissance' that Hamann postulated is an *ex post facto* assertion, which certainly is contradicted by the rest of the church: however we explain the crypt, there is no doubt that it looks chaotic. Why then should we assume a logical plan for the façade? None of the elaborate reconstructions are very satisfactory, and it seems much more reasonable to argue that although a few pieces, notably the socles, may have been prepared for an earlier scheme, when the façade was finally erected (an event which only happened once) a rather different plan was adopted.

The façade of S. Gilles is by any standards a curious work; magnificent in scale, it appears disjointed on closer inspection, and also iconographically unclear. The iconography of the actual façade (as opposed to that of the various hypothetical reconstructions)

[13] For the plan of the crypt see *Revoil*, vol. ii, Pl. LVI.

[14] (AN)NO DNI MCXVI HOC TEPLV (A)EGIDII AEDIFICARI CEPIT M APL FR II IN OCTAB PASCHE

[15] *C.A.* (1909), pp. 168–81.

[16] M. Schapiro, 'New Documents on St. Gilles', *Art Bulletin*, xvii, (1935), 415–30. I do not think it is possible to use the inscriptions in the cloister at Arles as evidence for dating, while rejecting those of S. Gilles, or *vice versa*. It may also be noted here that the excellent ashlar masonry of the lower west wall at S. Gilles proves my contention that such construction is not necessarily a sign of a later-twelfth-century date.

[17] It should be observed that Hamann's reconstruction makes no sense of this projection.

[18] For the sectional drawing see Hamann, *St. Gilles*, p. 18, Fig. 20.

has never been closely studied, and it certainly deserves further attention. It is surprising that the programme does not include any representation of S. Gilles himself. At Arles St. Trophimus and St. Stephen occur both on the façade and in the cloister; at Conques Ste Foy figures on the tympanum, while at Compostela St. James was represented on both the original west door and on the Puerta de las Platerias.[19] An explanation of the S. Gilles programme may perhaps lie in the concern with and reaction against heresy in the Midi in the course of the twelfth century. One of the most interesting of these heretics, Petrus Brusus, was burned at S. Gilles. Knowledge of his doctrines comes almost exclusively from Peter the Venerable, Abbot of Cluny, whose tract *Contra Petrobrusianos Hereticos* was written between 1138 and 1141.[20] S. Gilles became a Cluniac house in 1066,[21] and although it appears to have escaped direct dependence early in the twelfth century[22] no doubt some connections were maintained.[23] At any rate it is clear that S. Gilles was an orthodox centre, frequently visited by influential churchmen, from the pope downwards. It was here that Pierre de Castelnau was buried in 1207.[24] Thus one can probably assume that the *Contra Petrobrusianos* was well known at S. Gilles. In this work the abbot of Cluny refutes what he sees as the five central errors of the heresy; the reasons for his concern are obvious, and the far-reaching and highly disruptive nature of these beliefs is clear. The five are:

1. That infants should not be baptized.
2. That churches are unnecessary and should not be built.
3. That crosses should be broken (one should not venerate an instrument of torture).
4. That the sacraments are of no effect.
5. That prayers for the dead, the giving of alms, and the veneration of relics are of no effect.

The whole of the façade can be interpreted as a visual demonstration of Peter the Venerable's refutation of the heresy. A large and impressive church, greater than any other in the region, was a statement of opposition to the second point. The twelve Apostles and the Archangel witness the central truths of orthodox Christianity, portrayed on the frieze and tympana, just as they witness the truth of orthodoxy in Peter's refutation. Hamann's view that the angels fighting dragons, on the far right of the façade, is an overt reference to victory over heresy is altogether possible, but there is no indication that it is specifically Catharist heresy. The three tympana witness the

[19] The west door at Santiago originally had a representation of the Transfiguration. See Vielliard, *Guide*, p. 104.

[20] The most recent edition is J. Fearns (ed.), *Petri Venerabilis: Contra Petrobrusianos Hereticos (Corpus Christianorum, Continuatio Mediaevalis*, No. 10, 1968). There is a curious error on p. 5 of this text, where the editor glosses Sanctum Egidium as 'gallice S. *Gilles-les-Boucheries*'. Professor Colish of Oberlin College has made a detailed study of the relationship between Petrus Brusus and the iconography of S. Gilles, which is to appear shortly in *Traditio*. I am most grateful to Professor Colish for informing me about her work; her conclusions appear to coincide with mine and expand upon the views expressed here.   [21] Gouron, *C.A.* (1950), pp. 104–19.

[22] N. Hunt, *Cluny under St. Hugh, 1049–1109* (London, 1967), pp. 162–4.

[23] Peter the Venerable was himself there in 1130. See G. Constable, *The Letters of Peter the Venerable* (Cambridge, Mass., 1962), 2 vols.

[24] It is also this event which provides us with the first reference to an upper and lower church. See A. Fliche, *Aigues-Mortes et S. Gilles (Petites monographies*, Paris, 1961), p. 35.

divinity and majesty of Christ; His second coming in the centre, His crucifixion on the right (on a large and symbolic cross), and His divine birth, attested by the Magi, on the left. The meaning of the tympana is emphasized by the frieze devoted to the events of Holy Week, placed immediately below. This does not of course prove anything as regards the date of the programme, although to my mind a date after the appearance of the *Contra Petrobrusianos*, and after the burning of the heretic himself, seems most likely.

To return to the actual building of the façade, there is little evidence for the radical reconstructions which have been proposed. I suggest that the construction at S. Gilles was really quite straightforward; the major building campaign was begun in 1116. At this point the primary intention was to enclose the *confessio* chapel in a fitting manner. By the time the western wall was begun (before 1129) some form of superstructure was being envisaged, implied by the rectangular projection in the wall. Since this projection does not correspond precisely to the structure of the present façade, or to any of the proposed reconstructions, there is absolutely no reason to believe that the initial plan, whatever it was, was ever carried out, although it is quite possible that some of the sculpture on the socles was prepared for this early project. Whether or not Porter was right in terming these the work of the 'Angoulême Master', it is clear that their style is not Provençal.[25] The inconsistencies in the present façade are less significant than Hamann maintained. They only become important if we accept his conception of a Proto-Renaissance, and of the necessary adoption of an ordered and logical solution because of this. However, there is little reason to believe this contention, and at any rate it is clear that alongside a monument such as the Puerta de las Platerias the façade of S. Gilles is already an object-lesson in order and lucidity.

The upper church was built from west to east, but after the completion of the crypt. The façade must be seen as part of this upper church and not of the crypt. This church was of apse and ambulatory plan, unparalleled in the region.[26] The major piers of this nave were square with half-columns attached—again not found in Provence until the building of the Cistercian churches.

What all this adds up to is that the internal evidence suggests fairly clearly that the construction of the upper church, including the major sculpture of the façade, can hardly have been undertaken before *c.* 1150. The appearance of the name Petrus Brunus, 'artifex in opere ligneo et lapideo', in a Nîmes document of 1186, in conjunction with that of the same name in a S. Gilles document of 1171, has very reasonably been associated with the Brunus who signed two of the façade apostles, and this of course fits neatly with the conclusions reached here.[27]

---

[25] Porter, *Romanesque Sculpture*, pp. 273–4.

[26] The church of Montmajour did of course have an apse and ambulatory, but I have already argued that this church dates from the second half of the twelfth century. In addition, the S. Gilles plan involves chapels of two different sizes, arranged alternately, and this particular form is certainly unique in the region.

[27] M. Gouron, *La Cathédrale romane de Nîmes*; M. Aubert, 'Les dates de la façade de S. Gilles', *B.M.* (1936), pp. 369–72.

This is still not the real point, although it is worth stating. The point is that if the conclusions of the preceding chapters are more or less right, then a building of the type of the upper church at S. Gilles is practically inconceivable in this area in the first half of the twelfth century. The standard, in so far as it exists for major churches, was the Avignon/Cavaillon type. It is very hard to conceive of S. Gilles being built at the same time as these, but apparently influencing them in no way.

Of course S. Gilles is not without influence. Most directly it influences Arles, and indirectly all the buildings discussed in Chapter 8. The significance of the Avignon/Cavaillon group is not only that they are not influenced by S. Gilles, but equally they cannot be regarded as reactions against S. Gilles: it is clear that their designers and builders simply had no knowledge of the existence of S. Gilles, and in an area of this size this can only mean that when they were built the upper church there did not in fact exist. It is this that distinguishes such 'traditional' buildings as Carpentras, Rosans, and Le Thor from the earlier group, for they all reveal in some degree the influence of Arles, and so in turn of S. Gilles. In addition, the analysis of Provençal buildings undertaken here illustrates that those which show Arles influence are later than those which do not— but this conclusion is not based upon the fact of Arles influence itself, or on any assumptions about its date. There does seem to be a good case for saying that the concept of the elaborately decorated portal only emerges in Provence in the latter part of the twelfth century, and that when it does so it is directly the result of the influence of S. Gilles and Arles.

No view of Provençal sculpture would be complete without some consideration of S. Gilles. Equally important, but much more frequently neglected, are the group of marble capitals which represent the surviving traces of the cloisters of S. Ruf and Notre-Dame-des-Doms, Avignon. Curiously enough one of these capitals, that showing Samson, ranks among the best-known and most frequently reproduced pieces of Romanesque sculpture.[28] At the same time there is only one systematic study of the group as a whole, and there exists no detailed assessment of their place in the development of Provençal Romanesque.[29]

This Avignon work is totally unrelated to the nave capitals of Notre-Dame, but it is related, though not in any very clear manner, to the capitals of the north gallery of the cloister at Arles and those of the apse of Les-Saintes-Maries-de-la-Mer. The surviving fragments fall into two main groups, one attributable to S. Ruf, the other to Notre-Dame. They are stylistically related, but those from Notre-Dame are more developed than those from S. Ruf and may safely be placed later. It is possible to establish some sort of *terminus post quem* for the S. Ruf work, on the basis of the famous

[28] Now in the Fogg Art Museum, Cambridge, Mass.

[29] Stockhausen, *Die Kreuzgänge*, ii, 122–34. See also Labande, *Avignon*, pp. 340–60; A. K. Porter, 'The Avignon capital', *Fogg Art Museum Notes*, vol. i (Jan. 1923); R. de L. Brimo, 'A Second Capital from Notre-Dame-des-Doms at Avignon', *Bulletin of the Fogg Art Museum*, vol. v (1935–6); A. Borg, 'A Further Note on a Marble Capital in the Fitzwilliam Museum, Cambridge', *Burlington Magazine* (June 1968), pp. 312–16; L. Seidel Field, in S. Scher (ed.), *The Renaissance of the Twelfth Century* (Providence, 1969), pp. 132–3.

letter of Pope Adrian IV, dated 1156, relating to the members of the S. Ruf community who have gone to Carrara to fetch stone for their cloister.[30] This is backed up by the fact that the Avignon capitals can be closely related to the sculpture of Vienne, where the church of S. André-le-Bas contains a dated base of the year 1152.[31] A date in the 1150s can therefore be accepted for the S. Ruf capitals, and this coincides with the date proposed here for the façade of S. Gilles. Thus at two different places we find figural sculpture of excellent quality, unrelated to previous Provençal work, appearing at about the same time. Both represent in some sense outside influences, but once introduced they exerted a profound influence upon the internal development of the region. The major Provençal enterprise of the sixties and seventies, the cloister and façade of Arles, was almost inevitably influenced by both of them.

I do not wish to examine the nature of these outside influences here. Suffice it to say that the Avignon capitals are closely related to the development of sculpture in the Rhône valley, and that the origins of this style are themselves highly complex. Ultimately, as the letter of Adrian IV suggests, we should look to Italy, and probably to the vicinity of Pisa itself, for the genesis of this style. The façade of S. Gilles must be seen as consciously Antique in conception (see below), but its execution reveals stylistic influences from western Languedoc and from Burgundy.

The question of origins is less germane to the present study than the problem of influences. The two cannot of course be entirely divorced, and indeed confusion between them has given rise to many of the conflicting interpretations which have been proposed. My present task is not to support or oppose any of the previously formulated views, nor to propose new ones, but merely to see whether the interpretation of Provençal developments proposed here is tenable in the light of the external relationships which undoubtedly exist.

The problem of the relationship between the sculpture of Provence and the development of early Gothic styles in the north has been widely debated, ever since Vöge first defined the question.[32] It is obvious from the preceding discussion that I discount the possibility of any direct influence of S. Gilles on the west front of S. Denis, since I believe the latter preceded the former.[33] The problem of Chartres is more complex. The Portail Royal is not firmly dated, but in terms of developments in the Île-de-France it can hardly be later than 1160 and is much more likely to be *c.* 1150. Two

---

[30] The text is given by V. Mortet and P. Deschamps, *Recueil des textes relatifs à l'histoire de l'architecture, XIIe–XIIIe siècles* (Paris, 1929), No. XXXVII, p. 96. The key passage reads:
'atque quosdam fratres ecclesiae Sancti Rufi, quos pro incidendis lapidibus et columnellis ad partes vestras dirigimus . . .'
It is, however, possible that this refers not to the church in Avignon but to that in Valence, which became the head of the order in 1158.

[31] For S. André-le-Bas see J. Vallery-Radot, 'Le style et l'âge du clocher de S. André-le-Bas à Vienne. Les étapes de la restauration de la nef', *B.M.* (1951), pp. 113–33.

[32] *Die Anfänge des monumentalen Stiles im Mittelalter* (Strasbourg, 1894).

[33] I am here assuming that we can accept a date of 1140 for the sculpture of S. Denis, despite the fact that Suger himself makes no reference to it. See W. S. Stoddard, *The West Portals of St. Denis and Chartres. Sculpture in the Île-de-France from 1140 to 1190* (Cambridge, Mass., 1952), and A. Lapeyre, *Des façades occidentales de S. Denis et de Chartres aux portails de Laon* (Paris, 1960).

separate questions are involved here. In the first place, what is the position and influence of S. Gilles in the general evolution of northern French façade design, and more specifically in the evolution of the column figure? Secondly, there is the hypothesis that sculptors from S. Gilles travelled north and actually worked at Chartres.

To take the second point first, the idea of a direct connection between S. Gilles and Chartres depends upon a stylistic analysis of the sort undertaken by Priest,[34] and it remains to my mind totally unconvincing. The similarities which exist in detailed treatment of things such as eyelids are not in any way characteristic or idiosyncratic; for this sort of stylistic analysis it is imperative to deal with highly distinctive features (e.g. the unmistakable eyes of the Master of Cabestany). The overall differences in conception between the sculpture of S. Gilles and Chartres are much more striking than the occasional similarities, and there seems to me to be no question that they are the work of different, indeed totally unrelated artists. The more general question of the position and influence of S. Gilles is much harder to deal with. In terms of the column figure as such it is hard to see any direct Provençal influence on the early northern developments. At S. Gilles we do not find column figures in the Chartrain sense (i.e. figures attached to columns); instead we have caryatid figures in the classical sense, standing on a base, with a capital at the head, the figure replacing the column entirely. This concept is not present at Chartres, but it does appear in some of the derivatives of Chartres, such as Bourges, Angers, and Le Mans. It is therefore significant that it is in these buildings that we begin to find more convincing evidence of Provençal stylistic influences appearing.

It is difficult in terms of dating to see S. Gilles as directly influencing either S. Denis or Chartres, and this contention is supported by the lack of significant stylistic connections. On the other hand, it does make sense to see the northern and southern developments as parallel achievements, whose similarities derive from common aims, and to an extent from common sources. There can be little doubt that in a general way both S. Denis and S. Gilles were meant to look Antique, and that for Abbot Suger the source of authentic Antique style was Italy.[35] The designers of S. Gilles could also look to Italy, but they had their own Antique models directly at hand. The precise nature of these models has yet to be thoroughly investigated, but for S. Gilles (and I suspect for S. Denis as well) the source of inspiration was most probably not the triumphal arch, as is frequently stated, but the *scaenae frons* of the Antique theatre. From this we can derive the three portal façade of S. Gilles, the placement of caryatid figures in niches, and the use of flanking columns. It is also possible that the concept of the *scaenae frons* can cast light on the problem of the original appearance of the façade and the manner of entry into the upper church.[36] In the Roman theatre the stage itself (*pulpitum*) was

---

[34] A. Priest, 'The Masters of the West Façade of Chartres', *Art Studies*, i (1922), 28–44. Priest's conclusions were accepted by Porter in *Romanesque Sculpture*.

[35] This view may be compared with that recently expressed by Dr. P. Kidson 'that Suger's aim was—in some sense of the word—to create an Italian church in France . . .', *The Medieval World* (New York, 1967), p. 97.

[36] This problem has been largely ignored, but it appears from the 1840 engraving of the west front that originally there was no extensive flight of stone steps such as exists today. Mr. C. Hohler has drawn to my attention the interesting statement of a notary, Jean Amignet, from an inquiry of 1622, to the effect that the Protestants destroyed a flight of

raised above the orchestra, and access to it from the front was limited to two small flights of steps. The front wall of the *pulpitum* was normally much less elaborately decorated than the *scaenae frons* at the back, and was sometimes left quite plain.[37]

The possibility of the *scaenae frons* influencing the design of the S. Gilles façade becomes greater when we recall that there were, and are, several large Roman theatres in Provence, at Vienne, Orange, and in Arles itself. The Arles theatre, of which considerable traces remain, seems to have had the normal elaborate *scaenae frons*, with a large central door set in an apsidal niche, and a pair of smaller side doors. The original composition was probably two or three stories high, with a series of figures in niches and flanked by columns.[38] There is some doubt as to the state of the monument in the twelfth century; Constans assumes that it was largely destroyed in the fifth and sixth centuries, but, although it was undoubtedly pillaged then, there is no reason to assume it was destroyed. The question is, however, largely academic, since the similar theatre at Orange remains splendidly preserved today.

As has been stated, the stylistic origins of the S. Gilles sculptors remain far from clear. All that is certain is that their styles did not come from within Provence. Equally it seems that none of the actual S. Gilles artists remained to work in Provence. The sculptors of the north gallery of the cloister at Arles, while closely related to the S. Gilles *ateliers*, did not work there. The only clear instances of direct S. Gilles craftsmanship occur at S. Guilhem-le-Désert (Hérault) and on the west front of S. Barnard at Romans.[39] The Arles sculptors are also curiously isolated in Provence itself; certain stylistic influences, and perhaps also two individual hands, have been traced from there in other monuments in the region, but some of the most direct connections lie further afield. It seems clear that some of the sculptors who worked on the north gallery of the cloister left Provence and travelled northwards. Arles influences appear in several monuments which seem to be otherwise derived from Chartres, notably Le Mans, Bourges, and La-Charité-sur-Loire. The nature of the connection with Arles is not altogether certain, but in each of these monuments the purely decorative motifs, especially the foliage capitals and abaci, can be directly related to the north gallery of the cloister of S. Trophime. As has been noted, the main sculptor of the north walk at Arles appears to have left the *atelier* before work was begun on the façade or on the east walk. On the basis of the dates proposed here, this can hardly have been before the late 1160s, and suggests that the Le Mans portal cannot be earlier than *c.* 1170. However, it has been widely held that this may be dated on the basis of a dedication of the cathedral in 1158.[40] This dating is by no means certain, and it becomes difficult to sustain in the light of Branner's dating of the sculpture at Bourges to *c.* 1172, since there are undoubtedly

---

steps which could be mounted by thirty men abreast. However, these steps were probably themselves 'modern' (?sixteenth century) and there is certainly no visible evidence of any medieval steps.

[37] See M. Bieber, *The history of the Greek and Roman Theater* (Princeton, N.J., 1961).

[38] For the Arles theatre see L. A. Constans, *Arles antique* (Bibl. des Écoles françaises d'Athènes et de Rome, vol. xcix, Paris, 1921).

[39] See Hamann, *St. Gilles*, pp. 234–58.

[40] For all these monuments see Lapeyre, op. cit., and the bibliography cited by him.

stylistic connections between Bourges and Le Mans.[41] To sort out this situation would require a comprehensive stylistic study of early Gothic sculpture—something which, despite all that has been written, has never really been undertaken. Le Mans, Bourges, and the related Burgundian monuments represent for the most part a direct continuation of the Chartrain mode, and they remain largely unaffected by the second major stylistic trend in early Gothic sculpture, in which Mosan influences predominate (as represented, rather differently, by the Porte des Valois at S. Denis and the Porte romane at Reims). It is tempting to regard these as successive developments, but there is more reason to think that they represent two coexisting strands which only occasionally interweave. Since there are almost no firm dates involved, we have to rely upon stylistic and iconographic analysis. The conclusion which this suggests is that *ateliers* working in the Chartrain tradition moved south and south-east from the Île-de-France,[42] and, coming into contact with artists who had come north from Provence, evolved a series of hybrid versions of the Chartrain manner. The column figure was retained, although it tended to become a true caryatid, replacing rather than adhering to the column. The decorative repertoire of Chartres was largely replaced by that of Arles, including characteristic acanthus forms and *rinceau* scrolls. Arles influence is less apparent in the figure styles, although some of the voussoirs at Le Mans and the lintel at La-Charité may be compared with the work in the north gallery at S. Trophime.[43]

Similarly complex problems are posed by the question of Provençal influences in Italy. Again it is clear that there are numerous connections, but the general lack of firm dates makes it difficult to specify the exact nature of the relationships. On the basis of the studies of Francovich and Quintavalle, the pontile at Modena can be accepted as being no earlier than the 1160s.[44] The inspiration for this work is clearly the frieze of S. Gilles, reinforcing the suggestion that this dates from the 1150s. On the other hand, the chronology adopted here excludes the possibility that the Arles styles are influential at Modena. The key to this argument lies perhaps with the Cagliari pulpit, which was formerly in the cathedral of Pisa, and which is dated between 1158–61.[45] The pulpit is often taken as proof of Provençal influence in Italy at this date, but in fact I suspect the reverse is true. The confusion arises from the assumption that the Arles sculpture represents 'Provençal' style. It has been argued that the Arles *ateliers* were the product of the combined influences of the S. Gilles façade and the Avignon cloisters. Both of these represented 'outside' styles, and the latter can be derived from Italian sources, both on documentary and stylistic evidence. Thus the idea that Arles was susceptible to Italian influence is both possible and probable, and is historically more likely than the

[41] R. Branner, 'Les portails latéraux de la cathédrale de Bourges', *B.M.* (1957), pp. 263–70.

[42] This was not of course the only direction in which Chartrain influences travelled, as Corbeil and S. Loup-de-Naud witness.

[43] The column figures in the crypt at Coire, from the destroyed west portal, are probably the closest approach to the figure style of S. Trophime.

[44] G. de Francovich, *Benedetto Antelami*, pp. 45–109; A. C. Quintavalle, *La Cattedrale di Modena* (Modena, 1965), pp. 247–61.

[45] Francovich, op. cit., pp. 47 ff.

one-way current which is normally assumed.[46] Finally there is Antelami, whose first dated work is the Parma Deposition panel of 1178. He was certainly aware of developments in Provence, and this tends to confirm the dates proposed here; an artist of Antelami's stature was surely more likely to be influenced by recent, up-to-date work in Provence than by things which were, according to some scholars, over half a century old.

All these problems have here been passed over in a very summary fashion. It would be foolish to deny that many real questions still demand to be answered, and that much further detailed research will have to be carried out. However, it has perhaps been demonstrated that the development of Provençal sculpture here proposed is not out of step with what is known and what can be deduced of Provençal influence to the north and to the south. It may also be added that the Arles *ateliers* appear to have been extremely influential in Spain, and although this aspect has been almost entirely neglected,[47] such influence appears to be confined to works dating from the last quarter of the twelfth century.

POSTLUDE

Iт is difficult to close with any resounding conclusions, and it would probably be unwise to try and do so. I have provided a revised view of the evolution of the Romanesque style in Provence, and I have tried to show more clearly some of the connections between major Provençal monuments. Within this limited context, and despite numerous unsolved problems of detail, a fairly clear picture has emerged. This suggests that, while it was not as spectacular as developments in western Languedoc, Burgundy, or Italy, Provence too played its part in the revival of sculpture and architecture which took place in the decades immediately before and after 1100. From this point a coherent development can be traced, in which the forms established at Avignon and Aix were evolved to the point in the middle of the century when new architectural, decorative, and stylistic concepts were introduced. In the second half of the century we find a continual interplay of these two strains, resulting in a series of monuments in which what can now be seen as indigenous Provençal forms are combined with the newer architectural and decorative elements. Yet what I have just termed the 'indigenous' Provençal forms are themselves largely the result of external influences, and the characteristic 'anti-classicism' of the nave capitals never really took firm root. The incipient classicism of the eleventh-century decorative tradition eventually found fulfilment in the mid-twelfth century, but this was not a straight-line development. Nor were the churches of the nave capital group without influence. On the contrary, they established the plan and form of the Provençal church which was to survive to the end

---

[46] The picture is further complicated by the close connection between the animal friezes on the façades of Pisa cathedral and S. Gilles. As Mr. C. Hohler has pointed out, the latter is clearly the later, and provides more evidence of the complexity of the relationships between Italy and Provence in the mid-twelfth century.

[47] A rare exception is the article by V. Lassalle, 'L'influence provençale au cloître et à la cathédrale de Tarragone', *Mélanges offerts à René Crozet* (Poitiers, 1966) ii, 873–9.

of the century and beyond. They revived the techniques of stone-cutting and of masonry construction which contribute so much to the elegance and sober beauty of the region's buildings. All this survived the mid-century innovations, and it is notable that the taste for overflowing decoration, sometimes verging on vulgarity, which came in with S. Gilles and Arles, never really established itself in the church buildings themselves, but found its most acceptable outlet in the embellishment of cloisters. In buildings such as S. Paul-Trois-Châteaux the new sculptural conceptions were transformed into architectural decoration which preserved much of the harmony and sobriety of the earlier tradition. This essay will have made its point if these conclusions are accepted, and if buildings such as Notre-Dame-des-Doms at Avignon and the Corpus Domini at Aix are allowed to resume their rightful position as major monuments not only of the Provençal but also of the total European achievement in the development of Romanesque art.

Bibliography

The bibliography is divided into three sections:

A. Publications of documents relating to Provence.

B. Secondary works on Provence (including some monuments in the Gard).

C. General works which refer to or relate to Provence.

Section B comprises for the most part works on the medieval art and architecture of the region, but it also includes those books and articles on the political, social, and economic development of the region which I have found useful. Section C is the most eclectic and incomplete, since nearly every general work of history or of art history devotes at least some space to Provence. I have therefore included only those which have contributions on the region that I have found particularly interesting or stimulating. In addition, I include in this section a number of books and articles which, though they do not deal with Provence specifically, have a direct bearing upon conditions in the region and upon the problems considered here. Finally, it should be pointed out that not every book or article referred to in the footnotes is listed here, and conversely many of the books listed are not referred to in the notes.

A: PUBLISHED DOCUMENTS

ALBANÈS, J. H., and CHEVALIER, U. (eds.), *Gallia christiana novissima. Histoire des archevêchés, évêchés et abbayes de France*, 7 vols., 1899–1920.

BENOIT, F. (ed.), *Recueil des actes des comtes de Provence appartenant à la maison de Barcelone, 1196–1245*, Paris–Monaco, 1925, 2 vols.

CAIS DE PIERLAS, E. (ed.), *Cartulaire de l'ancienne cathédrale de Nice*, Turin, 1888.

DEVIC, C. L., and VAISSETE, J., *Histoire générale de Languedoc*, Toulouse, 1874–92, 14 vols.

DIDIER, N., DUBLED, H., and BARRUOL, J. (eds.), *Cartulaire de l'église d'Apt (835–1130?)*, Paris, 1967.

DUPRAT, E. (ed.), *Cartulaire du chapitre de Notre-Dame-des-Doms*, vol. i (1060–1263), Avignon, 1932.

FEARNS, J. (ed.), *Petri Venerabilis: Contra Petrobrusianos Hereticos. Corpus Christianorum, Continuatio Mediaevalis*, No. 10, 1968.

FONT-RÉAULX, J. de (ed.), *Cartulaire de l'évêché de S. Paul-Trois-Châteaux*, Valence, 1946.

GUÉRARD, B. (ed.), *Cartulaire de l'abbaye de Saint Victor de Marseille. Collection des cartulaires de France*, vol. ix, Paris, 1857, 2 vols.

JAFFÉ, P., *Regesta pontificum Romanorum ab condita Ecclesia ad annum 1198*, Leipzig, 1885–8, 2 vols.

LEROY, E. (ed.), *Cartulaire de S. Paul-de-Mausole à S. Rémy-de-Provence*, S. Rémy, 1961.

MANTEYER, G. de (ed.), *Les Chartes du pays d'Avignon (439–1040). Mémoires de l'Académie de Vaucluse*, vol. ii. (Mâcon, 1914).

MÉRIMÉE, P., *Correspondance générale*, Paris, 1941–64, 2 series, 17 vols.

MORTET, V., and DESCHAMPS, P. (eds.), *Recueil des textes relatifs à l'histoire de l'architecture*, XIIe–XIIIe *siècles*, Paris, 1929, 2 vols.

POTTHAST, A., *Regesta pontificum Romanorum*, Berlin, 1875, 2 vols.

POUPARDIN, R. (ed.), *Recueil des actes des rois de Provence (855–928)*, Paris, 1920.

POURRIÈRE, J., *Recherches sur la première cathédrale d'Aix*, Paris, 1939.

PROU, M., and CLOUZOT, E. (eds.), *Pouillés des provinces d'Aix, d'Arles, et d'Embrun. Recueil des historiens de la France; Pouillés*, vol. viii, Paris, 1923.

RIPERT-MONCLAR, M. le marquis de (ed.), *Cartulaire de la Commanderie de Richerenches de l'ordre du Temple (1136–1214). Mémoires de l'Académie de Vaucluse*, vol. i, Avignon–Paris, 1907.

VIELLIARD, J. (ed.), *Le Guide du pèlerin de Saint Jacques de Compostelle*, Mâcon, 1963.

B: SECONDARY WORKS ON PROVENCE

ACHARD, M., *Géographie de la Provence*, Aix, 1787.

    Description historique, géographique et topographique des villes et bourgs de la Provence, Aix, 1788.

AGNEL, abbé A., 'Notice archéologique sur le prieuré de Ganagobie', *Bulletin Archéologique*, 1910.

AINAUD DE LASARTE, J., 'Rapports artistiques entre St. Victor et la Catalogne'. Recueil des actes . . . S. Victor, *Provence Historique*, xvi, 1966, pp. 341–6.

ALLÈGRE, abbé A., *Monographie de Beaumes-de-Venise*, Carpentras, 1888 (reprinted Paris, 1967).

AMY, P., DUVAL, P., FORMIGÉ, J., HATT, J., PICARD, C., PIGANIOL, A., *L'Arc d'Orange. Supplément à Gallia*, No. xv, 1962, 2 vols.

ANDRÉOLI, E., and LAMBERT, B. S., *Monographie de l'église cathédrale de S. Siffrein de Carpentras*, Paris–Marseille, 1862.

AUBERT, M., 'Un édifice du premier art roman en Provence, la cathédrale de Vence', *Mélanges offerts à Nicolas Iorga*, Paris, 1933.

    'La porte romane d'Estagel au musée du Louvre', *Mon. Piot*, xxxiii, 1933, pp. 135–40.

    'Les dates de la façade de S. Gilles', *B.M.*, 1936, pp. 369–72.

BALTY, J., *Études sur la Maison Carrée de Nîmes. Collection Latomus*, No. xlvii, Brussels, 1960.

BARATIER, E., 'La fondation et l'étendue du temporel de l'abbaye de S. Victor'. Recueil des actes . . . S. Victor, *Provence Historique*, xvi, 1966, pp. 395–441.

BARRUOL, G., 'L'église Notre-Dame-des-Doms d'Avignon au XIIe siècle', *C.A.*, 1963, pp. 44–58.

    'Notre-Dame-de-Nazareth à Pernes', *C.A.*, 1963, pp. 328–36.

BARRUOL, J., *Ste Anne d'Apt d'après une documentation nouvelle*, Apt, 1964.

BÉCHET, L., *Notice historique et descriptive de la cathédrale de S. Paul-Trois-Châteaux*, Vaison, 1966.

BENOIT, F., *Arles: ses monuments, son histoire*, Lyon, 1917.

    L'Abbaye de Montmajour. Petites Monographies, Paris, 1928.

    Voyage en Provence d'un gentilhomme polonais, 1784–5 (A. F. Moszynski). Bibl. de l'Institut Historique de Provence, vol. v, 1930.

    'Marseille', *C.A.*, 1932, pp. 157–206.

    'Cathédrale S. Sauveur d'Aix', *C.A.*, 1932, pp. 9–29.

    'La tombe de saint Césaire et sa restauration en 883', *B.M.*, 1935.

    Les Cimetières suburbains d'Arles dans l'antiquité chrétienne et au moyen âge, Rome–Paris, 1935.

    'L'église des Saintes-Maries-de-la-Mer', *B.M.*, 1936.

    L'Abbaye de S. Victor et l'église de la Major à Marseille. Petites Monographies, Paris, 1936.

    'Chapiteau byzantin à têtes de bélier du musée d'Arles', *B.M.*, 1938, pp. 137–44.

    L'Art primitif méditerranéen de la vallée du Rhône. La sculpture, Paris, 1945.

    'Cimetières paléochrétiens de Provence', *Cahiers Archéologiques*, 1947, pp. 7–15.

    'La légende d'Hercule à S. Trophime d'Arles', *Latomus*, 1950, pp. 67–71.

    'Le sarcophage de Lurs en Provence. Situation dans l'art géometrique', *Cahiers Archéologiques*, 1959, pp. 27–30.

    Provence. L'Art roman en France, Paris, 1961.

'Les reliques de S. Césaire, Archevêque d'Arles', *Cahiers Archéologiques*, 1962, pp. 51–62.

'L'abbaye de S. Ruf', *C.A.*, 1963, pp. 152–60.

BENOIT, F. (ed.), *Histoire de Lérins*, Nice, 1965.

BENOIT, F., FEVRIER, P., FORMIGÉ, J., ROLLAND, H., *Villes épiscopales de Provence: Aix, Arles, Fréjus, Marseille et Riez. Congresso internationale di archeologia cristiana*, No. V (Aix, 1954), Paris, 1954.

BERENGUIER, R., *Églises et abbayes du Var*, Paris, n.d. (*c.* 1967).

BERNARD, l'archiprêtre, *Histoire de la basilique S. Trophime; le cloître de S. Trophime*, Avignon, 1879. *Les reliques conservées dans la basilique S. Trophime*, ?Arles, n.d.

BERNOULLI, R., *Die romanische Portalarchitektur in der Provence*, Strasbourg, 1906.

BESSE, J. M., *Abbayes et prieurés de l'ancienne France*, ii, *Provinces ecclésiastiques d'Aix, Arles, Avignon et Embrun. Archives de la France monastique*, No. VII, Paris, 1909.

BLANCARD, L., *Iconographie des sceaux et bulles des archives des Bouches-du-Rhône*, Paris, 1860, 2 vols.

BLIGNY, B., *L'Église et les ordres religieux dans le royaume de Bourgogne aux XIe et XIIe siècles*, Paris, 1960.

BONNET, E., 'Les bas-reliefs de la Tour de S. Restitut', *C.A.*, 1909, ii, pp. 251–74.

BORG, A., 'The Cloister of the Cathedral of St. Sauveur, Aix-en-Provence', London University M.A. Thesis, 1967, unpublished.

'A Further Note on a Marble Capital in the Fitzwilliam Museum, Cambridge', *Burlington Magazine*, June 1968, pp. 312–16.

BOUCHES-DU-RHÔNE, *Encyclopédie Départementale*, vol. iv, Pt. 1, 'Archéologie', Paris–Marseille, 1932.

BOUDIN, J. L., 'Renseignements divers sur la foire de Beaucaire', *C.A.*, 1897, pp. 333–40.

BOURRILLY, V. L., *Essai sur l'histoire politique de la commune de Marseille des origines à la victoire de Charles d'Anjou (1264)*, Aix, 1925.

BOURRILLY, V. L., and BUSQUET, R., *La Provence au moyen âge (1112–1481)*, Marseille, 1924.

BRAIVE, M. F., *Avignon, Villeneuve-lès-Avignon. Collection Sites de France*, ?Paris, n.d. (?1949).

BRIMO, R. de L., 'A Second Capital from Notre-Dame-des-Doms at Avignon', *Bulletin of the Fogg Art Museum*, vol. v, 1935–6.

BRION, M., *Provence*, London, 1956.

BRUN, L., 'Présentation de la Provence romane', *Centre International d'Études Romanes*, 1962, ii, pp. 5–10.

BRUN, R., *La Ville de Salon au moyen âge. Publications de la Société d'Études Provençales*, vol. vi, Aix, 1924.

BRUN-DURAND, J., *Dictionnaire topographique du département de la Drôme*, Paris, 1891.

BUHOLZER, J. H., 'Notes sur quelques églises romanes du Gard', *Annales du Midi*, 1962, pp. 121–37.

BUSQUET, R., 'Rois de Bourgogne et comtes de Provence', *Provence Historique*, 1951.

BUSQUET, R., BOURRILLY, V. L., and AGULHON, M., *Histoire de la Provence. Que sais-je*, No. 149, Paris, 1966.

CAHEN, E., *Les monuments de l'art gallo-grec en Basse-Provence*, Marseille, 1932.

CADIX, G., *S. Jean du Gard — nos pays et nos villes de France. Série de notices historiques locales*, Paris, n.d.

CARLIN, M. L., *La pénétration du droit romain dans les actes de la pratique provençale (XIe–XIIIe siècles). Bibl. d'histoire du droit et droit romain*, vol. xi, Paris, 1967.

CARRIÈRE DE BELLEUSE, A., *Abbayes et prieurés de l'ordre de S. Ruf*, Romans, 1933.

CAURON, abbé, *Valbonne, Aiguebelle, Sénanque, Bonpas, etc. . . . ou notice sur ces monastères*, Avignon, 1850.

CHAUVEL, A., 'La crypte de Vilhosc (Basses-Alpes)', *B.M.*, 1931, pp. 437–43.

CLAIR, M. H., 'Iconographie du portail de S. Trophime', *C.A.*, 1876, pp. 607–31.

CLÉBERT, J. P., *Provence antique, des origines à la conquête romaine*, Paris, 1966.

CLERC, M., *Massalia; Histoire de Marseille dans l'antiquité*, Marseille, 1927, 2 vols.

COLLIER, R., and EHRMANN, J. P., 'L'art roman primitif en Haute-Provence', *Provence Historique*, xv, 1965, pp. 3–24.

COLLIER, R., *Monuments et art de Haut-Provence*, Digne, 1966.

COMBES, J., 'Les foires en Languedoc au moyen âge', *Annales-Économies-Sociétés-Civilisations*, 1958, pp. 231–59.

CONSTANS, L. A., *Arles antique. Bibl. des Écoles françaises d'Athènes et de Rome*, No. 119, 1921.

CONSTANTIN, abbé M., *Les Paroisses du diocèse d'Aix*, vol. i, *Paroisses de l'ancien diocèse d'Aix*; vol. ii, *Paroisses de l'ancien diocèse d'Arles*; vol. iii, *Paroisses des anciens diocèses d'Arles, d'Avignon et de Marseille*, Aix, 1890–1911, 3 vols.

COSTE, J. P., *Études régionales: Aix et la Provence*, Aix, 1964.

COURTET, J., *Dictionnaire géographique, historique, archéologique et biographique des Communes du département de Vaucluse*, Avignon, 1857.

CRÉMIEUX, A., 'Les Juifs de Marseille au moyen âge', *Revue des Études Juives*, 1903.

DEVIC, C. L., and VAISSETE, J., *Histoire générale de Languedoc*, Toulouse, 1874–92, 14 vols.

DIDELOT, chanoine, 'Le pape Adrien IV à Valence', *Bull. de la Soc. départementale d'archéologie de la Drôme*, 1891.

DIDIER, N., *Les Églises de Sisteron et de Forcalquier du XIe siècle à la Revolution*, Paris, 1954.

DORÉ, R., *L'Art en Provence, dans le Comtat Venaissin et le comté de Nice*, Paris, 1929.

DUBY, G., 'Le port de Marseille et la civilisation provençale au moyen âge', *Revue de la Chambre de Commerce de Marseille*, 1955.

'Les villes du Sud-Est de la Gaule du VIIIe au XIe siècle', *La Città nell'alto medioevo. Centro Italiano di Studi sull'alto medioevo*, Spoleto, 1959, pp. 231–76.

DUPRAT, E., 'Les origines de l'église d'Avignon', *Mémoires de l'Académie de Vaucluse*, 1908–9.

La Provence dans le Haut Moyen Âge (406–1113), Marseille, 1923.

DURAND, A., 'La tour de Ribas et les monuments historiques de S. Laurent-des-Arbres', *C.A.*, 1897, pp. 257–66.

L'Église Sainte-Marie ou Notre-Dame de Nîmes, Nîmes, 1906.

DURANTY, J., 'Relation entre Marseille et Arles au moyen âge', *Congrès des sociétés savantes de Provence*, 1910.

ENGELMANN, E., *Zur städtlichen Volksbewegung in Südfrankreich (Kommunefreiheit und Gesellschaft, Arles 1200–1250)*, Berlin, 1959.

ESPITALIER, H., *Les Évêques de Fréjus du VIe au XIIIe siècle*, Draguignan, 1894.

ESTRANGIN, J. J., *Études archéologiques, historiques et statistiques sur Arles*, Aix, 1838.

FEVRIER, P. A., 'Les baptistères de Provence pendant le moyen âge', *Actes du Ve Congrès International d'Archéologie Chrétienne*, Paris–Vatican, 1957, pp. 423–32.

'Fragments romans de la collégiale de Barjols (Var)', *B.M.*, 1959, pp. 203–20.

'Sculpture paléochrétienne de S. Julien d'Oule', *Cahiers Archéologiques*, 1962, pp. 89–97.

'Venasque', *C.A.*, 1963, pp. 348–64.

Le Développement urbain en Provence de l'époque romaine à la fin du XIVe siècle, Paris, 1964.

FLICHE, A., *Aigues-Mortes et S. Gilles. Petites Monographies*, Paris, 1961.

FONTANA, M., *La Réforme grégorienne en Provence orientale. Publications de la Faculté des Lettres d'Aix, Travaux et mémoires*, vol. viii, Aix, 1957.

FORMIGÉ, J., 'Note sur l'appareil des voûtes en cul-de-four romanes de Provence', *B.M.*, 1923, pp. 197–201.

'Remarques diverses sur les baptistères de Provence', *Mélanges Fr. Martroye*, Paris, 1940, pp. 167–90.

FOURNIER, I., 'Le passage du Rhône entre Tarascon et Beaucaire au moyen âge et jusqu'à 1670', *Revue des Études Anciennes*, ix, 1907, pp. 21–6.

FOURNIER, P., *Le Royaume d'Arles et de Vienne (1138–1378)*, Paris, 1891.

GAGNIÈRE, S., *Une visite aux églises et chapelles d'Avignon*, Avignon, n.d.

GANSHOF, F., 'Notes sur les portes de Provence du VIIIe au Xe siècle', *Revue Historique*, 1938.

GERMAIN DE MAIDY, L., 'L'inscription de la cathédrale de Vaison; une autre interprétation', *B.M.*, 1905, pp. 460–5.

GIRARD, J., *Catalogue illustré du Musée Calvet de la ville d'Avignon*, Avignon, 1924.

GIRAUD, H., and IGOLEN, J., *Pernes, ancienne capitale du Comtat Venaissin*, Paris, 1927.

GOIFFON, abbé, *Dictionnaire topographique, statistique et historique du diocèse de Nîmes*, Nîmes, 1881.

GOLB, N., 'Monieux', *Proceedings of the American Philosophical Society*, cxiii, 1969, pp. 67–94.

GONTIER, L., *Notice sur S. Donat. Souvenirs historiques*, Valance, 1857.

GOURON, M., *La Cathédrale romane de Nîmes. Extrait du Bulletin Archéologique*, 1936–7.

    Note sur l'ancienne navigation dans la Petite Camargue. Extrait du Bull. de la Soc. d'Histoire et d'Archéologie de Nîmes, Nîmes, 1939.

    'S. Gilles', *C.A.*, 1950, pp. 104–19.

    'La découverte du tympan de l'église S. Martin à S. Gilles', *Annales du Midi*, lxii, 1950, pp. 115–21.

GUILLEMAIN, B., *La cour pontificale d'Avignon (1309–76). Étude d'une société. Bibl. des Écoles françaises d'Athènes et de Rome*, No. 201, Paris, 1962.

HAMANN, R., *Deutsche und französische Kunst im Mittelalter*, vol. i, *Südfranzösische Protorenaissance und ihre Ausbreitung in Deutschland auf dem Wege durch Italien und die Schweiz*, Marburg, 1922.

HAMANN, R., 'Ein unbekannter Figurenzyklus in St. Guilhem-le-Désert', *Marburger Jhb. f. Kunstwiss.*, ii, 1925–6, pp. 71–89.

    'Der Schrein des Heiligen Aegidus', *Marburger Jhb. f. Kunstwiss.*, vi, 1931, pp. 114–36 (republished in *S. Gilles*, pp. 299–319).

    'The façade of St. Gilles: a reconstruction', *Burlington Magazine*, 1934.

    Die Abteikirche von St. Gilles und ihre künstlerische Nachfolge, Berlin, 1955, 3 vols.

HIGOUNET, C., 'La rivalité des maisons de Toulouse et de Barcelone pour la prépondérance méridionale', *Mélanges . . . dédiés à la mémoire de Louis Halphen*, Paris, 1951, pp. 313–22.

HORN, W., *Die Fassade von St. Gilles. Eine Untersuchung zur Frage des Antikeneinflusses in der südfranzösischen Kunst des 12. Jhs.*, Hamburg, 1937.

HUBERT, J., 'La topographie religieuse d'Arles au VIe siècle', *Cahiers Archéologiques*, 1947, pp. 17–27.

JOLY, M., *L'Architecture des églises romanes du Vivarais*, Paris, 1967.

JOUVE, abbé, 'Notice sur la chapelle funéraire monumentale et sur l'église romane de S. Restitut', *B.M.*, pp. 182 ff.

    Statistique monumentale de la Drôme, Valence, 1867.

JULLIAN, R., 'L'art de la draperie dans la sculpture romane de Provence', *Gazette des Beaux Arts*, 1928, pp. 241–58.

KIESS, W., *Montmajour, eine Stätte provencalischer Romanik. Schriften der Staatsbauschule Stuttgart*, No. 31, 1965.

LABANDE, L. H., *Études d'histoire et d'archéologie romane. Provence et Bas-Languedoc*, Avignon–Paris, 1902.

    'Étude historique et archéologique sur S. Trophime d'Arles du IVe au XIIIe siècle', *B.M.*, 1903–4.

    'Le baptistère de Venasque (Vaucluse)', *Bull. arch. du Comité*, 1904, pp. 287–304.

    'La cathédrale de Vaison', *B.M.*, 1905, pp. 253–321.

    'Nouvelles remarques sur la même inscription' [i.e. Vaison], *B.M.*, 1905, pp. 466–8.

    'L'église Notre-Dame-des-Doms d'Avignon des origines au XIIIe siècle', *Bull. arch. du Comité*, 1906, pp. 282–365.

    'Guide archéologique du Congrès d'Avignon', *C.A.*, 1909.

    'L'église de Marseille et l'abbaye de S. Victor à l'époque carolingienne', *Mélanges . . . F. Lot*, Paris, 1925, pp. 50 ff.

    L'Église S. Trophime d'Arles. Petites Monographies, Paris, 1930.

LABANDE, L. H., and AGNEL, A., 'S. Sauveur d'Aix. Étude critique sur les parties romanes de cette cathédrale', *Bull. arch. du Comité*, 1912, pp. 289–344.

LASSALLE, V., 'Fragment roman d'un Sacrifice d'Abraham au Musée archéologique de Nîmes', *Revue du Louvre*, 1965, pp. 165–70.

'L'influence provençale au cloître et à la cathédrale de Tarragone', *Mélanges offerts à René Crozet*, Poitiers, 1966, ii, pp. 873–9.

'Les restes du décor d'un cloître roman au Musée archéologique de Nîmes', *Revue du Louvre*, 1966, pp. 123–34.

'La façade de l'abbatiale de S. Gilles', *Bull. annuel de l'École Antique de Nîmes*, 1966, pp. 79–93.

'Un chapiteau roman décoré de scènes de l'enfance du Christ au Musée archéologique de Nîmes', *Revue du Louvre*, 1970, i, pp. 1–8.

LASTEYRIE, R. de, 'Études sur la sculpture française au moyen âge', *Mon. Piot*, vol. viii, No. 1, 1902.

LEFÈVRE-PONTALIS, E., 'L'église Notre-Dame-du-Thor', *C.A.*, 1909, ii, pp. 275–98.

LEROY, E., *S. Paul-de-Mausole à S. Rémy-de-Provence*, S. Rémy, 1948.

LOUIS, M., 'La façade de la cathédrale de Nîmes', *Mémoires de l'Institut Historique de Provence*, xi, 1934, pp. 81–3.

MAITRE, L., 'La tour funéraire de S. Restitut', *Revue de l'Art Chrétien*, 1906, pp. 361 ff.

MANTEYER, G. de, 'Les légendes saintes de Provence et le martyrologe d'Arles-Toulon (v. 1120)', *Mélanges d'archéologie et d'histoire*, xvii, Rome, 1897, pp. 467–89.

La Provence du premier au douzième siècle, Paris, 1908.

MARIGNAN, A., 'L'école de sculpture en Provence du XIIᵉ au XIIIᵉ siècle', *Moyen Âge*, ii, No. 3, 1899, pp. 1–64.

MARIN, F. de, 'Des rapports d'Arles avec l'abbaye de Montmajour', *C.A.*, 1876, pp. 632–42.

MARTIAL, G., 'S. Trophime d'Arles: études de la sculpture romane du portail et du cloître', thesis for the École du Louvre, 1950, unpublished.

MARTIN, R., 'Abbaye de Sénanque, ses règles de construction', *Connaissance des Arts*, 1964, pp. 82–91.

MAZEL, A., *Notes sur la Camargue et les Saintes-Maries-de-la-Mer*, Vaison, n.d. (c. 1935).

MÉRIMÉE, P., *Notes d'un voyage dans le midi de la France*, Brussels, 1835.

MESSIÉ, J., *Bourg-S. Andéol: Notice historique et guide*, Bourg-S. Andéol, n.d. (c. 1965).

MICHEL, R., 'Les chevaliers du château des arènes de Nîmes aux XIIᵉ et XIIIᵉ siècles', *Mélanges d'histoire et d'archéologie*, Paris, 1926, pp. 115–35.

MILLE, abbé, *Notre Métropole ou Monographie historique et descriptive de la basilique métropolitaine S. Sauveur*, Aix, 1833.

MILLIN, A. L., *Voyage dans les départements du Midi de la France*, Paris, 1807–8, 5 vols.

MISSONE, D., 'La législation canoniale de S. Ruf d'Avignon à ses origines', *Moissac et l'Occident au XIᵉ siècle. Actes du colloque international de Moissac*, Toulouse, 1964, pp. 147–66.

MOYNE, abbé, *L'Abbaye de Sénanque, une notice historique et archéologique*, Avignon, 1857.

PALANQUE, J. R., 'Sur l'emplacement de la cathédrale d'Aix-en-Provence', *Revue Histoire Église de France*, 1941, pp. 31 ff.

PAPON, I. B., *Histoire générale de Provence*, Paris, 1727–86, 4 vols.

PAULET, L., and FASSIN, E., *La primatiale, ou monographie historique et descriptive de la basilique de S. Trophime*, Bergerac, 1910.

PERNOUD, R., *Histoire du commerce de Marseille, publiée par la Chambre de Commerce de Marseille*, vol. i, Pt. 2, *Le Moyen Âge jusqu'au 1291*, Paris, 1949.

PEROSSIER, C., *Recueil des mémoires, notices, et documents sur S. Donat*. MS. Bibl. de la Société Humbert II, Romans.

PEZET, M., *Les Alpilles: Eygalières et Mollèges des origines au XVIᵉ siècle*, Cavaillon, 1949.

PICARD, C., 'Les caryatides du Théâtre de Vienne et les caryatides monumentales des théâtres occidentaux', *Anthemon* (Florence), 1955, pp. 273–80.

PILLEMENT, G., *Défence et illustration d'Avignon*, Paris, 1945.

PORTER, A. K., 'The Avignon Capital', *Fogg Art Museum Notes*, vol. i, Jan. 1923.

POUILLON, F., *Maître d'œuvre: architectures cisterciennes — Sénanque, Silvacane, Le Thoronet*, Paris, 1967.

POUPARDIN, R., *Le Royaume de Provence sous les Carolingiens. Bibl. del'École des Hautes Études*, No. 131, Paris, 1901.

POURRIÈRE, J., *Recherches sur la première cathédrale d'Aix*, Paris, 1939.

    L'Achèvement de S. Sauveur d'Aix-en-Provence, Aix, 1949.

    Aix-en-Provence, rues et monuments, Aix, 1952.

PRADEL, P., 'Vestiges d'un zodiaque-calendrier Nîmois du XIIIe siècle', *Mon. Piot*, lv, 1967, pp. 105–13.

RAMBAUD, M., 'Le quatrain mystique de Vaison-la-Romaine', *B.M.*, 1951, pp. 157–74.

REYNAUD, M., 'Le Vernègues et la chapelle de S. Césaire', *C.A.*, 1876, pp. 657–72.

REVOIL, H., *Architecture romane du midi de la France*, Paris, 1874, 3 vols.

RIGORD, A., *Les Monuments religieux d'Orange depuis les débuts du Christianisme*, Orange, n.d. (*c.* 1964).

RIVOIRE, H., *Statistique du département du Gard*, Nîmes, 1842.

ROLLAND, H., 'Le baptistère de S. Rémy-de-Provence', *Gallia*, i, 1943, pp. 207–28.

    Fouilles de S. Blaise (Bouches-du-Rhône), Supplément à *Gallia*, iii, 1951; vii, 1956.

    Monnaie des comtes de Provence, XIIe au XVe siècles, Paris, 1956.

ROUSTAN, F., *La Major et le premier baptistère de Marseille*, Marseille, 1905.

ROUX, A., *La Cathédrale d'Apt d'après des documents inédits*, Apt, 1949.

ROUX, C., *Arles, son histoire, ses monuments, ses musées*, Paris, 1914.

SAGNIER, A., 'Le pont S. Bénézet', *C.A.*, 1882, pp. 259–382 [note the pagination is incorrect, and should read 259–282].

SAINT-ANDÉOL, F. de, 'Les cathédrales du Dauphiné. Église cathédrale de Notre-Dame de S. Paul-Trois-Châteaux', *Bull. de la Soc. d'Archéologie de la Drôme*, 1869, pp. 313–38.

SAINT VICTOR, *Recueil des Actes du Congrès sur l'histoire de l'abbaye S. Victor de Marseille, 29–30 Janvier, 1966. Provence Historique*, vol. xvi, 1966.

SALLUSTIEN-JOSEPH, frère, 'Quelques églises romanes du Gard', *C.A.*, 1897, pp. 305–18.

SAUREL, M., 'Anciennes églises des Bouches-du-Rhône', *C.A.*, 1882, pp. 102–11.

SAUTEL, J., *Les Villes romaines de la vallée du Rhône*, Avignon, 1926.

    Les Chapelles de campagne de l'archevêché d'Avignon et de ses anciens diocèses, Avignon–Lyon, 1938.

    Les Origines de la cathédrale de Notre-Dame-de-Nazareth à Vaison-la-Romaine, Lyon, 1950.

    'Nouvelles remarques sur les origines de la cathédrale Notre-Dame à Vaison-la-Romaine', *Actes du Ve Congrès International d'Archéologie Chrétienne*, Paris–Vatican, 1957, pp. 573–6.

    Vaison-la-Romaine. Sites, histoire et monuments, Lyon, 1955.

SAYONS, A., 'Le commerce de Marseille avec la Syrie au milieu du XIIIe siècle', *Revue des Études Historiques*, 1929.

    'Le commerce terrestre de Marseille au XIIIe siècle', *Revue Historique*, vol. lxiv, 1930.

SCHAPIRO, M., 'New Documents on S. Gilles', *Art Bulletin*, xvii, 1935, pp. 415–30.

SEIGNOLLE, C., *Le Folklore de la Provence. Contributions au folklore des provinces de France*, vol. vii, Paris, 1963.

SIGROS, H., 'Notre-Dame d'Aubune', *C.A.*, 1963, pp. 407–32.

    'Église de Noves', *C.A.*, 1963, pp. 442–59.

SITES ET MONUMENTS DE HAUTE PROVENCE, volumes in the series *Les Alpes de Lumière*, published at Apt.

STOCKHAUSEN, H. A. von, 'Die romanischen Kreuzgänge der Provence. I, Die Architektur; II, Die Plastik', *Marburger Jhb. f. Kunstwiss.*, vol. vii, 1933; vol. viii–ix, 1936.

THIRION, J., 'L'église S. Dalmas de Valdeblore', *B.M.*, 1953, pp. 157–71.

    'Note sur trois chapelles polygonales de l'ancien diocèse de Grasse (Alpes-Maritimes)', *Actes du Ve Congrès International d'Archéologie Chrétienne*, Paris–Vatican, 1957, pp. 589–97.

THIRION, J., 'Un témoin du premier art roman en Provence; La Madone de Levens', *B.M.*, 1961, pp. 345–51.

'S. Siffrein de Carpentras', *C.A.*, 1963, pp. 283–306.

'Notre-Dame-de-Cavaillon', *C.A.*, 1963, pp. 394–406.

'L'ancienne cathédrale de Nice et sa clôture de chœur du XIᵉ siècle, d'après des découvertes récentes', *Cahiers Archéologiques*, 1967, pp. 121–60.

'L'influence lombarde dans les Alpes françaises du Sud', *B.M.*, 1970, pp. 7–40.

TOURNIER, G., 'Pierres signées de Provence', *Centre International d'Études Romanes*, 1964, i, pp. 5–14.

TRICHAUD, J. M., *Histoire de la sainte église d'Arles*, Paris–Nîmes, 1857–64, 4 vols.

VALLERY-RADOT, J., 'Le domaine de l'école romane de Provence', *B.M.*, 1945, pp. 5–63.

'De Glanum à l'Avignon du XVIIIᵉ siècle. Remarques sur l'architecture', *C.A.*, 1963, pp. 9–43.

'L'église Notre-Dame de Mornas', *C.A.*, 1963, pp. 257–63.

'L'église S. Quenin de Vaison', *C.A.*, 1963, pp. 264–73.

VÉRAN, M., 'Visite de l'église S. Trophime', *C.A.*, 1876, pp. 563–9.

'Étude sur les voies romaines qui traversaient l'arrondissement d'Arles', *C.A.*, 1876, pp. 480–508.

VERNET, F., *La Cathédrale de S. Paul-Trois-Châteaux. La Drôme monumentale et archéologique*, Romans, 1930.

VIEILLARD-TROIEKOUROFF, M., 'Lurs-en-Provence et Ganagobie', *Cahiers Archéologiques*, 1966, pp. 221–5.

VILLARD, A., *Art de Provence*, Paris, 1957.

VINAY, L., *Essai sur les monuments et les anciens édifices de la ville de Romans*, Romans, 1903.

VIOLANTE, C., 'Les origines des fondations victorines dans la cité et au diocèse de Pise', Recueil des actes . . . S. Victor, *Provence Historique*, xvi, 1966, pp. 361–76.

VÖGE, W., *Die Anfänge des Monumentalen Stiles im Mittelalter*, Strasbourg, 1894.

'Der provencalische Einfluss in Italien und das Datum des Arler Porticus', *Bildhauer des Mittelalters; Gesammelte Studien von Wilhelm Vöge*, Berlin, 1958.

WUILLEUMIER, P., *Le Cloître de S. André-le-Bas à Vienne*, Vienne, 1947.

C: GENERAL WORKS

ADHÉMAR, J., *Influences antiques dans l'art du moyen âge français*, London, 1939.

AUBERT, M., *L'Architecture cistercienne en France*, Paris, 1948, 2 vols.

BAUM, J., *La Sculpture figurale en Europe à l'époque mérovingienne*, Paris, 1937.

BAUTIER, R., 'Les grands problèmes politiques et économiques de la Méditerranée mediévale', *Revue Historique*, 1965, pp. 1–28.

BAYERRI-BERTOMEU, E., *Los Códices medievales de la Catedral de Tortosa*, Barcelona, 1962.

BERGER, R., *Die Darstellung des Thronenden Christus in der romanischen Kunst*, Reutlingen, 1926.

BIEBER, M., *The History of the Greek and Roman theater*, Princeton, N.J., 1961.

BRESCIA, *Atti dell'ottavo congresso di studi sull'arte dell'alto medioevo. Stucchi e mosaici alto medioevali*, Milan, 1962, 2 vols.

BUCHWALD, H., 'Eleventh Century Corinthian-Palmette Capitals in the Region of Aquileia', *Art Bulletin*, 1966, pp. 147–58.

BUSCH, H., and LOHSE, B., *Pre-Romanesque Art*, New York, 1966.

BUTLER, H. C., *Early Churches in Syria. Princeton Monographs in Art and Archeology*, Princeton, N.J., 1929.

BYNE, M., *The Sculptured Capital in Spain*, New York, 1926.

CLAPHAM, A. W., *Romanesque Architecture in Western Europe*, London, 1940.

'The Renaissance of Architecture and Stone Carving in Southern France in the Tenth and Eleventh Centuries', *Proceedings of the British Academy*, 1932, pp. 4–66.

CONANT, K. J., *Carolingian and Romanesque Architecture, 800–1200*, London, 1959.

COTTINEAU, L. H., *Répertoire topo-bibliographique des abbayes et prieurés*, Mâcon, 1935–9, 2 vols.

CRESWELL, K. A. C., *Early Muslim Architecture*, Oxford, 1932–40, 2 vols.

CRIGHTON, G., *Romanesque Sculpture in Italy*, London, 1954.

CROSBY, S., 'Masons' marks at St. Denis', *Mélanges offerts à René Crozet*, Poitiers, 1966, ii, pp. 711–17.

CROZET, R., 'La corniche du clocher de l'église S. Hilaire de Poitiers', *B.M.*, 1934, pp. 341–5.

DEFOURNEAUX, M., *Les Français en Espagne aux XIe et XIIe siècles*, Paris, 1949.

DESCHAMPS, P., 'Étude sur la paléographie des inscriptions lapidaires', *B.M.*, 1929, pp. 5–86.

French Sculpture of the Romanesque Period, Eleventh and Twelfth Centuries, Florence–New York, 1930.

'La sculpture française en Palestine et en Syrie', *Mon. Piot*, vol. xxxi, 1930.

DUPONT, A., *Les Relations commerciales entre les cités maritimes du Languedoc et les cités méditerranéennes d'Espagne et d'Italie du Xe au XIIIe siècle*, Nîmes, 1942.

EBERSOLT, J., *Orient et Occident. Recherches sur les influences byzantines et orientales en France avant les croisades*, 1928, 2 vols.

ENLART, C., *Les Monuments des croisés dans le royaume de Jérusalem*, Paris, 1925–8, 4 vols.

ENLART, C., *Manuel d'archéologie française*, vol. i, Paris, 1927.

ESPINAS, G., 'Villes du midi et villes du nord', *Mélanges d'histoire*, vol. vi, 1944.

EVANS, J., *The Romanesque Architecture of the Order of Cluny*, Cambridge, 1938.

Cluniac Art of the Romanesque Period, Cambridge, 1950.

FABRE DE MORLHON and LACAZE, P., *La Cathédrale et l'île de Maguelone*, Montpellier, 1967.

FOCILLON, H., *L'Art des sculpteurs romans*, Paris, 1964.

FOURNIER, G., *Le Peuplement rural en basse Auvergne durant le haut moyen âge*, Paris, 1962.

FRANCOVICH, G. de, *Benedetto Antelami, architetto e scultore e l'arte del suo tempo*, Milan–Florence, 1952.

GILBERT, P., 'Caractères et origines du rinceau architectural romain', *Hommages à Léon Herrmann. Collection Latomus*, vol. xliv, Brussels, 1960, pp. 398–407.

GOMEZ-MORENO, C., 'The Doorway of San Leonardo al Frigido and the Problem of Master Biduino', *Metropolitan Museum of Art Bulletin*, 1965, pp. 349–61.

GRABAR, A., *Sculptures byzantines de Constantinople (IVe–Xe siècles)*, Paris, 1963.

GUILBERT, A., *Histoire des Villes de France*, Paris, 1844–5, 6 vols.

HASELOFF, A., *Pre-Romanesque Sculpture in Italy*, Florence, n.d.

HEYD, W., *Histoire du commerce de Levant au moyen âge*, Leipzig, 1885–6, 2 vols.

HIGOUNET, C., 'Mouvements de population dans le midi de la France du XIe au XVe siècle d'après les noms de personnes et de lieux', *Annales-Économies-Sociétés-Civilisations*, vol. viii, 1953.

HOLLAND, L., *Traffic Ways about France in the Dark Ages (500–1150)*, University of Pennsylvania, 1919.

HUBERT, J., 'Les routes du moyen âge', *Les Routes de France depuis les origines jusqu'à nos jours. Collection Colloques, Cahiers de Civilisation*, Paris, 1959.

'La "crypte" de S. Laurent de Grenoble et l'art du sud-est de la Gaule au début de l'époque carolingienne,' *Arte del Primo Millennio. Atti del IIo convegno per lo studio dell'arte dell'alto medio evo, Pavia, 1950*, Turin, n.d.

L'Architecture religieuse du haut moyen âge en France. Plans, notices et bibliographie, Paris, 1952.

'L'archéologie chrétienne en France depuis 1939', *Actes du Ve Congrès International d'Archéologie Chrétienne*, Paris–Vatican, 1957, pp. 97–108.

HUTTON, E., *The Cosmati: the Roman Marble Workers of the Twelfth and Thirteenth Centuries*, London, 1950.

JALABERT, D., 'De l'art oriental antique à l'art roman, II. L'aigle', *B.M.*, 1938, pp. 173–94.

La Flore sculptée des monuments du moyen âge en France, Paris, 1965.

JULLIAN, R., 'Sculpture lyonnaise et sculpture viennoise à l'époque romane', *Mélanges offerts à René Crozet*, Poitiers, 1966, i, pp. 563–8.

KAUTZCH, R., *Kapitellstudien. Studien zur Spätantiken Kunstgeschichte*, vol. ix, Berlin–Leipzig, 1936.

KING, G., 'Fact and Inference in Jamb Sculpture', *Art Studies*, 1926, pp. 113–46.

KRAUTHEIMER, R., *Early Christian and Byzantine Architecture*, London, 1965.

LAPEYRE, A., *Des façades occidentales de S. Denis et de Chartres aux portails de Laon*, Paris, 1960.

LASSUS, J., *Sanctuaires chrétiens de Syrie. Institut Français d'Archéologie de Beyrouth*, vol. xlii, Paris, 1947.

LASTEYRIE, R. DE, *L'Architecture religieuse en France à l'époque romane*, Paris, 1929.

LAVAGNINO, E., *Storia dell'arte medioevale italiana*, Turin, 1936.

LE BLANT, E., *Inscriptions chrétiennes de la Gaule antérieures au VIIIᵉ siècle*, Paris, 1856–65, 2 vols.
    Les Sarcophages chrétiens de la Gaule, Paris, 1886.

LEWIS, A., *The Development of Southern French and Catalan Society, 718–1050*, Texas University, 1965.

MERCKLIN, E., *Antike Figuralkapitelle*, Berlin, 1962.

MESSERER, W., *Romanische Plastik in Frankreich*, Cologne, 1964.

MICHEL, A., *Histoire de l'art*, vol. i, Paris, 1905.

MONNERET DE VILLARD, U., *Le Chiese della Mesopotamia. Orientalia Christiana Analecta*, No. 128, Rome, 1940.

MUNDY, J., *Liberty and Political Power in Toulouse, 1050–1230*, New York, 1954.

PANAZZA, G., 'Lapidi e sculture paleocristiane e pre-romaniche di Pavia', *Arte del primo millennio. Atti del IIº convegno . . . di Pavia*, Turin, n.d.

PIRENNE, H., *Les Villes et les institutions urbaines*, Paris, 1939, 2 vols.

PORTER, A. K., *Romanesque Sculpture of the Pilgrimage Roads*, Cambridge, Mass., 1923, 10 vols.
    'Iguacel and More Romanesque Art of Aragon', *Burlington Magazine*, March 1928, pp. 115–27.

PRIEST, A., 'The Masters of the West Façade of Chartres', *Art Studies*, i, 1922, pp. 28–44.

QUINTAVALLE, A., *La Cattedrale di Modena*, Modena, 1965.

RENOUARD, Y., 'Les voies de communication entre pays de la méditerranée et pays de l'atlantique au moyen âge', *Mélanges . . . dédiés à . . . Louis Halphen*, Paris, 1951, pp. 587–94.

REY, R., *Les Vieilles Églises fortifiées du midi de la France*, Paris, 1925.
    L'Art des cloîtres romans; étude iconographique, Toulouse, 1955.

SALMI, M., *L'Architettura romanica in Toscana*, Milan–Rome, n.d.

SALVINI, R., *Il Chiostro di Monreale e la scultura romanica in Sicilia*, Palermo, 1962.
    Wiligelmo e le origini della scultura romanica, Milan, 1956.

SCHAFFRAN, E., *Die Kunst der Langobarden in Italien*, Jena, 1941.

SINCERUS, I. (pseudonym), *Itinerarium Gallicae*, Lucerne, 1617.

SOUTHERN, R. (ed.), *Life of St. Anselm, Archbishop of Canterbury, by Eadmer*. Nelson Medieval Texts, London, 1963.

STENTON, F. (ed.), *The Bayeux Tapestry*, London, 1957.

STODDARD, W., *The West Portals of St. Denis and Chartres. Sculpture in the Île-de-France from 1140 to 1190*, Cambridge, Mass., 1952.

STRZYGOWSKI, J., *L'Ancien Art chrétien de Syrie*, Paris, 1936.

VERZONE, P., *L'Arte pre-romanica in Liguria*, Turin, n.d.

VEZIN, J., 'Un calendrier franco-hispanique de la fin du XIᵉ siècle', *Bibl. de l'École des Chartes*, vol. cxxi, 1963, pp. 5–25.

VIEILLARD-TROIEKOUROFF, M., 'Survivances mérovingiennes dans la sculpture funéraire du moyen âge', *Arts de France*, i, 1961, pp. 264–9.

VIOLLET-LE-DUC, E., *Dictionnaire raisonné de l'architecture française du XIᵉ au XVIᵉ siècle*, Paris, 1859–68, 10 vols.

VOGÜÉ, le comte de, *Architecture civile et religieuse du 1ᵉʳ au VIIᵉ siècle en Syrie*, Paris, 1865–77, 2 vols.

Index

S. Pierre, Montmajour. Interior.

-3. S. Pierre, Montmajour. Capitals.

4   5   6

4–6. S. Pierre, Montmajour. Capitals.

7

7–9. S. Philibert, Tournus. Cloister capitals.

8   9

10

11

12

10–13. Venasque. Capitals in the baptistery.

13

14–15. Gordes. S. Pantaléon. Capitals.

14

15

16

17

18

16–18. Bourg-S.-Andéol. Capitals now in the south transept.

19–20. Vaison-la-Romaine, cathedral. Apse capitals.
21. S. Victor, Marseille. Porch capital.

19

20

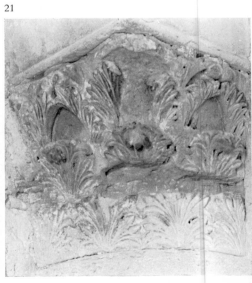

21

22. S. Restitut. South
porch.

23–4. S. Restitut. Frieze
panels.

23

24

25–7. S. Restitut. Frieze panels.

8–9. S. Paul-Trois-Châteaux. Reliefs on the south
ansept.

. Salon-de-Provence. Tympanum of West door.

31. Notre-Dame-des-Doms, Avignon. North side.

32. Notre-Dame-des-Doms, Avignon. Interior of nave.

33. Notre-Dame-des-Doms, Avignon. Exterior of the lantern tower.

34. Notre-Dame-des-Doms, Avignon. Cupola bay, south side.

35

36

35–8. Notre-Dame-des-Doms, Avignon. Nave capitals.

37

38

39–40. Notre-Dame-des-Doms, Avignon. Nave capitals.

41–3. Notre-Dame-des-Doms, Avignon. Lantern capitals.

39

41

40

42

43

Somno plasma dat
capit os ds eua creat .
parte pi patri duo
fert lat aula polit .
tusca sed alba rube
uirgo mariae e quoqz
mater .
Cuius floreut lac pane
mel dat acetum .
huic doces exemplo
euuo sita formula
templo .
Ut petra muroru
fuit humo dempta
duoru .
Qd cu trigenis sacra
rent qnqz getarchis .
Cu ustuf athetis
undena ecce uesu
d uno milleno bis
Qgeua noueno .
fsisumtu uerbum
qd gustaret a
cerbum .

biis eu flectere nonpossee · primo cotur nos confisofiele
uis uestiri eum fecit · & noue milibus ante se durare ·
Post modum insen tentia fixum manere uidens decd
Lri uissit · Quem tunc xpiani eode loco sepelierunt
Paruo tepi interposito · beatu baccum aloco quotu
mulatuis fuerat eleuantes · honorabili martyrib; loco
uixta sem sergiu com posuerunt · Ubi & uirgo iulia
que sub martiano preside · martyru consumauit · so
ciata martyribus sepulta quiesci · Eode die scou
martyrum · marcelli & epulei · qui qu de primo ad
heserunt symoni mago · sed uidentes mirabilia que
dns operabatur p aptum suu petrum · relicto symone
doctrina aptice se tradiderunt · Et post martyriu
aptou · confessione xpi & ipsi de corati · aureliano con
sulari uiro sententia ferente martyrii corona repor
tauerunt · sepulti nonlonge ab urbe roma ·
VIII · Id oct · Apud creta urbem cortina beati phy
lypi epi · magnis uirtutibus & optimis studiis predia
aum · Et te salonice · natalis sci de mayru martyris
Eodem die senis symeonis · qui dnm suscepit in ulnis
dicens · nunc dimittis dne seruum tuu in pace · Item
eode die apud cesarea · passio sce reparate uirginis
& martyris sub elacio preside · Apud auennica urbe
VII · Id oct · Ab urbe patriarche · Apud parisiu
natalis scou martyru · dyonisii epi · eleutherii pri
bzteri & rustici dyaconi · Qui beatus epi apon ifice

45. S. Sauveur, Aix. Nave, south side.

46. S. Sauveur, Aix. South transept (site of the oratory of S. Sauveur).

47. S. Sauveur, Aix. The Corpus Domini.

48. S. Sauveur, Aix. Cupola of the Corpus Domini.

49

50

49–52. S. Sauveur, Aix. Corpus Domini, nave capitals.

51

52

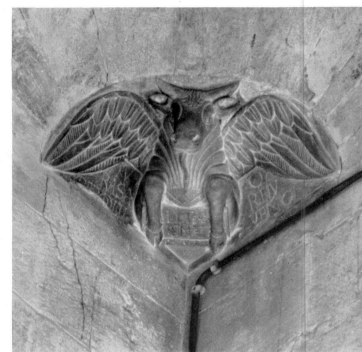

53

54

53. S. Sauveur, Aix. Symbol of S. Matthew in squinch of cupola.

54. S. Sauveur, Aix. Symbol of S. Luke in squinch of cupola.

55

56

55–6. S. Sauveur, Aix. Corpus Domini, pier imposts.

57. S. Trophime, Arles. Interior.

58. S. Trophime, Aries. South transept.

59

60

61

62

59–64. S. Trophime, Arles. Nave capitals.

63 64

65. S. Trophime, Arles. Remains of octagonal crossing-tower.

66. S. Trophime, Arles. Gable of west façade, detail.

67. S. Trophime, Arles. Gable of west porch, detail.

68. Notre-Dame, Cavaillon. Exterior from the west.

69. Notre-Dame, Cavaillon. Exterior, south side.

72

74

73

72–4. Notre-Dame, Cavaillon. Exterior frieze, south side.

75

75. Cavaillon. The arch of Marius.

76. Notre-Dame, Cavaillon. Apse, exterior.

77. Notre-Dame, Cavaillon. Apse capital.

78. Notre-Dame, Cavaillon. Nave capital.

79. Notre-Dame, Cavaillon. Nave.

80–1. Notre-Dame, Cavaillon. Nave capitals.

82–3. S. Restitut. Nave.

84–5. S. Restitut. Nave capitals.

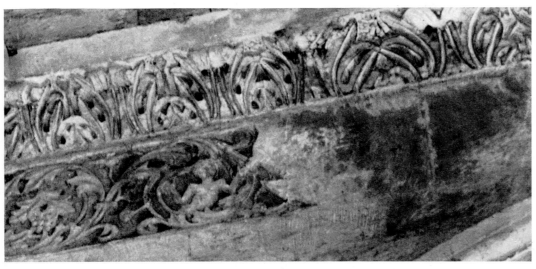

86–7. S. Restitut. Nave frieze.

88. S. Restitut. Base of tower, west side.

89. S. Restitut. Apse capital.

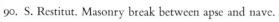

90. S. Restitut. Masonry break between apse and nave.

91. S. Restitut. Apse capital.

92. Pernes. Exterior, south side.

93. Pernes. Nave.

94

95

94–9. Pernes. Nave panels.

96

97

98

99

100. S. Siffrein, Carpentras. Nave.

101. S. Siffrein, Carpentras. Nave capital.

103. S. Siffrein, Carpentras. Symbol of S. Mark from the cupola.

102. S. Siffrein, Carpentras. Nave frieze.

104

104. S. André-de-Rosans. Nave looking west.

105

105-7. S. André-de-Rosans. Pier imposts.

106

107

108

109

108–11. S. André-de-Rosans. Nave capitals.

110

111

112. Notre-Dame-d'Aubune. Tower capitals.

113-14. Vaison-la-Romaine, cathedral. Nave panels.

115. Vaison-la-Romaine, cathedral. Corbel.

116

117

118
119

116–17. Vaison-la-Romaine, cathedral. Nave capitals.

118. Vaison-la-Romaine, cathedral. North side.

119. Vaison-la-Romaine, cathedral. Frieze, south side.

120. Vaison-la-Romaine, S. Quénin.
Exterior, east end, detail.

121. Vaison-la-Romaine, S. Quénin.
Apse capital.

122. Notre-Dame-du-Groseau,
Malaucène. Apse capitals.

123. S. Paul-Trois-Châteaux. Façade.

124. S. Paul-Trois-Châteaux. North transept.

25. S. Paul-Trois-Châteaux. Nave, south side.
26. S. Paul-Trois-Châteaux. Nave cornice, south side.
27. S. Paul-Trois-Châteaux. Remains of buttress on the south transept.

26

128. S. Paul-Trois-Châteaux. Interior.

129–30. S. Paul-Trois-Châteaux. Apse capitals.

131. S. Paul-Trois-Châteaux. Nave capital.

132. S. Paul-Trois-Châteaux. Symbol of St. Mark in the nave.

133-4. S. Paul-Trois-Châteaux.
Nave frieze.

135–6. S. Paul-Trois-Châteaux. Nave frieze.

137. Nîmes, cathedral. Frieze.

138. Nîmes, museum. Capital fragment.

139. Les Saintes Maries-de-la-Mer. Apse capital.

140. Les Saintes Maries-de-la-Mer. Apse capital.

141. Les Saintes Maries-de-la-Mer. Apse capital.

142. S. Trophime, Arles. Capital from the north gallery of the cloister.

143. Les Saintes Maries-de-la-Mer. Apse capital.

144. S. Trophime, Arles. Capital from the north gallery of the cloister.

145. Les Saintes Maries-de-la-Mer. Apse capital.

146. S. Trophime, Arles. Capital from the north gallery of the cloister.

147. Les Saintes Maries-de-la-Mer. Apse capital.

148. S. Trophime, Arles. Capital from the north gallery of the cloister.

149. Les Saintes Maries-de-la-Mer. Apse capital.

150. S. Trophime, Arles. Capital from the north gallery of the cloister.

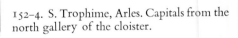

151. S. Paul-Trois-Châteaux. West door, detail.

152-4. S. Trophime, Arles. Capitals from the north gallery of the cloister.

155. S. Paul-Trois-
Châteaux. West door,
detail.

156. S. Gabriel. Oculus of
west façade.

157. S. Gabriel. Façade.

158. S. Gabriel. Tympanum.

WITHDRAWN-UNL